Realism and Racism

Taking as its starting point the contemporary unease about the status and possibilities of a social science, *Realism and Racism* argues that a realist approach to social research and concept formation offers a distinctive alternative. The book begins by examining the continuing difficulties within social science surrounding concepts of race. Bob Carter suggests that these difficulties stem from the uncertain ontological and epistemological status of race ideas, itself a consequence of the recognition that race concepts have all but lost their relevance as sociologically significant descriptions of genotypical and phenotypical distributions among human populations.

The book examines some of the ways in which social scientists have responded to this lack of an objective referent for race notions, before setting out to develop an alternative approach based on the recent work of realist authors, namely Archer, Layder, Pawson and Sayer. It argues that such an approach offers a radical revision of the orthodox debates about race concepts, about the possibility of a social science and about the nature of empirical research. These themes are well illustrated through two policy examples: an account of postwar Commonwealth and colonial migration to the UK, and debates about transracial adoption in the UK and the USA. Carter goes on to conclude that, although not without problems of its own, realism is a fruitful resource for those wishing to defend a 'modest objectivity' within the social sciences.

Bob Carter is Lecturer at the Centre for Research in Ethnic Relations, University of Warwick.

Critical Realism: Interventions

Edited by Margaret Archer, Roy Bhaskar, Andrew Collier, Tony Lawson and Alan Norrie

Critical Realism

Essential readings

Edited by Margaret Archer, Roy Bhaskar, Andrew Collier, Tony Lawson and Alan Norrie

The Possibility of Naturalism

A philosophical critique of the contemporary human sciences

Roy Bhaskar

Being and Worth

Andrew Collier

Quantum Theory and the Flight from Realism

Chris Norris

From East to West

Odyssey of a soul

Roy Bhaskar

Realism and Racism

Concepts of race in sociological research

Bob Carter

Realism and Racism

Concepts of race in sociological research

Bob Carter

London and New York

For Edna and Bob

First published 2000
by Routledge
11 New Fetter Lane, London EC4P 4EE

Simultaneously published in the USA and Canada
by Routledge
29 West 35th Street, New York, NY 10001

Routledge is an imprint of the Taylor & Francis Group

© 2000 Bob Carter

Typeset in Baskerville by Keystroke, Jacaranda Lodge, Wolverhampton
Printed and bound in Great Britain by Clays Ltd, St Ives plc

British Library Cataloguing in Publication Data
A catalogue record for this book is available from the British Library

Library of Congress Cataloging in Publication Data
Carter, Bob, 1949–
      Realism and racism : concepts of race in sociological research / Bob Carter.
         p. cm. — (Critical realism—interventions)
      Includes bibliographical references and index.
         1. Race. 2. Race—Research. 3. Sociology—Research. I. Title. II. Series.

HT1521 .C364 2000
305.8—dc21   00–042480

ISBN 0–415–23372–0 (hbk)
ISBN 0–415–23373–9 (pbk)

Contents

Acknowledgements

Writing acknowledgements is rarely easy, but a recognition of the profoundly collaborative nature of all academic work is necessary and desirable. Let me begin by identifying some major debts. It was Derek Layder's work which drew me to realism to begin with and he has proved a continuing source of intellectual and, no less importantly, moral support. Annie Phizacklea was a great encourager, and without her enthusiasm a project which is contentious in parts would not have been completed. Margaret Archer has never been less than generous with her time, support and advice. Doug Porpora undertook (voluntarily!) the unenviable task of reading and commenting on the entire manuscript in draft form.

Thanks must also go to several people who have had to listen to these arguments over the years and have always responded with generosity and in a spirit of intellectual comradeship, namely Marci Green, Ian Grosvenor, Rick Halpern, Clive Harris, Shirley Joshi, Kevin Magill, Robert Miles, Caroline New and Sabby Sagall. Alan How, in particular, shared an enthusiasm for social theory and a commitment to intellectual endeavour which, though frequently ruinous to our timekeeping, was nevertheless indispensable to developing many of the ideas found here. Dilwyn Porter kindly read Chapter 7 and provided helpful commentary and useful references. Malcolm Williams read Chapters 3 and 4 at very short notice and, despite his teaching and other responsibilities, still managed to produce several pages of helpful commentary. I also owe thanks to Alan Norrie for his suggestions on an earlier draft and to Joan Woodward for helping me to get writing in the first place. The staff at the Public Records Office, Kew were always helpful and accommodating.

Any author who has to combine writing and research with a full-time teaching post cannot fail to recognize their indebtedness to colleagues. A good deal of the book was completed whilst I was working as a Senior Lecturer in Sociology at University College Worcester and the intellectual and practical support of my colleagues in the Sociology department, especially Alan How, Ellie Hedges and Lesley Spiers, was crucial. The later stages were finished whilst in my current post at the University of Warwick, where I have enjoyed similar support, especially from Danielle Joly. My postgraduate students at CRER have also prompted various refinements in the arguments offered here. Of course, none of the above can be held responsible for any shortcomings in the final text. Part of Chapter 4 appeared previously in M. Lloyd and A. Thacker (eds), *The Impact of Michel Foucault on the Social Sciences and the Humanities*, London: Macmillan and I thank the editors and publishers for permission to use it here.

Finally, I owe a particular debt to Alison Sealey. Her intellectual companionship, emotional support, and sane view of the relevance of the academic enterprise have shaped this book in more ways than she knows.

Introduction

This is a book about social theory. More particularly, it is about the extent to which social theory can provide a compelling defence of a notion of social science. This begs the question of whether such a defence is necessary. After all, social science seems always to have been preoccupied with the uncertainty of its disciplinary status and boundaries so that talk of a crisis often seems little more than a case of in-house melodrama.

Nevertheless, I would suggest that the shift from Gouldner's 'coming crisis' to Mouzelis's 'what went wrong' indicates more than a shift in publishers' marketing taste for apocalyptic titles (Gouldner 1970; Mouzelis 1995). There is a sense now that the very idea of a social science is somehow anachronistic or passé, and insufficiently sensitive to the 'politics of truth' (Barratt 1991). The abstract rationality it putatively privileges is frequently seen as a Trojan horse of phallocentric, ethnocentric narratives and values (see, for example, Harding 1997; Hekman 1994; Outlaw 1996; Pittman 1997a).

Accordingly, a major task of the book is to delineate the theoretical conditions for a science of the social. These conditions are provided by a view of the social world as comprising not only human beings, but also the social relations and structures that are the products of human social interaction. There is nothing novel in this particular ontological claim; it informs the work of Marx, Durkheim and Weber, although with differing emphases and degrees of significance. However, in line with more recent usages, I shall refer to this central ontological claim, and the epistemological insights that it generates, as sociological or social scientific realism.

An important consequence of the questioning of a notion of social science has been an acceleration of the divorce between social theory and empirical research. There are many reasons for this estrangement, but it is not hard to recognize that the key functions of empirical research, namely measurement and evaluation, rely on a credible conceptual framework capable of specifying what is to be measured and how. Poststructuralist and postmodernist emphases on narratives and the discursively determined nature of theory tend to make empirical measurement supererogatory. Too often, as a result, social science has had little to say about issues of policy: if social phenomena can merely be interpreted rather than explained there is little incentive for policy makers to prefer expensive research to inexpensive prejudice. A second ambition of the book, then, is to demonstrate the ways in which a sociological realism can restore the relevance of empirical research to social science.

This nexus of social theory, empirical research and social policy making is explored in the book through an examination of the uses made by social scientists of concepts of race. Race concepts within sociology are an especially fruitful field of inquiry for several reasons. Their topicality is obvious, at least within academic and policy debates within the USA and Britain, but more importantly, the employment of race concepts within social theories vividly illustrates the pitfalls that follow from an under-theorized notion of science. The book takes its organizational cue from this and uses an exploration of the difficulties sociologists have encountered in using a theoretical concept of race to adumbrate a distinctively sociological realism.

What is the source of these difficulties? Why is it not possible for sociologists to define a theoretical concept of race, embedded within a web of competing and complementary concepts or propositions, as they do, for example, with terms such as bureaucracy or social class or social mobility? A major reason, the book suggests, is to do with locating a consistent referent for the term race. Sociologists can, and frequently do, disagree about, say, how social class is to be defined or measured, but there is usually agreement that there is *something* to be described, measured and explained, namely systematically reproduced and regular outcomes to do with the generation and distribution of material and cultural resources. When it comes to a concept of race, not even this minimal agreement is evident.

Partly this is a result of the rather inglorious scientific career of race terms. Although commentators vary in their assessment of the etymology of race categories, there is little doubt that the major impact of such categories was felt in the eighteenth and nineteenth centuries when they emerged as natural scientific terms for dividing human populations (Banton 1997; Barkan 1991; Kohn 1996; Malik 1996; Miles 1989; Stepan 1982). Scientific racism, as it came to be called, held that races were ontologically valid, biological categories which accurately described and identified discrete groupings of the human species. Furthermore, one's race conferred unalterable characteristics and qualities that, precisely because of their biological provenance, were not prone to melioration. Unsurprisingly, this view of things proved highly adaptive. The arguments of scientific racism were widely applied in Britain and in the USA to defend, amongst other things, slavery, the denial of the franchise to women and the working classes, and the denial of education to those races for whom it was considered pointless or inessential (Bederman 1995; Bolt 1971; Higham 1994; Lorimer 1978). Nor were such ideas confined to Europe and the USA (Dikotter 1992).

The ideas of scientific racism, particularly the claim that humankind was naturally divided into biologically discrete races, came under increasing scrutiny during the early twentieth century from scientists themselves, initiating what Barkan describes as the 'retreat from racism' (Barkan 1991). The central finding of the scientific critique was that differences between so called races were literally only skin deep. That is, classifying human populations into races was a theoretical exercise that only corresponded to superficial differences between human beings. Contemporary science has only confirmed this. It does not really matter, then, how groups are assigned to race classifications since '. . . the differences between major "racial" categories, no matter how defined, turn out to be small' (Rose, Kamin and Lewontin 1984: 126–7). Race categories have far more to do with politics than they have to do with science.

The most obvious illustration of this is the assertion made in popular (common sense and academic) discourses of race in the USA that race categories are based on colour differences. Borderline cases, where colour is indeterminate, are distributed among these or are assigned on the basis of incoherent claims about blood and inheritance (Davis James 1991) or made into new races. In this way race again finds new life as an analytical concept, with many of the consequences for theoretical understanding identified in this book. (See, for example, the debates about transracial adoption considered in Chapter 8.)

Even biologists who recognize the force and implications of the critique of traditional race concepts find it hard to abandon them. Thus Jones, after acknowledging that 'the average genetic difference between blacks and whites is smaller than that between individuals', still insists that it would be foolish to say that race does not exist:

> If people from different places can be seen to be distinct they can, on any rational classification, be placed in separate categories. Even though the term imposes a false unity on diverse groups it is worth preserving, if only because any alternative is so unsatisfactory.
>
> (Jones 1997: 183)

But, of course, people from different places cannot always be seen as distinct and the classifications we impose on them will depend on which differences are chosen to be regarded as significant. Calling these classifications races does far more than impose a 'false unity on diverse groups': it imposes the ideological and discursive baggage that accompanies the concept of race as a description of significant human difference. What is a concept of race worth preserving for? Why do we need an alternative?

This is the starting point of the book. Despite the recognition that, as Kohn (1996) puts it, race ideas are a scientific solecism, sociologists still employ a concept of race. More than that, the concept remains something of a prospector's paradise; new claims are lodged all the time – 'race' and the Enlightenment, 'race' and the body – even while the older seams – 'race' and class, 'race' and gender, 'race' and nation – continue to maintain a prodigious output. There is no escaping the unease and uncertainty, however, that surround the use of race notions following their fall from scientific grace. Uniquely in the pantheon of social scientific terms, 'race' is rarely allowed a public appearance without its minders, represented by the accompanying collar of inverted commas. Chapters 1 and 2 explore some features of this crisis of the race concept, but before introducing these it might be appropriate to indicate the approach to terminology used in the book.

First, ideas and propositions about race – that there are races, for example, or that some races have natural, unalterable aptitudes or characteristics, or that history is the history of race struggle – have a social reality, embodied in texts of various kinds and in the practices of social life. Thus they have a definite ontological status, and I therefore do not propose to use inverted commas when discussing them. Race ideas, concepts, terms are ontologically no different from, say, Buddhist ideas or Renaissance ideas or Green ideas and, it seems to me, no more deserving of being shackled by inverted commas.

Second, I shall use the terms racist (race-ist) and racism (race-ism) as the means of describing those actions and ways of thinking that are explicitly based upon, justified or motivated by, ideas about race. (The methodological difficulties of determining the extent to which actions and thoughts can be said to be racist are dealt with in Chapters 6, 7 and 8.) This may seem an idiosyncratic manoeuvre, but it is fully consistent with the realist position that is developed in Chapter 4 and which views race ideas and propositions as ideational resources.

Chapters 1 and 2 examine the most common ways in which the lacklustre, common sense notion of race is transmuted into a glittering analytical concept. Briefly, it is suggested that there are two alchemical strategies at work. The first is to claim that race refers to certain forms of mutual knowledge which may be used by social actors in their routine 'ways of going on', and as such it constitutes a viable object of sociological analysis. The second is to argue that race is discursively construed and that it plays a key role as a signifier in accounts of cultural difference and definitions of Other-ness.

Beginning with the work of Rex, Chapter 1 demonstrates how a redefinition of race in terms of the meanings assembled and deployed by social actors in everyday interaction and in judgements about access to resources such as housing and employment, gives fresh vitality to a sociological concept of race. Thus the claim is made by Rex and later authors, particularly in the USA, that when actors use race ideas to make sense of social relations, then those relations can be understood as race relations. This broadly interactionist, humanist approach, Chapter 1 suggests, remains widely influential, although its theoretical assumptions are rarely made explicit.

The postmodern contributions examined in Chapter 2 provide a major alternative to those of the interactionists. The work of Foucault in particular has had a far reaching impact, both on sociology's claims to scientific status and on disputes surrounding the concepts of race and ethnicity and their relevance to accounts of social identities and political movements. Chapter 2 contends that Foucault's ideas may be fruitfully applied to sociological accounts of race ideas and racism, questioning, as they do, the ontological status of race categories, and the conventional view of social identities often derived from them. The various postmodernists considered in Chapter 2 develop a strong form of Foucault's ideas, but their position is compromised by a neglect of empirical attention to social relations of inequality and exclusion.

This larger argument is pursued in Chapters 1 and 2. Here it is argued that the persistence of race ideas within social science both reflects, and is a consequence of, a wider equivocation about the nature of social science itself and particularly its claims to provide a specific form of knowledge about the social world. This raises the question of whether a viable notion of social science is defensible. Chapter 3 answers this question affirmatively by turning to the traditions of realism within sociology. On the basis of a critical review of the work of Bhaskar and others, it identifies a number of key principles for a realist social science based on the recent contributions of Archer, Layder, Pawson and Sayer, namely:

1   a belief in the externality and objectivity of structured social relations and a belief therefore in a social reality relatively independent of individual social actors;
2   as a corollary to this, a methodological commitment to analytical dualism, that is a commitment to the notion that structure and agency are analytically distinct and irreducible to each other;
3   a claim that social reality constrains but does not determine how we interpret the world so that knowledge is neither random, arbitrary or free-floating, nor governed mechanically by material circumstances.

However, although forms of sociological realism have received increasingly sophisticated theoretical explication and development in recent years, its implications for those interested in social research have had less attention. There are, as yet, few examples of realist sociology at work, either informing empirical research or being applied to substantive areas of sociological inquiry.

Accordingly, Chapter 4 begins to draw out some of the possibilities of a realist approach to the study of race concepts and racism. Two particular contributions are seen as crucial: the morphogenetic perspective developed in the work of Archer and the domain theory of Layder (Archer 1989, 1995, 1996; Layder 1990, 1997). Together they provide a powerful foundation for a realist social science and allow a distinctive take on sociological views of race. Some elements of this are picked out in Chapter 4.

The chief claim advanced is that race concepts, ideas and propositions are items in the cultural system of a society. Certain properties of race concepts, ideas and propositions are identified, namely that:

1   as elements in the cultural system, they are the products of sociocultural interaction and are generated by social actors;
2   over time, though, race concepts, ideas and propositions, like all cultural system items, have the capacity to escape the clutches of their originators and acquire an autonomy as denizens of the cultural system. At this point we can examine how they constrain and influence subsequent social actors.

One of the first benefits of a realist account, paradoxically, is this restoration of attention to the *content* of race ideas and propositions and to their logical relations of non-contradiction and entailment with other ideas and propositions. The realist insight that race ideas have powers and properties whose reach extends temporally and spatially beyond extant social actors, is explored in detail in Chapter 5. The relationship between culture, structure and agency that lies at the core of analytical dualism is examined using as an empirical example the role played by race concepts and ideas in the development of immigration and nationality legislation in the UK. Inter alia, Chapter 5 also notes the unwillingness to offer an intellectual critique of race ideas, often on the mistaken grounds that to do so is to challenge the hermeneutic authenticity of actors' beliefs.

Having established the relevance of sociological realism for a theoretical critique of concepts of race, Chapters 6 and 7 consider its potential for generating sociologically adequate accounts of specific sequences of social change. Sociological realism is pre-eminently a historical sociology, one whose concern with temporality is fundamental. The realist notion of a stratified social ontology, with its emphasis on causal relations, generative powers and emergent properties, makes history indispensable to social science (see Burke 1992; Dunn 1978; Evans 1997; Gellner 1973; Jenkins 1995 for various views of the relationship between history and social theory), hence the morphogenetic model outlined in Chapter 4, which provides the basic methodological principles of a realist approach to social change. Analysis proceeds in the form of three stage cycles. Stage one starts from a configuration of structural (and cultural) conditions, antecedent and so partially autonomous from social actors and agents. It is within these conditions that, in stage two, social actors and agents pursue interests. The social and cultural interaction that results culminates in a stage three of structural (and cultural) elaboration, where in pursuing their interests social actors, both consciously and unintentionally, modify or reproduce the conditions they encountered at stage one. This brings us to the start of another morphogenetic cycle with a new stage one. Chapters 5, 6 and 7 apply this model to an empirical instance of social change.

The example used is the shift in government policy between 1945 and 1981 from the endorsement of the unrestricted entry to the UK of colonial and Commonwealth subjects and citizens to the introduction of discriminatory and restrictive immigration and nationality legislation. These chapters examine how this legislation contributed to, and defined, emerging notions of citizenship and how these were mobilized by social actors and agents, often in ways unintended by those drafting the legislation. A central argument is that immigration and nationality legislation, and the formal and informal notions of citizenship generated by it, becomes an important structural condition for social action which deploys race ideas. Such action – from discrimination to physical violence and genocide – is inexplicable without an account of these structural conditions.

The discussion of government responses to colonial and Commonwealth migration to the UK after 1945 is based on primary source material located at the Public Record Office. PRO documents are used illustratively to explore the stratified dimension of agency, that is the different powers and capacities accruing to actors and agents from their various social locations.

Of course, in the sense that I am proposing a particular view of social science, examples from any aspect of social life would have served as well. However, the postwar case illustrates handily some themes central to the argument for a sociological realism. This argument, it will be recalled, extends over several different levels. First, there is the issue of theoretical concepts and ideas and how these should be identified, developed and applied within social science discourses. The claim is that a concept of race does not qualify as a sociological concept. It is a misdescription of the social world and a concept which, partly for that reason, cannot be easily connected to the developed frameworks of theoretical concepts and meanings established by social scientific theory. The example of government discussion of possible legislative responses to postwar migration enables the book to draw some interesting contrasts and parallels between the uses made of race by sociologists and the uses made of it by politicians. This further reinforces the distinction advanced in Chapter 3 between lay and social scientific language and the key role played by theory in concept formation in the latter.

Second, there are the uses made in social policy and empirical research of race concepts. Chapters 5, 6 and 7 provide plenty of evidence about the impact of race ideas and especially the ways in which these have informed notions of citizenship and entitlement in the UK. These chapters also suggest an alternative morpho-genetic approach to explaining concrete instances of social change (and social stasis). However, the deployment of race concepts and categories in contemporary policy debates in the UK and the USA, their embodiment in the titles of government and private agencies, their role as a feature of political identities and as a basis for political mobilization raises further issues.

Perhaps the most obvious of these is how we account for the continued use of race concepts not only by large numbers of lay actors but also by sociologists. A second question has to do with the role played by race ideas as intersubjective meanings, as sources of psychological sustenance and personal expression of identity, and as interactional resources employed by people in accomplishing the routines of everyday life. This involves a consideration of the symbolic forms of race ideas and their embeddedness in social contexts and processes such as public ceremonies or the construction of 'the national interest', as well as their role in the sustenance of other symbolic forms which circulate in social life (Billig 1995; Thompson 1990).

Finally, there is the question of what it is exactly that is being measured by empirical and policy studies that use race categories? How might the realist offer an alternative? These are especially pertinent questions for research on racism and discrimination in the USA, where the term *race* refers overwhelmingly to distinctions of colour. Research investigates correlations between the categories of black and white and life chances, job opportunities, education and so on. The theoretical insights, even the political force, of much research into race might be enhanced by a more appropriate emphasis on colour discrimination and colour-based racism. These topics are examined in Chapter 8.

Using Layder's domain theory (1997), Chapter 8 argues that the role and relevance of race ideas and concepts will vary across different social domains and that this requires a sociological approach sensitive to these variations. An exami-nation of social policy research in the area of 'transracial adoption', a policy debate conducted almost entirely in race terms, is then used to identify some of the pitfalls associated with the use of an under theorized notion of race.

It is one thing to note the effects of race research, quite another to offer an alternative means of researching discrimination, exclusion and the effects of race ideas. Yet this is what any plausible social theory must be able to do. Chapter 8 points to the work of Pawson (1989a) and Pawson and Tilley (1997) as providing a basis for a realist model of measurement and evaluation. This suggests avenues for social research into discrimination, inequality and racism which require no concept of race; not only is the abandonment of a sociological concept of race necessary for social science but doing so opens the way for a properly realist social research. Of course, this in no sense whatsoever implies that social researchers should not continue to investigate racism and discrimination, merely that they should not do so using a notion of race as an analytical category.

In an important sense this brings the argument full circle, since the book begins with the question of what is wrong with the concept of race. The arguments for abandoning the concept and expelling it from the discourse of social science have always been shadowed by larger debates about the future of social science and particularly its claim to privileged knowledge; indeed some would question strongly the very notion of a science of the social. It is to these doubts and debates that the final chapter turns.

One of the problems facing realist sociology lies in developing a body of methodological work. Whilst realism has established a respectable foothold as a philosophy of science, its impact within the practice of social science has been much less significant. The advent of various forms of relativism associated with the rise of postmodern and post-structuralist ideas has also impeded the development of a sociological realism along the lines argued in this book. Amongst other things, this has led to a waning of confidence amongst social scientists in the ability of their discipline to offer anything much beyond 'stories and narratives'.

The concluding chapter reviews and extends my central argument that realism provides the basis for a claim to privileged knowledge. This claim rests on several distinctive features of sociological realism. First, realism provides a cogent defence of objectivity and an evolutionary view of the growth of knowledge. The insistence that social scientific knowledge is knowledge *of* an ontologically stratified social reality avoids the solipsism that follows from the claim that our theories are entirely self-referential.

However, and second, realism is resolutely post-empiricist in its stress on the theory driven nature of social scientific knowledge. The prominence of theory leads to both a distinctive view of empirical research as the identification of mechanisms and contexts responsible for regularities, and to a sharp break with those sociologies which insist on the commonality of social scientific and lay languages or discourses. Whilst acknowledging their common sources, realism retains the view that theoretical languages serve different purposes to the languages of everyday life.

Serving a different purpose from everyday communication need not mean that the discussion of theoretical issues has to be expressed in obscure or difficult ways. Although the book deals with some complex topics within social science, I have attempted to ensure that it does so in a clear and perspicuous manner. This is not simply because I want to increase sales by widening the appeal of the book (although this is not necessarily a poor motive). It is also because I think that the arguments it advances need testing amongst an audience beyond that of professional theory mongers (like myself).

1   A sociological concept of race

Concepts of race continue to appeal as theoretical categories for sociologists both in Britain and the USA. Those who criticise the use of such concepts within sociology are confronted by a range of objections which typically include some or all of the following: that a critique of race concepts within social science amounts to a denial of racism and discrimination and is therefore politically inappropriate or objectionable; that it amounts to a sort of rationalist bullying, implying that once we stop using the wrong words, then we will stop arriving at wrong ideas; and finally, that in the end it does not matter a great deal, since we all know what we are talking about when it comes to race. The effect of these objections is to ensure that the concept evades serious sociological scrutiny.

I shall consider the biography of the race concept later. For the moment, though, my concern will be to examine the efforts of sociologists to account for race in specifically sociological terms, that is, to define for social scientific purposes the kinds of social phenomena designated by the term *race*. It is part of my case that the use of a concept of race is an attempt to capture certain structural, objective, onto-logically real features of social reality and to apprehend real social relations of difference. However, the notion of race makes the apprehension and explanation of these relations more, not less, difficult because of the elision it effects between common sense thinking and social scientific thinking. (This distinction is pursued further in Chapters 3 and 8.)

This leads to serious difficulties. The concept of race, as a category rooted in the forms of phenomenal experience, is ill-suited to the tasks of theory (it is not alone in this, of course). Yet it displays a remarkable tenacity and longevity in lay and social scientific discourses. The persistence of a concept of race within social science both reflects, and is a consequence of, a wider equivocation about the nature of social science itself and particularly its claims to provide a specific form of knowledge about the social world. This is why I think that an examin-ation of how sociology has theorized the notion of race can tell us a great deal not only about racism and racialized social relations but also about social science itself.

A major contribution to the development of a sociological concept of race has come from those writers influenced by, or drawing upon, the work of Robert Park. In particular the work of Michael Banton and John Rex has utilized Park's core insights about the meaningful nature of social interaction and the role played by the ideas and beliefs of social actors in constituting social relations to develop a distinctively sociological concept of race.

RACE AS A FORM OF COMMON UNDERSTANDING

Park's work on race arose out of his more general critique of biological reductionism. His work as a journalist and as publicity officer for Booker T. Washington had demonstrated convincingly to Park the inutility of biological notions of race in accounting for patterns of racism and discrimination in the USA. Drawing upon the theoretical tradition of Symbolic Interactionism developed by Charles Cooley (Cooley 1964), Park elaborated a notion of race as a social category, a symbolically constituted, culturally embedded coding of conflict and competition among groups (Lal 1986). It is therefore relational (an emergent product of relations between groups) and to be distinguished from individual attitudes.

Park's approach rested on the key neo-Kantian philosophical assumption that we interact with others not directly but on the basis of our ideas about them. The proper 'facts' of society are therefore the imaginings we have of each other. Such a claim emphasizes the fluidity and negotiated-ness of social order as a product of actors' symbolic resources and interpretative strategies.

Park's core concept of race relations is derived from this and describes those situations of group conflict and competition which social actors interpret in race terms. Hence we can talk of a race relations situation when:

> racial differences enter into the consciousness of the individuals and groups so distinguished, and by so doing determine in each case the individual's conception of himself as well as his status in the community . . . Race relations, in this sense, are not so much the relations that exist between individuals of different races as between individuals conscious of these differences.
>
> (Park 1950: 81)

There are several features of this formulation that are worth examining. First, race relations are an emergent feature of group conflict and therefore possess a certain autonomy from individual social actors. This autonomy enables Park to distance his approach sharply from various forms of biological or psychological reductionism by, second, constituting race relations as an ontologically distinct object of analysis. Thus Park's race relations cycle, consisting of the four stages of contact, conflict, accommodation, and assimilation, strongly implies a structural sequence ('progressive and irreversible' according to Park) in some measure independent of actors' conscious accounts and imaginings:

> All this suggests that the term race relations, as here conceived, includes relations which are not now conscious or personal, though they have been; relations which are fixed in and enforced by custom, convention, and the

routine of an expected social order of which there may be at the moment no very lively consciousness.

(Park 1950: 83)

Race notions and ideas, as conscious interpretative strategies developed and pursued by social actors in the course of everyday life, thus become 'fixed' through routine and tradition and so part of a society's symbolic resources, available for use by subsequent social actors. The fact that race is a social category, not a biological one, does not make its social force any less effectual. For Park, Wacker notes, 'If . . . racial pride was based upon illusion, that did not make the pride any less real or less a healthy reaction to prejudice' (Wacker 1983: 65). Race may refer to a symbolic categorization rather than to a biological classification, but a belief in it carries real social effects.

There have been many critiques of Park's account of race relations (see, for example, Lal 1986; Omi and Winant 1994; Wacker 1983). My concern is with its adequacy as a theoretical description suitable for social science (especially as a Parkian defence of the concepts of race and race relations still carries a deal of credibility, as we shall see presently). Here I want to establish two points. First, there is a tension within Park's argument between his commitment to some version of interactionism, in which actors' understandings shape the form of social relations, and his recognition that symbolic and cultural resources have a distinctive ontological status that allows, for example, for the identification of a race relations cycle. In other words, the relationship between structure and agency in Park's formulation of race relations is indistinct.

The second point is directly related to this. If race relations are those relations interpreted by social actors in terms of race ideas and imaginings, how might we account for these ideas and imaginings? In order to avoid triviality (race relations are those relations understood in terms of a notion of race), Park insists that actors' understandings become embedded in routines, customs and conventions which shape the imaginings of subsequent actors. Now we have a distinct category of social relations not reducible to actors' understandings and presumably capable of shaping such understandings. Why, then, does Park give primacy to actor interpretations in the sense of seeing these as the source of race relations? After all, to note that one element of a society's symbolic resources comprises ideas, propositions, beliefs and values to do with notions of race does not explain why some people make use of them when others do not.

This leads to an equivocation about the term *race* itself in Park's work. On the one hand it is an interpretive social category employed by people in making sense of their milieux; on the other hand it appears to describe extra-discursive differences between people so that race relations arise when social actors become conscious of these differences:

> Race relations . . . are the relations existing between peoples distinguished by marks of racial descent, particularly when these racial differences enter into the consciousness of the individuals and groups so distinguished . . . Race relations,

in this more inclusive sense, might comprise, therefore, all those situations in which some relatively stable equilibrium between competing races has been achieved and in which the resulting social order has become fixed in custom and tradition.

(Park 1950: 81–2)

Here Park seems to imply that race relations are those relations where social actors attach significance to (already existing?) race differences or use 'marks of racial descent' as the basis for distinguishing groups and individuals. Of course, the 'mark of racial descent' that preoccupied Park was skin colour and it might be queried whether Park needed a notion of race at all to address the problems of racism and discrimination with which he was primarily concerned. I shall return to this issue of terminology in later chapters. For the moment, I have pointed to some of the difficulties facing a sociological account of race relations that sets out from an interactionist perspective. Park's work is notable precisely because he initiates the idea of race as a social, rather than a biological, category and then attempts to build a compelling model of race relations on the basis of it. I have sought to argue that the problems he encountered in doing this stem in significant measure from the unbalanced relation of structure and agency in interactionist sociology.

I want now to turn to another significant, and more contemporary, effort to develop a sociological concept of race relations, namely John Rex's key text *Race Relations in Sociological Theory* (Rex 1983). There are important differences between the approaches of Park and Rex. Most significantly, Rex is able to provide an account of the structural conditions that are favourable to the development of a race relations situation, identifying, for example, the role played by colonial relations in shaping the newly arrived migrants' entry into the housing and employment markets. This means that the ambiguity surrounding Park's references to 'marks of racial descent' and to 'races' as the source of common sense race classifications is avoided. Nevertheless, Rex, like Park, places a critical emphasis on the meanings social actors attach to certain sorts of social relations, regarding them as defining how such relations should be described theoretically.

Earlier work than Rex's within sociology in Britain had focused largely on the problems experienced by migrants to the UK, particularly those from former colonies in the Caribbean, India, Pakistan and Africa. These problems were designated racial because they involved relations between 'black' and 'white' people. Studies such as Sheila Patterson's *Dark Strangers*, first published in 1963 and Anthony Richmond's *The Colour Problem*, first published in 1955, both written from a critical and concerned liberal perspective, epitomized the approach.

Richmond's book was a comparative assessment of the relations between 'blacks' and 'whites' drawing on material from South Africa, Kenya, Britain and the Caribbean, whilst Patterson's was a careful, mainly empirical, study of the difficulties facing newly arrived migrants from the Caribbean. As she saw it, these difficulties were exacerbated by the skin colour of the migrants, which placed them in particular sorts of social relation to the indigenous 'white' population. For Richmond a central concept was the notion of the 'colour bar', which he defined as the imposition of 'social and psychological barriers between the races' (Richmond 1961: 18). Patterson, on the other hand, characterized the situation in Britain as an 'immigrant' one, 'not, or not yet, basically a colour or race one' (Patterson 1963: 17). For both authors, the notion of race, signified by colour, was, analytically speaking, taken for granted, although both disputed its pejorative use as a means of imputing inferiority. Neither of these studies discussed the status of race as a theoretical concept in social science.

This, then, is the central importance of the work of Rex, and particularly his text *Race Relations in Sociological Theory* (hereafter *RRST*). Rex identifies the historical conjuncture that led to his writing the book as the meeting of the UNESCO Experts Committee on the Nature of Racism and Race Prejudice in 1967 (Rex was a member of the Committee). The Committee reiterated the conclusions of previous meetings which was that 'the concept of race as biologists used it had no relevance to the political differences among men' (Rex 1983: viii). Rex draws out the implications of this by pointing to the fact that in popular discussion notions of race are overwhelmingly concerned with these political differences and thus sociologists are obliged to reframe their questions (Rex 1983: 4). That is, since race, as a biological term, has no relevance to the explanation of social differences then sociological explanations of such differences, which employ a notion of race, are, ipso facto, inadequate. Principally, this is because, as Rex notes, they take as given what needs to be explained, or, as Rex puts it, 'the question we have to face is what the characteristics are of those situations which men call racial' (Rex 1983: 4).

This leads Rex's account in a fresh direction and opens up the distinctively sociological issue of how to provide 'an adequate explanation of how it is that men come to be classified as racially different' (Rex 1983: 5). Here, it would seem, is a clear rejection of accounts that begin from the assumption that race is an accurate scientific description of human populations, in favour of interpretations which recognize the socially mediated nature of race categories. Put somewhat differently, we no longer derive a knowledge of race relations from a given object *race*, but instead proceed from the insight that race is itself a theoretical construct whose production (and very 'taken-for-grantedness') needs to be examined. However, *RRST* does not take this step. This leaves the critical terms 'race' and 'race relations' hanging ambiguously between the open arms of full blown constructionism – if races do not exist, then our constructions of them are entirely arbitrary – and the reassuringly firm grip of structural sociology – there are 'situations which men call racial'.

This ambiguity is reflected in the claim in *RRST* that race relations consist of three elements. The first two refer to social structural conditions, whilst the third emphasizes the relevance of actors' accounts. The first element is the necessary, but not sufficient, existence of a situation of 'severe competition, exploitation, coercion or oppression'. This is the structural condition for race relations. Second, this competition must occur between groups, not individuals, and there must be limited opportunities for inter-group mobility. Third, these two structural prerequisites can be defined as a race relations situation when they are interpreted, or, 'rationalized ideologically', by social actors in terms of a deterministic theory of human attributes

(Rex 1983: viii). On the basis of this description, Rex concludes that race relations 'refers to a distinct group of social phenomena, with demonstrably different attributes from other phenomena' (Rex 1983: 7).

It is unclear, though, in what sense this is the case. Despite the insistence on the significance of structured social relations, what marks out a race relations situation, say, from a class or gender situation is the way in which social actors interpret it. The two structural features Rex identifies are characteristic of most, even all, societies and most, even all, group relations. They apply with equal force and accuracy to class relations as well as to gender relations. The crucial factor which marks out such features as a race relations situation is then actors' interpretations of these structural conditions in race terms.

This basically Weberian focus of *RRST*, in which the structural conditions of market capacities and situations are already present, awaiting the galvanizing current of actors' beliefs and dispositions to give them significance, tilts causal priority towards the structuring conceptions of social actors. It is actors' accounts that actively define a competitive situation as one thing rather than another: a 'true race relations situation exists when men have beliefs of a certain kind' (Rex 1983: 9). Now, although Rex acknowledges that such beliefs are associated only with a limited range of structures and so not arbitrary or adventitious, he does not specify the nature of the links between structure and actors' beliefs or rationalizations.

This leaves *RRST* with a somewhat undifferentiated notion of social action and social actors. This results in a loss of depth and complexity. For example, which social actors need to interpret competitive situations in race terms for these situations to be defined as ones of race relations? Clearly some sorts of actors are more influential in the reproduction of racist discourses and discriminatory practices than others, but which ones? How many of them need to rationalize market situations in race terms for a race relations situation to exist? Is the strategic relevance of these actors connected with the structures of the competitive situation itself? These are also the sorts of questions that Park found difficult to answer convincingly.

There is a further problem. The emphasis that Rex places in *RRST* on the meanings actors use to make sense of certain structural situations is predicated on a broader claim about the ontological status of such structures. It is not possible, claims Rex, 'to make an absolute distinction between structures of social relations as they really are uninterpreted by participant actors' theories and concepts, and the ideas and concepts and theories in terms of which interpretations are made' (Rex 1983: 8). Much rests here on the phrase 'absolute distinction', but Rex uses the (sociologically unexceptionable) claim that social knowledge is concept dependent to support the (sociologically contentious) argument that it is actors' interpretations that define social scientific descriptions of social relations.

This is a crucial point. Miles has drawn attention to one paradoxical consequence of this epistemological privileging of actors' accounts, namely the reification of race. As Miles puts it, race is:

> given an objective status as an active subject . . . By creating a sociology of 'race relations', one is creating a form of analysis which simply reflects back the

phenomenal, everyday world, and, in so doing, the world of appearances is legitimated. Thereby, the sociology of 'race relations' becomes a moment in the reproduction of the appearance of the social world.

(Miles 1982: 33)

The significance of this for sociological accounts of racism will be dealt with later. For the present I want to concentrate on some further implications for social theory which flow from the claim that since people believe there are races, then social relations between groups so categorized can be identified as race relations. These implications also apply to Park's approach which, as we have seen, rests on a similar claim about the relationship between actor beliefs and the sociological description of social relations.

There are two implications in particular that I wish to explore (although there are others: see Miles 1982). First, the emphasis on actors' interpretations as determinative of whether a 'race relations' situation exists not only raises the question, mentioned above, of which actors are referred to, but also the question of temporality, that is the relationship between contemporary and past interpretations of structural conditions as 'race' based. Second, Rex's insistence on the primacy of such interpretations makes it difficult to investigate structures as causally antecedent to these interpretations. Let me elaborate on these points.

Although Rex takes history to be a central element in his analysis in *RRST*, for instance with his account of colonialism and its consequences for the creation of potential 'race relations' situations, it is also true that a historical account of the emergence of 'race relations' situations is problematic for his approach. This is because if it is the presence of actors' beliefs about race that determines the categorization of certain sorts of social relations as 'race relations', then 'race relations' situations must be contemporaneous with beliefs about race. We arrive, in Archer's words, at the 'autonomy of the present tense' (Archer 1995: 86). The consequences of this for Rex's argument (and for Park's) are serious.

For instance, take one of the key characteristics of Rex's definition of 'race relations' situations, that 'they refer to situations in which one or more groups with *distinct identities and recognisable characteristics* are forced by economic and political circumstances to live together in a society' (Rex 1983: 160, my emphasis). In what sense, it may be asked, are these identities distinct and those characteristics recognizable? The assumption is that 'race' somehow fastens on to these already constituted distinct identities and recognizable characteristics and uses them as the basis for the ascriptive allocation of roles and rights (Rex 1983: 160). This leaves the social and political construction of 'distinct identities and recognisable characteristics' unaccounted for and implies that distinguishable groups pre-exist 'race' thinking since they are precisely what such thinking interprets deterministically in a 'race relations' situation. It seems to me that *RRST* here comes close to saying that race relations exist in terms of 'distinct identities and recognizable characteristics' before they exist, that is have come to be understood as such by actors. The object of action – social relations – and action itself – agents' conceptions of race – are folded into each other.

Yet several writers (see, for example, Carter, Green, and Halpern 1996; Fields 1990; Higham 1994; Miles 1982; Small 1994; Webster 1992) have demonstrated how 'races' have to be made and, relatedly, how race thinking precedes temporally the 'seeing' of people as distinct and different. These accounts abandon an undifferentiated notion of the social actor in favour of recognizing that actors occupy different strategic positions. Higham, for instance, provides an account of the transformation in the USA of the specific cultural features of immigrants into a general fear of immigration. This was a transformation for which 'race thinking' was particularly well suited and which was 'largely the work of cultivated minds rather than a simple derivative of popular instincts' (Higham 1994: 94). Further, he notes that:

> Sharp physical differences between native Americans and European immigrants were not readily apparent; to a large extent they had to be manufactured. A rather elaborate, well-entrenched set of racial ideas was essential before the newcomers from Europe could seem a fundamentally different order of men.
>
> (Higham 1994: 133)

So then, some recognition of the temporally a-synchronic relations between the beliefs of different social actors – 'popular' and 'cultivated' – and between these and the process of 'race making' would seem to be essential for an adequate history.

This would entail abandoning the 'autonomy of the present tense' but this is exactly what Rex has difficulty doing in so far as he is committed to the position that what actors believe is what makes a 'race relations' situation. This vulnerability is also evident when *RRST* attempts to deal with the relationship between structural conditions and 'race relations' situations. First, Rex's account does not clearly specify under what circumstances such general structural features of the social order come to be accounted for in race terms, although Rex does identify other structural features, such as colonial relations, likely to have a potential to become 'race relations' situations. Second, the investigation of structures as causally antecedent to actor interpretations is difficult if you start from an assertion of the primacy of actors' interpretations in defining a 'race relations' situation. Thus Higham's tracing of the ebb and flow of anti-immigrant currents of thought in US politics not only identifies their varying spatial and social distribution but is also able to recognize both their internal limits – ideas about discrimination clash with ideas about democracy – and their external limits, critically conditioned by the confidence of US capitalism and the need for foreign labour. In effect, Higham shows how 'race thinking' emerges from definite historical and political conditions and social interests (Higham 1994). This sort of historical tracing, or genealogy, of the development of 'race thinking' is difficult in Rex's scheme because, in viewing 'race relations' situations as constituted by actors' beliefs, it encourages an approach focused on the present, one with a restricted, even inactive, notion of temporality.

Rex's key text represents an influential, subtle and rare effort to conceptualize race as a social relational form and to develop appropriate sociological methods of analysing it. I have argued that in important ways it fails to do this, principally because it does not develop a thorough critique of the race concept and so reproduces within social science the same problems and inconsistencies that beset the term in its everyday usage. Yet its core claim, shared with the work of Park and of Banton (Banton 1997), namely, that people believe there to be races and that these beliefs define how certain sorts of social relations are to be defined by the sociologist, is still influential within both British and American sociology. Indeed, it is not implausible to claim that it remains, in its various local guises (and invariably less cogently expressed), one of the dominant approaches within sociology, a case I shall argue more fully later.

For now, I want to point to some of the consequences for social theory of accepting Rex's arguments for a field of 'race relations' within sociology. Miles has developed a sophisticated critique of the 'race relations' problematic from a Marxist perspective (Miles 1982; Miles and Phizacklea 1984). He suggests strongly that by identifying a transhistorical field of 'race relations' as an object of study and starting point for sociological analysis, Rex 'in common with sociology as a method of investigation' abstracts social relations from production (Miles 1982: 29). Miles' point is twofold. The first issue is that 'race relations' is an abstract category that does not correspond to any social scientific object. The second point is that for Miles it is a characteristic feature of sociological method to proceed through a rationalist definition of objects of study which are then applied to concrete social reality. Miles contrasts this with Marx's method of rooting concepts firmly within the analysis of the relations of production, an ontologically privileged realm invested with correspondingly greater explanatory weight.

By pointing to some of the consequences of race thinking in sociology, I want to extend Miles's critique. And by indicating an alternative sociological approach to the study of racism, I want to defend 'sociology as a method of investigation'. (Miles's own work, and particularly his use of the notion of racialization is considered more fully in Chapter 4; I have not dwelt on it here since Miles does not regard his work as a sociology of race or race relations.)

A RACE BY ANY OTHER NAME . . .

Although Miles published his critique in 1982, and repeated it in a number of subsequent texts, a cursory glance at recent texts and publishers' catalogues would seem to indicate that its key point – that race itself does not do anything or have any consequences – has been missed. Moreover, the attempt by Rex to develop an adequate sociological conception of race relations seems to have been neglected. Race continues to flourish as an autonomous, active variable within sociology. Several examples will suffice to make the point.

In their popular text *Introduction to Race Relations* (published in its second edition in 1990) Cashmore and Troyna discuss the term *race*. Having noted its customary fragility when subjected to scientific scrutiny, they go on to observe that 'the belief in race has been – and still is – a powerful force' (Cashmore and Troyna 1990: 32).

This is an accurate, even uncontentious, claim as far as it goes (although we might wonder what a 'belief in race' actually looks like), yet the authors immediately argue from this 'that race is real . . . for, if people recognize that race exists . . . it is real' (Cashmore and Troyna 1990: 32). This is a version of the interactionist approach considered earlier: from the prosaic observation that many people continue to believe in the existence of races we come to a sociology based not on the equally prosaic notion that therefore, sociologically speaking, the *belief* in races is real (a claim not without its own empirical and epistemological strains) but on an altogether different claim that *race* is real. This is a common consequence of the (usually implicit) view that structure and agency are mutually constitutive.

As a consequence, structures of discrimination and disadvantage become the *effect* of the beliefs held by actors about difference, hence their frequent description as 'racial'. 'A racial group', note Cashmore and Troyna 'is a label stuck on a collection of people by others . . . who feel themselves to be different, maybe superior, to those people' (Cashmore and Troyna 1990: 28). As *effects*, therefore, it is difficult to see how these structures can be causally efficacious or influential. Of course, it is possible to adopt the Parkian solution and regard such effects (customs, traditions, conventions) as a distinct order of social phenomena. But in this case we have an issue of the relation between structure and agency rather than simply a process in which some social actors symbolically construct other social actors as different, and without some account of the ways in which structure influences agency actors' interpretations or beliefs attain a free-floating, undetermined status. Thus the notion that a racial group is merely any collection of people so labelled by others becomes shallow and unhelpful. Which people are labelling whom? Why are some people's labels more powerful than other people's labels? How do you 'stick a label' on a collection of people?

A similar line of argument is followed by Guibernau, in a recent volume exploring nationalisms in the twentieth century (Guibernau 1996). After again noting 'the substantial arguments that question the scientific validity of the concept of race', Guibernau contends that 'classification according to physical differences maintains an indisputable strength which derives from the visibility of physical traits' (Guibernau 1996: 86). Once more, the conflation of agency and structure obscures the ways in which actor's understandings are shaped by structural contexts. So, Guibernau's contention begs several important questions: why are only some physical traits – such as skin colour – visible when others – such as eye colour, or hair colour – are not? In what sense are they visible and to whom? How does the 'visibility' of certain *physical* traits generate specific *cultural* systems of classification? What about systems of classification that do not rely on 'visible' physical traits, such as anti-Irish racism in Britain or the conflicts in Rwanda or former Yugoslavia?

An adequate sociological answer to these questions requires some means of examining how pre-existent structures condition, without determining, the repertoire of accounts available to social actors in making sense of social interaction. This, in turn, rests on making an analytical distinction between agency and structure in order to grasp how agency is structured. I am arguing that the use of a concept of race makes such a distinction problematic. Significantly, within a page or two,

Guibernau is re-presenting race in its new, autonomous form: 'Class, gender and race reflect power structures within a given society and play a crucial role in the constitution of individual identity' (Guibernau 1996: 89).

Here is a final example to close the point. The study of local politics in Birmingham by Solomos and Back has as an aim the explanation of the 'power of ideas about race and ethnicity in shaping political mobilisation and participation' (Solomos and Back 1995: ix). Here then is an undertaking to explore the ways in which agency, particularly political agency in the form of participation and mobilization in the public political domain, is structured by ideas, even ideology.

The authors go on to quote approvingly the work of Goldberg and his recognition of the ways in which categories such as race and ethnicity work to 'define populations, groups and, by extension, social agents as self and other at various historical moments' (Solomos and Back 1995: xi). Again, a little imprecision goes a long way. It is not the categories themselves that do the work, they are merely concepts, but social actors, and this returns us four-square to the question of how such categories, or discursive struggles, come to be socially organized, to have a determinate relationship with particular social conditions. If this question cannot be raised then a familiar reification occurs: categories and ideas become independent things, capable of dynamically interacting with 'class and social change' and 'shaping political identities, party politics and political representation' (Solomos and Back 1995: 3).

To repeat: it is not that *ideas* about race do not influence political mobilization, identities and the like, but that the social and historical grounding of this way of seeing social relations is masked if race is reified. Instead of being able to explore these groundings in an adequate, social scientific manner, we are instead confronted by a variable with an independent ontological status. Revealingly, Solomos and Back then proceed with numerous subheadings in which 'race' has precisely this status – 'class, race and ethnicity', 'race, community and conflict', 'Smethwick, race and electoral politics'.

These examples are by no means isolated ones, and my purpose here is not to identify these as texts that are in some way defective. Nevertheless they illustrate the continuing reluctance of sociologists within a sociology of race and race relations to confront what they mean by the term race. Indeed, I have argued that, through a tacit commitment to some loosely interactionist assumptions, these writers transform claims about race as an idea into a reified concept of race as sociologically real and capable of dynamically interacting with other variables such as gender and class. It comes to be seen as a universal category and, as we shall see in Chapters 8 and 9, this often inclines researchers to assume that in any society their initial conceptual task is merely a question of deciding which relations are to be termed racial.

If sociologists working within the field of race and race relations have not come fully to grips with the ontological status of race and the epistemological problems that it raises for social science, what of sociologists working outside these fields who have had something to say about race and racism? Two areas are of special relevance here: feminism and postmodernism. Although these will be dealt with in greater detail in the next chapter, I want to suggest here that they too display an aversion to social scientific critique of race notions.

In striking contrast to the bashfulness of race sociology, feminists have subjected the key categories of sex and gender to sharp and sustained scrutiny (see, for example Butler 1990; Segal 1990) and combined this with an assault on 'mainstream/ malestream' sociological knowledge (see, for example, Bhavnani 1994; Harding 1987, 1991; Hekman 1994). More recently, and in response to debates within feminism itself, there has been a growing interest in issues of racism and race amongst feminist writers. Similarly, amongst those influenced by postmodernism (and this includes, of course, a number of feminists) there has also been an increasing concern with issues of identity and difference and these have also touched upon race (Afary 1997; Bederman 1995; Brah 1996; Maynard 1994; Skeggs 1997; Ware 1996).

Again, my contention would be that both these perspectives (with some important qualifications and exceptions that will be dealt with later) use race in very much the same way as orthodox sociology and so encounter similar problems and reproduce similar shortcomings. Once more, one or two examples will have to suffice at this stage.

In a recent volume Afshar and Maynard define race as an ascriptive category that is socially constructed and temporally, spatially and culturally specific. As we have seen this is a common depiction: (some) social actors use race, as they might use sexist notions, as a means of ascribing characteristics to other social actors. The actual characteristics being ascribed and the specific ways in which they are ascribed will vary from time to time and from place to place.

This is a well-established and sociologically unremarkable claim. In view of this, one might expect a critical sociology to develop some account of how actors come to see the world in this way. Such an account would be the proper object of sociological knowledge rather than the fallible, partial appreciation which actors have of their structural setting. After all, feminists (rightly) tend not to take actors' versions of what is 'masculine' or 'feminine' at face value. In recognizing that these are historically variable, socially constructed ascriptive categories they properly direct analytical attention to the processes of social construction rather than endow the categories themselves with a separate ontological status.

However Afshar and Maynard argue for a distinction between race and racism (Afshar and Maynard 1994). The basis for this distinction appears to be simply that race can be chosen as an affirmative identity by individuals or collectivities (so too can masculinities, presumably). Race is therefore a means of political mobilization and resistance and, they argue, its subsumption under the term racism does not permit this phenomenon to be interpreted or understood (Afshar and Maynard 1994: 2–3).

Now, to argue that you want to retain a notion of race to refer to those instances where social actors choose to affirmatively identify themselves, or make sense of their social milieu, in terms of race is possibly defensible, though not comfortably so (Is Nazism affirmation? Is it a race phenomenon in the sense that Rastafarianism might be viewed as a race phenomenon?). Nevertheless, race is swiftly put to tasks beyond this. There is talk of 'racial dynamics' and 'racial domination' (why not 'racist dynamics' and 'racist domination' since a self chosen category of affirmation can hardly generate dynamics and domination?). Maynard later poses the question of how race and gender interact (Maynard 1994: 12), but on her earlier definition it is difficult to see exactly what this means other than how understanding oneself in race terms affects, and is affected by, one's gender.

Further in the same article she makes the following claim: '"race" does not simply make the experience of women's subordination greater. It qualitatively changes the nature of that subordination' (Maynard 1994: 13). Race thus casts off its former minor, constricting garb as merely one of the ways we make sense of who we are and emerges resplendent as a fully fledged causal variable able to 'qualitatively change the nature of women's subordination'.

Although I will deal with the issues of appropriate terminology later, it is worth pointing out that Maynard's case would be compelling if she were to substitute *racism* for *race*. Indeed many of the examples she cites as evidence are examples of *racism and discrimination* not instances of race: 'It has been shown, for example, how "race" significantly affects black women's experience of and treatment in areas such as education, the health service and the labour market' (Maynard 1994: 14).

Those writers influenced by postmodernism (a description to be treated with more discernment in the next chapter) have addressed issues of race and racism via their more general concern with identity and difference. Indeed, a recent text recommends that sociologists abjure discussions about the ontological status of race, partly on the grounds that 'Reiterating that "there's no such thing as race" offers only the frail reassurance that there shouldn't be a problem. It cannot deal with the problems that do exist, because it fails to see them as a problem' (Donald and Rattansi 1992: 1). Instead, sociologists should be concerned with how race categories operate in practice, how 'racial logics and racial frames of reference are articulated and deployed' (Donald and Rattansi 1992: 3).

For Donald and Rattansi the retention of a notion of race is necessary to refer to the 'unstable and "decentred" complex of social meanings constantly being transformed by political struggle' (Donald and Rattansi 1992: 1). Race now becomes 'part of the process of constructing an operative symbolic and social reality: literally a common sense' (Donald and Rattansi 1992: 3). So critiques of the concept race seriously underestimate its power as a discursive category, targeting the irrationality of racist beliefs, whereas 'the fictional or metaphorical status of the category "race" in no way undermines its symbolic and social effectuality' (Donald and Rattansi 1992: 3). The concern with the ontological status of race as an object of sociological enquiry is therefore not only misplaced, but also misleading. Instead, sociologists should be addressing the analyses 'of contemporary political struggles over questions of representation, symbolic boundary formation, and identification. It is in this conflictual dialogue that the meanings of "race", racism and antiracism are forged, broken and remade' (Donald and Rattansi 1992: 4).

Central to this enterprise of 'getting to grips with an ever-changing nexus of representation, discourse and power' (Donald and Rattansi 1992: 3) is a concept of culture. Culture is not understood in its conventional sense as something that expresses the identity of a community. 'Rather it refers to the processes, categories and knowledges through which communities are defined as such: that is, how they are rendered specific and differentiated' (Donald and Rattansi 1992: 4). Culture thus acquires a more assertive, Foucauldian character, in which particular discursive knowledges or ways of knowing the world, such as race, also operate as the practical categories by means of which we define and place ourselves in relation to others. Knowledge is power; it organizes or maps the social world for us, enabling us to become effectual social actors. This claim that knowledges are productive in that they are the very means by which we are 'rendered specific and differentiated' carries several implications.

First, in common with much postmodern theorizing, it is strongly anti-essentialist; that is, in emphasizing the contingency of any instituted cultural authority, Donald and Rattansi challenge the fixing of characteristics which they hold to be the distinguishing feature of race discourses. Second, by insisting that race and identity are inherently contestable social and political categories they also offer a challenge to 'race thinking' within sociology that, as we have noted, often reifies race by representing it as a homogeneous cultural form. Indeed Rattansi argues strongly, in an essay later in the same collection, for a greater sensitivity to the complexity and ambivalence of discourses surrounding race (Rattansi 1992). It is worthwhile pausing to consider what Rattansi sees as the sources of this complexity and ambivalence.

Whilst recognizing that racist discourses (and it is not clear how these are to be distinguished from race discourses, if they are to be distinguished at all) are 'produced by a complex combination of social and psychic structures and forces' (Rattansi 1992: 37), Rattansi identifies two sorts of factors ensuring the complexity and ambivalence of such discourses. The first of these arises directly from the fact that racist discourses are 'contextually produced and differentially deployed in particular situations and institutional locations' (Rattansi 1992: 37). This situational and contextual logic allows for the possibility of inconsistency and incoherence amongst discourses and so offers a potential for (discursive?) conflict and change. Individuals will have different reasons for advancing or opposing racist discourses; different interests will be served or hindered, different ambitions realized or frustrated. The second source of instability arises from the inevitable admixing of racist with other sorts of discourses, particularly those of gender and class, so that it rarely operates or appears in a pure form but is 'fractured and criss-crossed around a number of axes and identities' (Rattansi 1992: 37).

This approach has a good deal to commend it and I am sympathetic to many of Rattansi's arguments against multicultural and antiracist education, or those forms of it which rely on homogeneous, unproblematic notions of culture, racism and ethnicity. Nevertheless, problems remain, some of which have to do with the employment of a particular notion of discourse, of which more later, others of which are specific to Rattansi and Donald and Rattansi's pragmatic decision to sweep issues about the status of race under the carpet. It is these that I shall deal with here.

The predicament of the carpet sweeping strategy is that there is always the risk that you do not manage to cover everything up and race, like dust, seems to get everywhere. So, having announced their brisk spring clean, Donald and Rattansi still find themselves discovering those tell-tale traces on the furniture. For instance, there is an oscillation in their text between the terms *race, racial* and *racism* and it is unclear what the distinctions between these terms are. Rattansi urges the necessity of separating racism from racial discrimination (Rattansi 1992: 36) on the (in my view correct) grounds that discriminatory outcomes cannot be transparently attributed to racist discourses. But what, then, are we supposed to make of racial discrimination? Is this discrimination based on a discourse of race? If it is, then why is this not *racist* discrimination, a formulation that implies a clear attribution of agency? If, on the other hand, we cannot tell whether race discourses were causally efficacious – because we do not have empirical or other sorts of evidence, say, or because such discourses are inextricably entangled with discourses of class and gender – what is the point of the prefix 'racial'? Similar queries can be addressed to other expressions used by Donald and Rattansi, such as 'racial' violence and 'racial' harassment. In all these cases, the concept of race reappears as an active subject, eliminating agency and forestalling the development of an adequate social scientific account of racism. Later, I want to suggest that this issue of agency is a recurring one for many who write within a broadly postmodern ambit.

SUMMARY AND CONCLUSION

In this chapter I have pointed to the continuing vitality of a concept of race within social science and to the privileged status it seems to enjoy in comparison with other denizens of the sociological realm. Since the Holocaust and the discrediting of race as a natural scientific category, sociologists have been confronted by the paradox that whilst science may have recognized the inutility of the concept, many human beings continue to employ it as a means of making sense of their lives and many political movements continue to exploit it as a means of gaining power.

Sociologists have responded to this paradox in several ways. Park regarded race as a social category employed by people as a means of making practical, everyday sense of group differences. His account, though, left the source of these group differences unaccounted for and so was undecided about the theoretical object of a concept of race. Rex, in his *Race Relations in Sociological Theory*, advanced a neo-Weberian sociological definition of race and argued a case for identifying certain sorts of social relations as race relations. A number of shortcomings to this approach were identified, largely deriving from the indeterminacy in Rex's account of the relations between agency and structure. Despite these, Rex's work remains one of the few systematic efforts to explore notions of race *within an explicit context of sociological theory*. Since then sociological theory and race concepts seem to have parted company. This move seems to have been all to the advantage of the concept; unaccompanied by its nagging partner of theory, it has enjoyed ready access to a much wider circle of social research.

The brief survey in this chapter illustrates this. Currently, race as an analytical category in social science is defended in one of two ways (although distinguishing between these two defences is not always easy). Either it is claimed that race refers to people's everyday, common sense classifications of human populations and that these constitute an adequate object of sociological knowledge; or race is defended as a discourse, a means of reading cultural difference and a mode of differentiation. Both positions thus easily acknowledge that race is a social category; both claim that debates about the meaning of race are largely beside the point. It is, however, those perspectives most closely associated with postmodernism that have run furthest with these last two balls, and which in many ways represent the most significant obstacles and objections to a realist view of social science. Chapter 2 turns its attention then to postmodernism and its impact on social scientific accounts of race.

2 Discourse, identity and difference: postmodernism and concepts of race

In Chapter 1 I pointed to a crisis in the use of a concept of race prompted by the abandonment of the race category in natural sciences and the revelations about its political and ideological uses in right wing political movements. This crisis placed the notion of race in an uneasy relation to social science, compelling various forms of corrective adjustment by those who wished to retain the concept. The most common strategy, already noted, was to abandon the use of race notions as adequate descriptors of biological divisions within humankind and instead to defend them as terms employed by lay actors in 'getting on in the world'. Race notions were simply an element in the everyday social lexicon used by social actors to negotiate daily interactions. This is the use of race ideas as phenomenological categories, as a 'frame' for the interpretation of routine social interactions.

Common though this position is, the defence of race ideas as interactional categories raises certain problems, as Chapter 1 noted. First, it reduces social relations to actors' conscious understandings of them – race relations are those relations understood in race terms by the actors involved (would we define class relations as merely those relations understood by actors in class terms?). Second, it makes it difficult to distinguish between social *relations* (as systemically reproduced, anterior distributions of material and cultural resources, including institutional roles and settings) and social *relationships* (the actual interactions between real individuals). Finally, it derogates the agential element in social interaction, that is the ways in which antecedent distributions enable and constrain through the generation of vested interests and particular situational logics. There is a marked tendency in sociological writing for race ideas to be hypostasized as *race*, whence they are endowed with all sorts of causal powers and an autonomous capacity to engage with social relations. There is an implicit reification and transhistoricization of race, such that specific ideational forms such as nationalism, xenophobia, Nazi anti-Semitism, apartheid in South Africa, objections to colonial immigration in postwar Britain, come to be grouped together on the grounds that they all have something to do with race.

Despite these shortcomings, the defence of a notion of race to refer to an interpretive category employed by social actors in routine encounters has received a new spin in the works of authors exploring race ideas as elements in discourses, as modes of signification and representation which can provide the bases for political and cultural identities. This has been especially, though not exclusively, associated with writers adopting a postmodern stance.

The present chapter considers such 'race as discourse' approaches within the wider setting of postmodernism. This is not to suggest that those writers using notions of discourse, difference and identity may all be regarded as postmodernists, a term that in any case has many, not always consistent, meanings. Nevertheless, the postmodern contribution to accounts of racism and race ideas is an important one, and its influence within current debates is undeniably wide. Furthermore, it is a contribution that in many ways is based on a rejection of orthodox approaches to social science and its alleged logocentrism and foundationalism. This chapter then provides a bridge between those sociological accounts drawing on the vitality of race concepts as part of the 'practical consciousness' of everyday life and the realist approach developed in the remainder of the book. Postmodern theorists reject both options, although for distinct reasons, and their objections therefore need to be assessed.

The chapter will begin by examining the work of Foucault on power and identity, since this has had a significant influence on postmodern writings. Some contemporary accounts of race will then be reviewed, and some central themes identified: race as a discourse, race as identity and as modalities of difference and positionality; race as belonging and as forms of imagined community; and the relationship between race and class and gender. Finally, the conclusion will draw up a balance sheet on the potential dividends and penalties accruing from postmodern approaches to racism and exclusion.

POSTMODERNISM AND SOCIAL SCIENCE

The term postmodernism, as one writer has recently noted, 'is employed so broadly that it seems to apply to everything and nothing all at once' (Rosenau 1992:17). Nevertheless, it is possible to identify some common themes that broadly define postmodernism in the social sciences, and after doing this I shall focus on what postmodern writers have contributed to sociological understanding of race ideas, racism and exclusion. Central to this contribution has been the work of Foucault and particularly his notion of discourse. Consequently I address this first. After that, I follow Rosenau's broad but useful division of postmodernists into sceptics and affirmatives.

Sceptical postmodernists are those theorists influenced principally by Nietzsche and Heidegger and whose critique of modernity culminates in a rejection of notions of objectivity, truth and reason. Affirmative postmodernists, on the other hand, are those writers who see the critique of modernity as prising open space for non-dogmatic, emancipatory projects, often based on visionary ethics or an identification with non-ideological political coalitions (Rosenau 1992). Of course, as Rosenau points out, there are many overlaps and convergences between these two camps, but this nevertheless remains a useful distinction.

Rosenau's claim is that the sceptics offer few prospects for the social sciences, since they reject most of the notions necessary for it to be practised at all. The affirmatives, on the other hand, whose political practice usually entails some normative commitment, have engaged with social science, often drawing upon it in pursuit of political or ethical choices and allegiances. This is particularly the case with race, where affirmative postmodernists have made some important contributions.

FOUCAULT, POWER AND DISCOURSE

The work of Foucault remains a strong source of inspiration for much postmodern writing on race, although Foucault himself was famously coy about his attitude towards postmodernism. My concern here is not with the whole Foucault oeuvre but more with the two key concepts that have exerted a powerful fascination for postmodernists, namely his concepts of power and discourse.

A central theme in Foucault's writings is his emphasis on the ways in which human beings are made into social actors, or, more formally, his concern with the construction of human subjectivities (Foucault 1982: 208). Foucault's stance is strongly anti-essentialist: he rejects not only the notion that the social world can be made intelligible by starting from the standpoint of individual consciousness, but also the idea that there is some essential self, some real 'me'. Instead his concern is with how social beings come to be made into certain types of subject – a consumer, a conservative, a parent, a heterosexual – through the various modes of seeing, knowing and talking about the world that are made available to them by society.

Foucault refers to such ways of seeing, knowing and talking as discourses; human subjectivities are thus discursively formed and profoundly historical. Rather than expressing the inner essence of an individual, subjectivities are the creation of specific discursive practices (Gordon 1980: 151). Systems of etiquette produce the 'well brought up' person, just as medical knowledges and practices produce the 'sane' person. Such a strategy renders problematic any politics based on transhistorical notions such as race, or indeed any concept resting on claims about putatively essential human characteristics. Hence Foucault's coolness towards those forms of feminism resting on some essential notion of 'woman-ness' (Hoy 1986: 195).

Discourses may come to congeal in specific ways, more or less loosely, often adventitiously, and in these cases they may constitute a regime of truth; that is they come to mutually sustain, support and validate a particular way of knowing about the world. Regimes of truth come to be powerful, even dominant, ways of seeing and knowing and, at the same time, the sources of their social and historical production are obscured: they become common sense, taken-for-granted, axiomatic, traditional, normal. Regimes of truth also become the means whereby what is to be regarded as true can be distinguished from what is to be regarded as false.

For Foucault, to be able to name something is also to be able to position it within particular discursive arrangements, to 'put something in its place' and thereby determine what is to constitute adequate or proper knowledge of it. This is what Foucault means by power as creative: it brings objects into the realm of acceptable knowledge but does so in ways that render them knowable only in terms of that knowledge. In this sense, too, knowledge and power become inextricably intertwined; to know something is also to be able to objectify it, to say definitively what it is. (See Foucault's discussion of the school examination as a 'normalizing gaze' for an illustrative account of this (Foucault 1977: 184–94)). Indeed, for Foucault, this is one of the most pernicious consequences of the human sciences, their panoptic laying claim to the knowing of more and more areas of social life, a knowing that controls through objectification (Foucault 1977).

Regimes of truth do not only have consequences at the level of knowledge or epistemology. They carry with them a whole range of practices issuing from their claims and assumptions. These practices Foucault identifies as moral technologies, an unusual coupling of terms whose meaning is perhaps best captured in Rose's phrase 'governance of the soul' (Rose 1989). Moral technologies are simultaneously modes of surveillance and the means through which social subjects come to be fabricated and individuated.

We come to see ourselves as students or parents or consumers partly through the social recognition of ourselves as students or parents or consumers gained through our complicity with the various calibrating measures of government. Thus to be a student means, amongst other things, registering with a recognized institution, appearing on mark sheets and official forms. To be a parent means, amongst other things, registering a birth, attending a clinic, changing tax arrangements; to be a consumer means, amongst other things, purchasing something, having access to money.

When Foucault talks of modes of subjectification, he is not merely describing the shaping of our mental selves, the ways in which we consciously come to understand what we are or assemble for ourselves some relatively coherent narrative of self. He is also insisting that moral technologies inscribe themselves upon the body. How we present ourselves physically, and how our physical, corporeal self is interpreted by others, is, to a greater or lesser extent, a product of the ways in which our subjectivities are determined by various moral technologies; only the superficial, as Oscar Wilde observed, refuse to judge by appearances. Moral technologies are also techniques of the body, disciplinary regimes for correct training. Being taught the correct way to eat with a knife and fork, to sit up straight, to raise your hand to ask a question, to queue properly, all are instances of moral technologies traversing the body and shaping it in specific ways. Foucault points, then, towards a semiotics of the body, seeing bodies as texts bearing, and baring, the inscriptions of a thousand tiny techniques of subjectification. 'A disciplined body,' he pithily notes, 'is the prerequisite of an efficient gesture' (Foucault 1977: 152).

These complementary processes of individuation and surveillance, in which the regulation of bodies and the formation of self go hand in hand, are designated by Foucault as governmentality (Foucault 1982: 219). Through governmental practices the self-regulating individual is produced, a subject with historically definite orientations and capacities, a person, in Nietzsche's phrase, 'able to make a promise'. This profoundly historical approach to an 'analytics of self' (Foucault 1982) was accompanied by Foucault's averral that governmentality and regimes of truth were to be studied 'genealogically'. This notion radically uncouples the practice of doing history from any teleological or transcendental purpose, through its insistence on the irreducible and inescapable contingency of history itself. History, in the big sense of evolution or progress, is going nowhere, has no final purpose or ultimate unity. In its place Foucault proposes an 'effective history' (Dean 1994), the uncovering or laying bare of the internal relations of particular regimes of truth and their associated practices of governmentality and self. This, for Foucault, is the appropriate method for the making of historical sense in the contemporary world (Rabinow 1984).

What might a genealogical approach to race look like? To begin with it would aim at evaluative neutrality. Once a notion of transcendental truth (a truth good for all times and all places) is abandoned then it would seem that with it disappears the point of critique, the site outside the objects of study from which such objects can be criticised.[1] A genealogical procedure would thus differ markedly from many conventional accounts of race and racism that do not problematize the site from which they judge – to regard a 'truth' as unscientific or irrational implies a notion of science or rationality. Rather than begin from the assumption that racism is pathological and aberrant, genealogy instead examines the ways in which discourses and practices generate an experience of race, make race a truth for us, an experientially valid means of interpreting social relations and negotiating the everyday social world.

Genealogy thus restores an important measure of hermeneutic credibility to 'race thinking', including racism, by posing the question of how social actors have come to understand who they are in terms of ideas about race. There is perhaps a danger here of giving too much credibility to racism by implying that racist and non-racist discourses are both just regimes of truth which, in the scrupulous pursuit of evaluative neutrality, one has no means of adjudicating between. Again, Foucault's unwillingness to abandon an epistemology that implicitly denies that knowledge can be assessed in terms of its relationship to its objects leads him to a potentially conservative politics.

The persistent relativism that such an epistemology entails is also expressed in Foucault's account of power. This has been noted elsewhere (see, for example, Dews 1989; Dreyfus and Rabinow 1982; Layder 1994; Owen 1994; Ramazanoglu 1993) but some central features of it are relevant to the present discussion. Foucault's main challenge is to what he describes as 'juridical – sovereign' notions of power. This is an orthodox conception of power that sees power as *held by* somebody and therefore *denied to* others. Foucault also refers to this as the repressive view of power, a model in which those who possess power are able to repress those who do not (Gordon 1980: 156).

Against this view, Foucault urges a model of power that regards it as diffusely distributed throughout social relations, and as constitutive of such relations. He explicitly rejects as contradictory a social world where power is absent.[2] Instead, Foucault argues, power should be regarded as productive. It generates knowledges and thus the distinctions between what is to count as true and what false. Power is also generally available – indeed, the power to resist is an unavoidable implication of power being exercised at all, since the exercise of power, for Foucault, is only necessary where resistance has to be overcome (Gordon 1980: 119). (See also Foucault 1977.)

Locked into this symbiotic relationship, power and resistance, like wrestlers vying for an advantage, goad each other into renewed effort (power and resistance thus have what Foucault terms an agonistic relationship). Power operates to overcome resistance whilst resistance prompts a more intense exercise of power (Foucault 1982: 221). In place of power as the struggle between those who have it and those who do not, Foucault offers an interpretation of power as 'spread throughout society in a capillary fashion' (Hoy 1986: 134).

Since power is not something that is possessed by a sovereign or a class, it is not manifested globally, nor is it concentrated at nodal points. Power, for Foucault, is omnipresent (Foucault 1978: 93); it is a 'machinery that no one owns' (Dreyfus and Rabinow 1982: 156). This is, as Layder has observed, a 'flat' view of power, one which sees it as permeating social relations at all levels and which characteristically expresses itself at local points as 'micro powers' (Layder 1994).

There are benefits to be gained from broadening our approach to power from a sole emphasis on the state and government to a concern with the diffuse ways in which social relations and social spaces, such as the school and the prison, are permeated by power. However, this may prove frustrating for those interested in practical politics, for whom the identification of points of greater and lesser strategic political significance is of paramount importance.

Let us suppose, for example, that you believe that poverty is a bad thing and ought to be abolished. It helps in reviewing possible political strategies to be able to distinguish key factors in the reproduction of poverty – such as the maldistribution of wealth – from the less essential ones – such as the amount of money the poor allegedly spend on cigarettes, alcohol or videos. A search for such a distinction is not necessarily incompatible with a concern for micro politics, of course. Yet it introduces a tension in Foucault's work, noted by others (the chapters by Smart and Said in Hoy 1986, for instance, as well as Dews 1987; Habermas 1987; Soper 1993), between the critical cast of his own outlook and the need for effective politics.

In summary, Foucault provides us with a distinctive procedure for analysing historical forms of truth, their moral technologies, forms of subjectification and practices of governmentality. The critical pull of these 'social analytics' (Dreyfus and Rabinow 1982) is to dislodge embedded truths by exposing their historical determinations, relocating them as discursive products of contingent processes. Foucault, in other words, reaffirms the social and historical character of knowledge.

In so far as this is taken to mean a rejection of the idea that knowledge, including racist knowledge, can have indubitable, universal foundations, it is sociologically unexceptionable. However, if it is taken to mean that knowledge, including non-racist or antiracist knowledge, is *merely* the product of the social conditions from which it arises, then the possibility of a critical social science withers. To the extent that my knowledge is different from your knowledge because my conditions are different from your conditions, there is a significant sense in which knowledge claims become incommensurable.

Despite this ambiguity, Foucault's writings have proved a rich resource for (affirmative) postmodernists wishing to investigate the contemporary construction of identities. Foucault's uncompromising hostility towards essentialist and reductionist notions of the subject have prompted several writers to explore racisms as discourses of representation (Goldberg 1990, 1993, for example), and would appear to terminally undermine the ontological status of the race concept.

Nevertheless, there are difficulties in applying Foucault's ideas to the study of race and racism, some of which derive from his more general philosophical position, others of which have to do with drawing a politics from Foucault's work. There are three difficulties in particular that I wish to consider.

To begin with, there is Foucault's claim that power operates as 'intentionality without a subject'. He does not mean by this that power relations do not affect individuals, nor that they operate independently of specific social actors. Indeed he argues that power relations are the 'possibility of action upon the action of others,' and are 'rooted in the system of social networks' (Foucault 1982: 222). What Foucault means by 'intentionality without a subject' is that power has no teleological source, no purpose 'above' society. So, for Foucault, as we have seen, power is not a thing, nor is it merely a product of class relations, a capacity held by the ruling class and deployed against the labouring class. 'A society without power relations can only be an abstraction', claims Foucault (Foucault 1982: 220–1) and it is in this sense that it has a subject-less intentionality. Power does not belong to anybody and does not serve any transcendental purpose; it necessarily emerges where social relations are antagonistic.

Although Foucault is careful to insist that such a view of power 'makes it all the more politically necessary' to analyse 'power relations in a given society, their historical formation, the source of their strength or fragility, the conditions which are necessary to transform some or abolish others' (Foucault 1982: 221), it is also clear that this approach presents significant obstacles to such an analysis. In particular, as Habermas has noted, Foucault develops a view of power 'no longer bound to the competencies of acting and judging subjects' (Habermas 1987: 274). Such a view makes it difficult to identify those political conditions favourable to the transformation of particular power relations and to recognize the stratified nature of social relations, the fact that social actors, individually or collectively, do not contribute equally to the construction of social life.

The neglect of social hierarchies of power that this involves has some damaging political effects, making the identification of strategic locations, of nodal points of power, a barren process (Layder 1994). Rather, Foucault directs us towards a politics based around those groups that have somehow evaded the unblinking panoptic gaze of Enlightenment surveillance – the criminal, the insane, the marginalized, the outcast: the draft dodgers of Western rationality offering an embattled resistance to the inexorable growth of disciplinary power. Such a strategy, it seems to me, finds it hard to escape the common bugbear of voluntarist politics: why bother at all? Why resist the growth of disciplinary power? On what basis could those of us thoroughly subjectified by contemporary regimes of truth unite with those who are less thoroughly subjectified? How are we to identify common interests? Although

Foucault sometimes brushed aside such questions as 'Enlightenment blackmail' (Miller 1993: 337), preferring to emphasize local struggles and the 'micro politics' of self, they still retain a good deal of pertinence.

Second, Foucault's distaste for, and lack of faith in, the great emancipatory narratives of the Enlightenment left him little to say about nationalism, either within Europe or outside it. This has two direct implications. One is that for Foucault's work the 'imperial experience', an experience that had deeply involved an earlier generation of French intellectuals such as Sartre, Camus and de Beauvoir, is 'quite irrelevant' (Said 1993: 47). A genealogical history of Foucault's own writings might yet reveal some complex filiations between French intellectual life in the 1960s and 1970s and the history of colonial subjugation (see Bhabha 1990: 243–4 for a discussion of the 'Eurocentricity of Foucault's theory of cultural difference', for example). Second, it makes it difficult to apply Foucault's ideas to the exploration of contemporary nationalisms and their ambiguous relations with historically specific modes of racism such as ethnic cleansing. It is hard not to see Foucault's eschewal of critique here as 'a swerve away from politics' (Said 1993: 336).

Third, there are the vexed, and related, issues in Foucault's work of agency and relativism. Baldly put, in the context of racism and antiracist politics: why, and to whom, should an antiracist politics matter? And to what purposes and ends should an antiracist politics be directed? Answers to these questions, I would argue, presuppose some evaluative purpose, since we would need to identify those political agents or constituencies with an interest in antiracism as well as those with an interest in resisting it. And evaluative purpose requires a critical social scientific practice able to assess the relative adequacy of different accounts of the world, of different regimes of truth, a practice Foucault is prevented from specifying by his idealist separation of knowledge from its object. Thus, although Foucault, by implication if not explicitly, relativizes racist knowledges, he cannot interrogate the object of such knowledges and identify them as misrepresentations of social phenomena that have structures and properties which exist independently of our individual understandings of them.

This suggests a renewed concern with structured relations of domination, and their connections with the real, material experience of inequality and difference characteristic of class societies, in accounting for what we might term the impulse of differentiation. In other words, racisms, as discourses that naturalize difference, both sanction inequality of practices and resource allocation and create practical hierarchies of exclusion and acceptability. Recognizing this, though, presupposes mechanisms and structures generating and reproducing material inequalities, scarcity and differentiation. The ways in which racisms interact with, as well as form part of, these mechanisms and structures remains a matter for empirical and theoretical investigation. Yet it is still the case that an account of such mechanisms and structures, and of the specific ways in which material inequalities are produced and reproduced, occupies a central place in any analysis of racisms.[3]

This is because without an account of structured social relations which recognizes their obdurate resistance to cognitive modification and their persistent asymmetries of power, our theoretical descriptions remain unconstrained by any reference to an extra discursive reality and float ineluctably towards voluntarism and identity politics. If we are unable to adjudicate between competing accounts of racism (and this is not to suggest that such adjudication is either simple or straightforward) it becomes impossible, as Geras (1995) has recently observed, to speak of truth and injustice; there are merely different (and incommensurable) versions of truth and injustice.

In summary, what is to be gained from a Foucauldian approach? A genealogical approach points to the (often contingent) connections between different discourses about, amongst other things, race, colour, difference, national identities, belonging, community, home, England, Great Britain, colonial empire. Scholars influenced by Foucault's work have developed analyses that bring together social features and phenomena that are often overlooked (the work of McClintock 1995; Said, 1983, 1993; Young 1990 provide good examples). They have, too, drawn attention to the discontinuities of what were previously considered seamless, monolithic narratives (Hall *et al.*'s 1978 insistence on novel forms of racism in postwar Britain, for instance).

Furthermore, the notion of racism as a moral technology, with an accompanying array of disciplinary techniques, can also throw new light on the relations between government deliberations, legislative action and everyday life. The regulation of notions of Self and Other, such a characteristic consequence of racist discourses, can thus be extended to an exploration of the forms of racialized subjectivities. Foucauldian approaches have much to say on how we become subjects for whom 'race thinking' is 'normal', for whom certain sets of cultural practices and ways of seeing come to seem naturally occurring qualities rooted in the psychic and physical 'truth' of the human subject.

In turn, the 'truths' of racist knowledges can be seen to constitute an element in the normative, disciplinary regimes of 'bio-power' (Foucault 1977; Martin, Gutman, and Hutton 1988). 'Bio-power', the governance of human populations through the production of 'docile bodies' – in prisons, schools, asylums – whose conduct can be guided by the state in the direction of its own administrative purposes, is central to modern political regimes. It is also a further instance of what Foucault refers to as the 'double bind' of humanism: the very knowledges that individuate us are also the very means by which our subjectivities are locked more securely into modern forms of power relations. While we continue to understand ourselves in terms of essentialized, racialized identities, themselves the product of racist knowledges, we simultaneously subjugate ourselves to the state's own political projects. Instead, Foucault insists that we do not:

> try to liberate the individual from the state, and for the state's institutions, but to liberate us both from the state and from the type of individualization that is linked to the state. We have to promote new forms of subjectivity through the refusal of this kind of individuality which has been imposed on us for centuries.
>
> (Foucault 1982: 214)

Leaving aside the suppressed yearnings for the humanist subject that appear to me clearly present here, it does indicate again Foucault's lack of sympathy with forms of transcendental politics rooted in 'shared meanings'. He offers instead an inquiry into the historical practices that have generated those modes of individuation – white, Aryan, black, Jewish, Croat – that recognize themselves in different types of shared meanings, again radically historicizing the question of how we come to believe some things to be real and not others. Immigration and nationality legislation in Britain may be regarded as just such a historical practice, playing a crucial role in reaffirming the facticity of race, reproducing racialized meanings of self and inserting these within discourses of nationhood and belonging, profoundly connecting relations of domination with the meanings of everyday life. Of course, this discursive reconstitution of national identities will always find itself confronted with contradictions precisely because those structures generating material inequalities will ceaselessly reproduce the differences that the homogenizing project of nationhood seeks to overcome.

Let me now summarize the main elements of Foucault's legacy for those seeking a postmodern account of race and racism. First, Foucault has provided a rich legacy of terms and ideas that have directed attention to the ways in which discourses are: temporally and spatially relative; embedded in, and reproduced by, ranges of practices or technologies; and the products of particular, historically contingent 'regimes of truth'. The anti-essentialist thrust of these notions, I have suggested, is blunted by Foucault's insistence that all identities – and this must also include non-racialized ones – are merely products of regimes of truth. The basis for a critique of actually existing, racialized identities, on the grounds that they misrepresent social relations and that therefore non-racialized identities are to be preferred, is lost.[4]

Second, this approach to identities leaves us with the difficulty of explaining why we have the sort of identities we have. We seem to have two choices. On the one hand, we go with the now unfashionable notion that identities are in crucial, yet broad, ways structurally shaped – so that, for example, being black in postwar Britain did imply a common experience of a second class citizenship. Or we go with the more fashionable, constructionist idea that we create our identities in some Nietzschean act of overcoming. This latter choice makes the task of understanding common struggles around the distribution of social goods much more formidable since the notion of commonality is rendered practically indeterminate. The connections between agency, resources and interests are left relatively unexplored.

Third, there is the issue of power. For Foucault, the key political struggle of modernity is the struggle against the hegemony of humanist discourses and 'the simultaneous individualization and totalization of modern power structures' (Foucault 1982: 216). These regimes of truth and their associated moral technologies possess the capacity to make individuals subjects. Indeed their power rests precisely in their ability to determine identities within specific, historically contingent knowledges, so that the more we reveal our identities, 'tell the truth' about who we are, within such knowledges, the deeper our attachment to them becomes. The more we construct truthful identities for ourselves within such knowledges – as mad, as criminal, as immigrant – the more intensely they come to hold the key to who we are. We thus become implicated, says Foucault, in an ethics of authenticity, an ethics based on notions of who we *really* are.

The problem with such ethics, for Foucault, is that they constrain our ability to transform ourselves by subjecting us to expert knowledges embedded in particular regimes of truth (such as psychoanalysis, criminology, medicine, racism). Placed in the seductive grip of such confessional technologies, we are always about to disclose the truth about our self and always under the subjugation of the expert. We are thus willing collaborators in shrinking the circle of autonomy and freedom, swirling centripetally towards the acme of Foucauldian discipline, the docile body.

Against this, Foucault sets the anti-humanist claim that there are no essential truths of what we are.[5] This means that the truthful identities of expert knowledge can be resisted, since they can be revealed, through genealogy, to be aesthetic constructs, imaginative narratives, 'armies of metaphors' to use Nietzsche's phrase, whose truths are necessarily partial. Instead, then, of an ethics of authenticity, characteristic of humanism and the human sciences and based on some notion of *the truth* about ourselves, we have an ethics of creativity. This entails a styling of the self, a styling which in order to strive towards autonomy must be transgressive of social practices based on humanist discourses and their attendant practices. We must, urges Foucault, reject 'truthful identities' such as homosexual, black, woman, heterosexual, Hutu, Serb, Jew, British.

This politics of transgression is not merely a matter of thinking about ourselves differently, since it must entail confronting not only the discourses reproducing, or making available, 'truthful identities' but also the practices that flow from those discourses and sustain them. Immigration controls in the UK, amongst other things, authenticated some notions of what it meant to be British; to transgress these requires not simply a refusal to accept their authenticity, it requires opposition to the discourses and practices of immigration control.

We arrive, then, at a politics aimed at resisting those discourses and practices that constrain or foreclose the possibilities for self-transformation, whilst encouraging those that heighten or extend our capacities for self-transformation and autonomy. For Foucault, 'Human dignity is our capacity to be otherwise than we are' (Owen 1994: 207). In so far as racism profoundly denies this capacity, it is a legitimate site of resistance and opposition for Foucault. It is inaccurate, therefore, to claim that Foucault does not offer grounds for a politics of resistance. However, this resistance must itself be a discursive social production, not one based upon, or derived from, what things *are* – unequal and exploitative social relations for example – or from what they are inherently capable of becoming.

I have suggested that this is not accidental, but is a consequence of Foucault's 'inadvertent idealist foundationalism' (Sayer 1995, personal communication) which leaves him unable not only to provide a critique of racialized identities but also failing to identify any transformative social agency other than the self styling subject. Foucault's fastidiousness with regard to the historical and discursive nature of what we can know, and his insistence that reality is undecideable and ordered through contingent truth regimes, leave him in a poor position to offer insights about the analysis of structural relations of domination. I now want to examine how successfully postmodern theorists deal with these deficiencies.

POSTMODERNISM AND THE CONCEPT OF RACE

The previous section has pointed to Foucault's ambiguous legacy for (postmodern) social science. In this section I shall consider the efforts of some contemporary theorists to apply Foucauldian insights to the study of race identities and racism. This survey is necessarily selective. First, because the area of race, identity and difference has been such a burgeoning one over the last decade or so that a thorough treatment of it would be impossible. Despite the proliferation of texts, however, certain themes – a focus on race as identity or a 'modality of difference', a rejection of what are regarded as class reductionist theories, and an anti-foundationalist view of sociological knowledge – stand out. Second, although not all the writers considered below would accept that their work has an explicit or identifiable Foucauldian provenance, nevertheless in so far as they explore these themes they may be taken as expressing certain postmodern attitudes towards the analysis of race and racism. I wish to include these as they represent significant currents in contemporary theory. (This is the case, for example with the work of Hall and Gilroy.) For ease of exposition I consider the various currents under three headings: race as discourse; race as identity, as a modality of difference and as positionality; and race as authentic experience or 'life world'.

Race as discourse

Before considering some examples of work utilizing a notion of discourse in the study of race, I want to return briefly to Foucault's use of the concept of discourse. Earlier I noted that Foucault used the term, roughly speaking, to refer to ways of talking, knowing and seeing. I want now to refine this definition, mainly because I think that Foucault's employment of a notion of discourse is more fastidious than is the case with some of his followers. Indeed, I want to suggest that Foucault's definition of discourse in *The Archaeology of Knowledge* is compatible with the realist account presented here in so far as it recognizes the irreducibility of discourse to either individual speakers or to linguistic structure in the Saussurean 'langue' sense (Foucault 1974).[6] In this sense, it posits, a stratified social ontology in which we have linguistic structure, discourse and individual speech activity, each with their distinctive properties and each irreducible to either of the others. Foucault expresses it thus:

> Discourse lies at the level of pure atemporal linguistic 'structure' (*langue*) and the level of surface speaking (*parole*): it expresses the historical specificity of what is said and what remains unsaid.
>   Discourses are composed of signs, but what they do is more than use these signs to designate things. It is this move that renders them irreducible to the language and to speech. It is this 'move' that we must reveal and describe.
>
> (Foucault 1974: 49)

It seems to me that this view of discourse has considerable relevance to sociological accounts of racism and race ideas and some of these have been indicated in the previous section; others will be drawn upon in Chapters 5, 6 and 7. Nevertheless, there is a certain 'openness' about this definition that allows for less moderate interpretations, examples of which I shall come to presently. For the moment, though, I want to identify two instances of this openness.

As we have seen, a discursive formation consists of 'rules of formation' for the particular set of statements which belong to it. In other words every discourse both enables and constrains actors and agents through the rules that govern its operation. These rules, to follow Fairclough's (1992: 41–9) useful typology, concern the formation of objects, the formation of enunciative modalities or 'subject positions', the formation of concepts and the formation of strategies. The last two of these refer to the ways in which intra- and inter-discursive relations of complementarity, competition, analogy and so on, operate to shape the meanings and possibilities available within a discursive formation. (Note that such relations are possible precisely because of the ontological status of discourse and its irreducibility, although there is little in Foucault's work to justify a strong claim that discursive relations may be realized independently of social agency.) However, it is the first two sets of rules of formation that have been subject to readings which have pushed Foucauldian discourse in a decisively postmodern direction.

Common to the discursive formation of both objects and of subject positions is Foucault's view of discourse as constitutive, 'as contributing to the production, transformation, and reproduction of the objects . . . of social life' (Fairclough 1992: 41). Race is one such object produced by the discourse of race ideas and the social practices enacted upon the basis of such ideas. So discourse is not only constitutive, in significant or important ways, of our ideas about reality, it is also productive of the ideas we have about all sorts of social relations and thus about the social practices – of measurement, accounting, examining and imprisoning – that we found upon these ideas.

Besides this constitutive role in the formation of objects, discourses also constitute subjects and their subjectivities. They accomplish this via the subject positions that are associated with discursive activity: for example, 'immigrant' and 'British' are two subject positions constituted by discourses about race and immigration in postwar Britain. Subject positions are historically specific, and therefore subject to change, and are able to exert a conditioning influence on those subjects positioned in particular ways.

Both of these constitutive functions can be interpreted in what I shall call 'weak' and 'strong' ways. In their 'weak' senses it seems to me that they have a great deal to offer sociological analysis. In particular, they can draw attention to what Taylor (1985a: 234) has termed the expressive aspects of language and the ways in which they serve to 'express/constitute different relations in which we may stand to each other: intimate, formal, official, casual, joking, serious, and so on'. Recognition of this expressive or constitutive role of discourse, I shall argue later, is centrally important in any social science account of race.

Reservations about the Foucauldian notion of discourse arise from the 'strong' interpretations. With these the de-centring of agency becomes the elimination of active social agency in any meaningful sense. The social world is seen as constructed by authorless discourses which themselves become agents; rather than tension between actors, agents and discourses, concretely negotiated in particular historical settings, there are merely discourses constructing objects and human subjects. It is this strong interpretation that is favoured by many postmodern authors and I want to argue that in their accounts the value of Foucault's ideas is seriously compromised. The examination of some postmodern texts deploying the strong interpretation will demonstrate this claim.

Knowles adopts an explicitly Foucauldian framework in her analysis of the role played by race discourses in labour politics. The term 'labour politics' is deliberately unspecific since Knowles herself does not define the term with any exactitude. Her focus is 'labourist discourse', which according to her account has constructed black communities in Britain (Knowles 1992: 27). Although this discourse is sometimes identified with 'Labour', it is unclear whether Knowles means by this the Parliamentary Labour Party, the Labour Party as a whole or the Labour movement generally or possibly some combination of all of these. This inattentiveness to agency, to who is doing what to whom, is not accidental. It follows directly from the strong interpretation of discourse where discourses themselves assume agential powers.

For instance, discussing the collapse of opposition to immigration controls amongst the Parliamentary Labour Party, Knowles notes that 'It was not the case that labourism, at this time, could not support the demands made upon it, to defend constituencies with reference to racial difference. It chose not to' (Knowles 1992: 116). The problem with this claim is the intentional role given to labourism, a discourse. Labourism as a discourse cannot choose; only human beings possess intentionality in this sense.

In Knowles' account there is a tension between the political need to identify who is responsible for what – a necessary prerequisite for examining 'whether the Labour Party may be an effective force for race equality' (Knowles 1992: ix) – and the role of authorless discourses as constructors of social reality. On the one hand we have the employment of a 'weak' notion of discourse to criticize essentialist claims about 'race'. Thus 'Notions of racial difference have no ontological existence. Like other concepts race is given meaning in the contexts in which it is used. It is constructed in the discourses in which it occurs' (Knowles 1992: 2). Or again, 'racial classifications are political constructs employed for specific purposes . . . Race . . . is used to organise a range of human distinctions construed in discourse' (Knowles 1992: 61). On the other hand, the use of a 'strong' notion of discourse ensures that the users and constructors pointed to are other discourses, which 'emerge around' race discourses and 'articulate' with them.

Not only does this leave the reader perplexed as to which groups, collectivities or individuals have actually enacted immigration controls, been guilty of discriminatory practices or opposed or promoted racist violence, but it vitiates Knowles' analysis in two important ways. First, in the absence of specifiable social agency, the 'strong' notion of discourse acquires an explanatory role by default. The result is a cartoon-like discursive animation in which discourses take on a life of their own; like cartoon characters, their features are exaggerated in order to emphasize particular qualities. Discussing the response of 'Labour' (again undefined – a discourse? A political party? A set of values?) to postwar colonial migration to the UK, Knowles comments that it 'actively constructed the significance of blackness in terms which made it an oppositional political community confronting Englishness, and requiring a defence of Englishness' (Knowles 1992: 88). The best that can be said of this is that it is an impressionistic claim: for who was blackness significant? In what senses? How, and by whom, might Englishness be confronted? Indeed, how, and by whom, might Englishness be defended? How does one confront a discourse? There is little room available here for the wide range of normative commitment actors and agents might adopt towards notions of Englishness, and a corresponding underestimation of the degree of reflexive interpretation available to social actors.

Second, and directly related to the animation of authorless discourses just mentioned, there is the difficulty of establishing a critical distance towards the social phenomena one is attempting to grasp. This is not so much of a problem for sceptical postmodernists, for whom the notion of critical distance is arrogant modernist meddling. However, for affirmative postmodernists such as Knowles it presents a particular problem, since without some evaluative stance it is difficult to see why the Labour Party's attitude towards 'race equality' should be of any political or academic interest. However, critical distance proves elusive in the world of authorless discourse precisely because discourses are not moral agents and so are unconvincing objects of moral disapprobation.

This is why Knowles' use of a notion of race is curiously anodyne. Because 'Racism, like race, is a concept constructed within specific discourses . . . Racism is whatever it is claimed to be in discourse' (Knowles 1992: 17). And this is as far as we get. We cannot arrive at a description of what might constitute a racist proposition or interpretation of the world since 'The question of what concepts race is associated with in political discourses is an empirical one' (Knowles 1992: 8). But neither can we make any judgements about its adequacy as an account of things since it is 'whatever it is claimed to be in discourse'.

Race as identity

Ideas of identity are central to postmodern discussions of race. However, there are a number of difficulties attached to their use. Conceptually, the notion of identity is rarely given an unambiguous meaning. Does it refer to those features of a person's beliefs and values that define who they consider themselves to be (their feminist identity, their academic identity, their Christian identity and so on)? Does it depict their 'positioning' within certain discourses of identity (as they are positioned or distributed across the 'discursive spaces' of sexuality, gender, race, class and so forth)? Or is it to do with the struggle over the qualities attributed, socially and institutionally, to individuals and collectivities?

Each of these questions brings its own problems. If identity is about how one chooses to identify oneself, then its usefulness for sociological purposes is sharply limited. What if you change your mind, or are rationalizing, or are mistaken, or are engaged in an exercise in wish fulfilment? On the other hand, side-stepping these issues in favour of a less subjective discursive distribution of subject positions diminishes the extent of actors' engagement with the cultural resources they encounter. That is why, as we have seen earlier, postmodern writers tend to fall back on some version of cultural integration where identities are held to be derivable from certain sorts of values. But which values? In what ways are they constitutive of our identities? Methodologically, these studies are generally compelled to rely upon large-scale descriptions of the doings of discourses that can rarely withstand serious historical scrutiny. Little wonder that Billig has argued that the notion of an identity is not helpful, since 'It is seldom clear what an identity is' (1995: 7).

I want to suggest that a viable notion of identity requires a richer notion of human agency than is permissible in the postmodern world of de-centred human subjects. We need a more complex view of social actors as human beings, one that is activist – that is, sees human beings as self interpreting beings who partially create a human self on the basis of their self interpretations – and stratified – that is, regards human beings as biological organisms, as persons, as social actors and as agents. I shall have more to say about a realist view of what for the moment I shall call selfhood in Chapter 8, but for the present let me propose a simple distinction between social identity and selfhood. In failing to make this distinction, many postmodern writers find themselves making extravagant claims about the relevance of identities and their apparently limitless plasticity.

Social identities are those symbolic descriptions actors and agents draw upon, or have imposed on them. They are therefore cognitivist in nature, since *somebody* must be actively doing the drawing upon, or doing the imposing, or resisting the imposing. Social identities have to do with the social organization and distribution of cultural resources and the ability of different actors and agents to mobilize these in pursuit of their interests. Clearly there will be limits both to what sorts of social identities can be created by actors and agents, and to the repertoire of viable social identities available. Here the notion of tradition or culture is fundamental since, in Fay's words,

> it is in terms of the contents of their tradition that people are the particular sorts of people they are and have the capacities and opportunities to engender the social and personal changes they can. The identity of humans is in part what they have appropriated from their past. They are constituted out of the historical heritage they make their own, and they transform themselves in terms of the material provided to them from this heritage. People are just those creatures which, among other things, take into themselves the conceptual and social resources of their societies.

(Fay 1987: 163–4)

Social identities are thus properly grasped in terms of the culture/structure – agency dualism that will be developed in Chapter 3. This approach allows social science to explore the determinate, historical relations between the particular cultural forms and resources within which human beings are set and the ways in which, in appropriating these, they partially define their identity. This is the sense in which, as postmodernists often observe, identities are socially constructed (although I would prefer to view them as being fashioned partly out of antecedent cultural resources). It is in this sense, too, that social identities belong fully within the purview of sociology.

However, not only do notions of social identity reach outwards towards the domains of tradition and culture, they also reach inwards towards the self, to what Layder has termed the domain of 'psycho-biography' (Layder 1997). Just as notions of social identity reach an upper explanatory limit where different sorts of social objects – institutions, class relations, property relations – come into play, they also reach an explanatory limit going the other way, where they encounter the individual psyche. It is this level of inner, existential experience which I shall refer to as selfhood.

Selfhood is my way of referring to the relatively autonomous area of inner experience, of recognizing it as a distinct ontological domain with its own properties and which places a limit on the reach of sociological explanation. It is this realm of subjective, inner experience that talk of self-identity tries to capture, so that, as Craib claims 'Social identities can come and go but my identity goes on as something which unites all the social identities I ever had, have, or will have. My identity always overflows, adds to, transforms the social identities that are attached to me' (Craib 1998: 4). This is another reason why we cannot see identity or experience as only a social construct, since to do so effectively denies the distinct characteristics of psychological phenomena and its own partly independent features. Two of these features in particular are pertinent to the discussion of identity.

First, there is the fundamentally ambivalent way in which we experience the world that arises from the human condition of being both of the world and yet separate from it in our sense of self, a struggle between separateness and connectedness (Layder 1997), between wanting to belong to the world yet at the same time wanting to preserve a sense of our own lived uniqueness. This ambivalence is a key element in making selfhood refractory to discursive influences. It also provides, as Craib has noted, a significant ontological objection to the achievement of identity, namely that in seeking determinate social identities individuals are engaged in a (futile) denial of the ambivalence of human experience (Craib 1998: 34). In fact, there is much to be said for Craib's suggestion that it is the politics of experience rather than the politics of identity that should claim our attention.

The second relevant feature of the psycho-biographical domain is that to be a full human agent is 'to exist in a space defined by distinctions of worth. A self is a being for whom certain questions of categoric value have arisen, and received at least partial answers' (Taylor 1985a: 3). Furthermore, this is not a contingent fact about us, one we happen to share in this place at this time, but is 'essential to what we would understand and recognize as full, normal human agency' (Taylor 1985a: 3).

In this sense, and contrary to the blighted human subject who barely casts a shadow in postmodern theory, how we strongly evaluate, how we decide what is important to us, is partly constitutive of our experience. Most importantly for Taylor:

That description and experience are bound together in this constitutive relation admits of causal influences in both directions: it can sometimes allow us to alter experience by coming to fresh insight; but more fundamentally it circumscribes insight through the deeply embedded shape of experience for us.

(Taylor 1985a: 37)

Note, too, the possibility of critique implicit in this formulation, for this constitutive relation of experience and description is itself conditioned and shaped by other social and cultural relations that are, as it were, beyond it. So all our descriptions 'are potentially under suspicion of distorting their objects [and] we have to see them all as revisable, . . . we are forced back, as it were, to the inarticulate limit from which they originate' (Taylor 1985a: 40). And this limit is, of course, the self.

To point to an ontologically distinct psycho-biographical domain of lived experience, necessarily ambivalent and authentic, is not to argue for some form of reductionism. Whilst a more elaborate answer to this must wait until Chapter 3, it should be apparent from the argument developed so far that to understand selfhood:

> involves seeing the individual in the context not just of the surrounding 'significant others' at different times of his or her life, but also in terms of position in the wider social structure and of the wider historical processes which provide us with the stage on which we act out our lives. We are each of us given a starting point and we do something with it.
>
> (Craib 1998: 28)

With these preliminary comments on an alternative approach to making sociological sense of notions of identity, let us turn to consider what postmodern writers have made of them.

An important source of contemporary concerns with identity derives from the work of Stuart Hall. Hall's writing has covered a diverse range of issues, but here I want only to consider his deliberations on identity and this as a preface to a more detailed consideration of Paul Gilroy's explicit efforts to defend a notion of race as identity. I am aware that the relationship of both authors to postmodernism is an ambiguous one (for example, they have carefully resisted extravagant claims about relativism and political values). However this relationship is understood, it is clear that their work has made a significant contribution to postmodern accounts of identity.

Hall was one of the first to recognize the problems raised by the critique of essentialist notions of race for cultural politics (although as writers such as Miles have noted, Hall's use of the term 'race' is not always consistent) (Miles 1993: 39–40). In particular this critique raises serious questions about the notion of a unitary black subject and experience and 'inevitably entails a weakening or fading of the notion that "race" or some composite notion of race around the term black will either guarantee the effectivity of any cultural practice or determine in any final sense its aesthetic value' (Hall 1992: 252).

If the black subject and black experience 'are not stabilized by Nature or by some other essential guarantee' (Hall 1992: 257), then what sense if any is to be given to notions of 'black identity'? In answering this question it is important to bear in mind what sorts of purposes we want any answer to serve. For instance, we might with consistency want to claim that if concepts such as 'black subject' and 'black experience' are not naturally existing nor defined by some supra-individual 'essential guarantee', then they are unreliable categories of social analysis. We might want to adopt a more moderate position, perhaps recognizing that the terms, whilst not capable of objective definition, nevertheless are used by politicians and other lay actors in a fairly loose way. As such they are a legitimate object of sociological analysis, although sociologists might want to adopt a critical attitude towards the terms themselves in trying to account for their use.

Hall's response is different from either of these. Since 'black' can no longer be seen as signifying or providing a common subject or experience, the task is to consciously construct alternative forms of identity, ones which can 'make common struggle and resistance possible but without suppressing the real heterogeneity of interests and identities' (Hall 1992: 255). This can be done through 'a new cultural politics which engages rather than suppresses difference and which depends, in part, on the cultural construction of new ethnic identities' (Hall 1992: 257).

This is a political notion of identity. Hall sees ethnic identities as replacements for the now discredited notion of race identities. What is called for now is:

> a positive conception of the ethnicity of the margins, of the periphery. That is to say, a recognition that we all speak from a particular place, out of a particular history, out of a particular experience, a particular culture, without being contained by that position . . . We are all . . . ethnically located and our ethnic identities are crucial to our subjective sense of who we are.
>
> (Hall 1992: 258)

This formulation does not take us very far. If we all speak from particular places, histories, cultures, experiences why do we need a notion of ethnicity and what do we need it for? And if ethnic identities are constructed 'historically, culturally and politically', presumably intentionally by social actors and agents, in what sense are we all 'ethnically located' and in what sense can ethnic identities be crucial to 'our subjective sense of who we are'? There is a further difficulty: the 'difference' that ethnicity is meant to transcend, yet without suppressing, is vague. Which differences are we talking about? Are some differences – wealth and income, say, or citizenship status – more significant than others such as the language we speak or our preferred religion or politics or the colour of our eyes? Which differences matter? In what circumstances?

Moreover, a notion of difference implies its opposite, similarity. Difference, as postmodernists remind us, is a binary term, defined in relation to its 'other'. However, Hall is unable to specify the basis of similarity since this requires some criterion of sameness. Either this is constructed too, in which case difference loses its force as an analytical category, or it refers to some essential features of human beings and we are back with claims about the non-discursive features of people which Hall understandably is reluctant to make.

This amounts, in effect, to a contradiction within the view that ethnic identities are socially constructed. Simply, if ethnicity is constructed it can only serve as a sociological concept under certain conditions, namely describing those situations in which actors come to interpret the world in terms of ethnic ideas, self under-standings, and so on. In this case a critical sociology remains possible since these ideas and understandings can be evaluated on the basis of a sociological account: we can examine the social and historical conditions of their production, assess their content, suggest and identify alternatives, make informed judgements about their consequences. Failing this, a notion of ethnicity has to rely on identifying certain invariant, extra-discursive features as significant.

There are two reasons why Hall cannot do this. First, because it acknowledges that there is something people share in common extra-discursively that justifies its description as ethnic identity. Second, this in turn requires some range of evaluative preferences that would enable us to decide what is significant, in what ways it is significant and for whom it is significant.

This tension between recognizing notions of ethnicity or race as socially constructed whilst simultaneously wanting to retain them for political purposes or sociological theory is also found in the work of W.E.B. DuBois at the turn of the century. DuBois argued for a viable notion of race identity in terms strikingly similar to those advanced by Hall for ethnic identity. Like Hall's claims for a positive notion of ethnic identity, DuBois rejects essentialist, biological notions of race, hinting that 'race identity' should be maintained only until the 'the ideal of human brother-hood has become a practical possibility' (DuBois 1966). Race identity has to be constructed, for DuBois, by 'race organizations', who through the education of the 'talented tenth' would provide political and intellectual leadership for the race as a whole. Without such leadership 'the best energy of the Negro people cannot be marshalled to do the bidding of the race' (DuBois 1966: 488).

Here we encounter again the incoherence that lies at the heart of Hall's formu-lation about ethnic identity. Like Hall, DuBois wants to substitute a social-historical concept for a biological one but this simply buries the biological one beneath the surface; it does not transcend it. He is thus compelled to face the same tension between race as a culturally and politically constructed identity and race as the essential, extra-discursive something that identifies it as a salient difference around which a political identity should be forged. Unsurprisingly, then, in answer to his own question 'What is the real meaning of Race?' DuBois, after running through the inconsistencies that arise from definitions based on physical and language differences, claims that there are 'subtle, delicate and elusive differences' that have divided human beings into races (DuBois 1966: 483–4). What, then, is a race? According to DuBois:

> It is a vast family of human beings, generally of common blood and language, *always of common history, traditions and impulses*, who are both voluntarily and

involuntarily striving together for the accomplishment of certain more or less vividly conceived ideals of life.

(DuBois 1966: 485 (my emphasis), see also DuBois, 1973.)

That this common-ness of purpose is far from self-evident (what we might call the question of agency) is recognized by Du Bois when he observes that 'No Negro . . . has failed to ask himself at some time: Who, after all, am I? Am I an American or am I a Negro? Can I be both?' (DuBois 1966: 488).

In other words, DuBois and Hall, despite their efforts to free race and ethnic identities from their essentialist moorings, find themselves unable to do so. To claim that such identities are historically, politically and culturally constructed, that is, free of any extra-discursive content, is to render them inutile as theoretical categories (although it may increase their political appeal). In order to avoid this both theorists are forced back to a tacit evaluation of significant difference ('common tradition', 'common history', 'common experience' where what identifies these things *as common* is precisely what needs to be explained). This is then used to supply the 'natural' basis for racial or ethnic identification. What makes our history common is our racial or ethnic identity; what defines our racial and ethnic identity is our common history. The circularity of this argument is obvious. 'The truth is', to use Appiah's formulation, 'that there are no races: there is nothing in the world that can do all we ask "race" to do for us' (Appiah 1986: 35).

Perhaps the most sustained contemporary effort to ask 'race' to do things for us in terms of identity and difference is found in the work of Paul Gilroy. In his earlier work (Gilroy 1987), the effort to use 'race' in the Hall–DuBois sense, namely as both a description (and constitutor) of common experience and as an analytical category, gave rise to some serious theoretical inconsistencies, cogently identified by Miles (Miles 1993: 40–3). More recently, Gilroy has endeavoured to steer a middle course between the two perspectives he regards as currently dominant. On the one hand, there is the 'volkish outlook' of various ethnic essentialisms in which 'overintegrated conceptions of pure and homogeneous culture . . . are construed as somehow automatically *expressive* of the national or ethnic differences with which they are associated'. On the other hand, there is the polyphonic celebration of diversity and difference associated with postmodernism (Gilroy 1993: 31–2).

Whilst Gilroy's grounds for rejecting the essentialist perspective are similar to those found in Foucault, the basis for his reservations about postmodern approaches is more distinctive and returns to the theoretical ambiguity in the earlier work about the meaning of race. In highlighting the social and cultural construction of race, the anti-essentialist postmodernists, for Gilroy, are in danger of becoming 'insufficiently alive to the lingering power of specifically racialised forms of power and subordination' (Gilroy 1993: 32).

The concept of racialization (discussed in Chapter 5) refers to those forms of social interactions and social relations that come to be understood by actors and agents in race terms, as Gilroy implies by his talk of race as a language, a discourse and an idea. However, it is hard to see why recognizing race ideas or discourses as social and cultural constructions should make theorists less alert to 'racialised forms of power and subordination'. Indeed, it might be argued that recognizing them as such is an indispensable condition for accounting for such forms of power and subordination, or is at least a significant element in such accounting.

Gilroy's counterposing of these two claims reflects the dilemma noted in the work of Hall and DuBois. Like Hall, Gilroy points to the 'inescapable fragmentation and differentiation of the black subject' (Gilroy 1993: 35); like Hall he is reluctant to let go of the notion of a common cultural experience, a notion threatened by the view of race as socially and culturally constructed. Now, though, the common-ness of this experience derives not from some putative 'race' essence but from 'racialised forms of power and subordination'. Races, that is, are a response to the experience of racism and discrimination.

So we still have race ideas (since how else are racialized forms of power and subordination possible), but no critical account of them *as ideas* (as opposed to expressions of biological capacities or differences). We can have a notion of black identities, but derived now from the experience of racism and discrimination and not from 'race' essences. '[B]lack identities are made,' says Gilroy, '– even required – by the brutal mechanics of racial subordination and the varieties of political agency which strive to answer them' (Gilroy 1993: 109).

I am not denying that the experience of racism and discrimination will generate common perceptions of interest amongst those who are on the receiving end of them. Nor am I denying that actors and agents can develop creative cultural and political responses to this experience. The question, however, is the place of race ideas and discourses in *sociological* accounts of these processes. Gilroy wants both to remove race, demoting it to a discursive resource that has no object, that is socially and culturally constructed, yet retain it as a description of the 'coherent . . . experiential sense of self' (Gilroy 1993: 102) that emerges from the effects of 'racialised forms of power and subordination'. This notion of black identities still hovers perilously close to those 'overintegrated conceptions of a pure and homogeneous culture' that Gilroy alerted us to earlier.

I have dwelt on the work of Hall and Gilroy because they represent the most sophisticated instances of the attempt to view ethnicity and race as political notions of identity. By this I mean that they view identity partly as an experiential response to racism and exclusionary practices. This is why such identity comes to be expressed in terms of ideas about race and ethnicity. Their defence of these terms is that they are experientially authentic, and therefore to be taken seriously as modes of political mobilization. There is much to be said for this, but my argument has been that this has left Hall and Gilroy unable to develop a *theoretical* critique of ideas of race and ethnicity and of their role in social theory. Without this the tendency to reify the concepts, to treat 'racial collectivities' as things in themselves capable of autonomous agency, will almost always prove irresistible. This is most marked in those writers who clearly align themselves with (affirmative) forms of postmodernism.

Brah, for example, argues that black refers to a political subject, 'a politics of solidarity against a racism centred around colour' (Brah 1996: 13). Freed by the thoroughgoing constructionism of postmodernism from needing to find a basis for shared experience in history, Brah is able to put further distance between her approach and a notion of race by the pre-eminent role given to discourse. 'Experience does not reflect a pre-given "reality"', she argues, 'but is the discursive effect of processes that construct what we call reality' (Brah 1996: 11).

This is the sort of thoroughgoing constructionist position that Gilroy sought to avoid and with good reason. After all, if our experience of the world is a discursive effect then it cannot reliably ground a politics, especially if the reality we 'experience' in this way is itself constructed by other processes. Brah's text embodies so well the key assumptions of the social constructionist approach to race that I shall deal with it in some detail and, to make it easier for the reader, identify these assumptions under separate sections.

Discourses as social agents

The key constructors of reality for Brah, as for Knowles, are discourses. Discourses construct experience and reality by providing 'fields of signification and representation' and 'inscribing social relations, subject positions and subjectivities' (Brah 1996). As we noted above, this 'strong' interpretation of Foucault invariably imparts to discourses an agential power. Thus 'ethnicist discourses seek to impose stereotypic notions of "common cultural need" upon heterogeneous groups with diverse social aspirations and interests' (Brah 1996: 100). Or again,

> the usage of 'black', 'Indian' or 'Asian' is determined not so much by the nature of its referent as by its semiotic function within different discourses. These various meanings signal differing political strategies and outcomes. They mobilise different sets of cultural and political identities, and set limits to where the boundaries of a 'community' are established.
>
> (Brah 1996: 102)

Let me emphasize that the issue is not whether this tells us something about the use of particular terms (it clearly does), but that it identifies discourses as the source of this usage rather than social actors. This point will be dealt with often enough in succeeding chapters, but it is worth stating it plainly here. Discourses, as emergent products of human consciousness, as ways of talking about and interpreting the world, are inert; by definition they cannot possess agency and the capacity to act in the world. As we shall see there are ways in which discourses can be said to condition and constrain what actors may say and do, but they cannot 'mobilise' or 'signal' or 'set boundaries'. All of these require intentionality and reflexivity – and discourses possess neither.

Voluntarism and the derogation of agency

The 'strong' role given to discourse creates acute problems for affirmative postmodern accounts such as Brah's, which want to argue for particular forms of political project (in this case antiracism). The most serious of these concerns the identification of a social agent or agents capable of critically evaluating their discursively constructed experience and shrugging off the subjectivities within which they have been inscribed in order to recognize some common interest in changing (or rearticulating?) discourses. Since even discourses cannot plausibly be expected to change themselves, Brah requires a *deus ex machina* to bring about the solidarity that is a necessary condition of such change. This she finds, as so many affirmative postmodernists do, in the myth of cultural integration (Archer 1989) or, to use the appropriate idiom, the myth of shared narratives.

Briefly, the myth equates propositions and ideas with normative commitment to those ideas and propositions. It consequently exaggerates the degree to which social actors internalize normative obligations and thus also the extent to which such obligations are shared. It is, though, a helpful device for imputing common interests and pointing up common projects, especially in the face of the postmodern emphasis on 'difference'.

In this way we can understand 'difference' as 'the historical and contemporary trajectories of material circumstances and cultural practices which produce the conditions for the construction of group identities' (Brah 1996: 118). But since authorless discourses are the only agents in this socially constructed reality, it is not human beings as social actors who construct these group identities; rather group identities 'refers to the interweaving of shared collective narratives within feelings of community' (Brah 1996: 118). Hence, although identity is neither fixed nor singular but is 'a constantly changing relational multiplicity', its (constructed) stability at any moment – 'our' construal of the 'self' as an 'I' – is itself the product of discourses of identity generating 'articulations of subjectivity' (Brah 1996: 123–5).

The concept of difference, then, refers not so much to the (constructed) cultural, material, political differences between groups, collectivities and individuals but to the 'variety of ways in which specific discourses of difference are constituted, contested, reproduced or resignified' (Brah 1996: 125). This is a formulation characteristic of 'strong' Foucauldian approaches in that it omits to mention who is actually doing the contesting, resignifying and so on, or to specify what is actually being contested. This is not accidental. It is a direct consequence of what I want to address in my third theme.

Stealthy grammar – transitivity and nominalization

Participants and processes are universal components of all human languages. In other words, for speakers to communicate with each other about the world and their experience of it the linguistic system must make it possible to identify who and what exists in the world, what people and things in the world do and to whom or what they do them. Typically, 'participants' are encoded as nouns and noun phrases, whilst 'processes' are encoded as verbs. Thus in the sentence 'The government excluded asylum seekers', 'The government' is a noun phrase representing the Actor, 'excluded' is a verb representing the Process and 'asylum seekers' is a noun phrase representing the Goal. (This terminology is consistent with the functional grammar associated with Halliday. See Halliday 1985.)

This is more than simply a matter of grammatical detail. The ways in which we put language together in order to express our ideas about the relationship between objects, processes and outcomes reflect in important senses how we conceptualize them theoretically. In grammatical terms this is reflected in the system of transitivity. Choices in transitivity show 'how speakers encode in language their mental picture of reality and how they account for their experience of the world around them' (Simpson 1993: 88). It is therefore concerned with the transmission of ideas, or what Halliday (1985) terms the ideational function of language.

Linguists in the Hallidayan tradition point out that there is a logical though not determining relationship between different kinds of processes and the kinds of actors which carry them out. Inanimate objects can be actors. For example, rain can fall, or lightning can incinerate your house. However, a great deal of action in the social world is necessarily brought about by people. The processes in which human beings engage include mental and verbal processes. The actor who carries out these kinds of actions 'must by definition be a sentient being: a human or at least animate creature (except in metaphorical or fantastic uses)' (Bloor and Bloor 1995: 118).

It is evident, then, that it is only in a 'metaphorical or fantastic sense' that an abstract entity, such as a discourse for example, could be said to engage in mental or verbal processes. Yet we find in Brah the claim that 'Black feminism prised open the discursive closures which asserted the primacy of . . . class or gender over all other axes of differentiation; and it interrogated the constructions of such privileged signifiers as unified autonomous cores' (Brah 1996: 114). It might be objected that this is simply a metaphorical, connotative description – that what is really meant is that black feminists challenged those accounts which sought to privilege class or gender and they did so by pointing out that these categories frequently excluded the experiences of black women. However, as I suggested a moment ago, the grammatical form in which authors choose to encode their accounts carries consequences. In this case what is altered by the particular form that Brah chooses?

First, whilst it is possible to engage with black feminists, to take issue perhaps with their ideas or to assess their relevance, it is much more difficult to take issue with 'black feminism'. Second, this is partly because the personification of black feminism – turning a descriptive category into an active agent capable of 'prising open' and 'interrogating' – imposes a retrospective unity, reinforced by the pronoun 'it'. In other words, this formulation makes it appear that 'black feminism' is an identifiable object, rather than a description of what (some) black feminists have argued. As such it allows little space for the pertinent sociological questions: which black feminists have done the challenging and in which ways? How have other black feminists responded? For whom has this interrogation been significant?

In Brah's discussion of racism, the linguistic choices (personification, transitivity) lead to further conceptual inconsistency. So whilst 'Structures of class, racisms, gender and sexuality cannot be treated as "independent variables" because the oppression of each is inscribed within the other – is constituted by and is constitutive of the other', racisms are yet able to 'articulate with patriarchal class relations in specific ways under given historical conditions' (Brah 1996: 109–10).

Once more, the derogation of agency in these accounts gives rise to a peculiar inversion. The plethora and diversity of racist ideas and their protean adaptability to different sorts of political and cultural projects is viewed as a quality of the ideas rather than of actors and agents seeking to accomplish particular ends. Instead of racist representations being deployed for specific purposes by politicians or governments, say, thus producing the frequently noted inconsistencies, evasions and lacunae of racist ideologies, we have instead different racisms. Moreover, these racisms are 'not simply parallel racisms but are intersecting modalities of *differential racialisations marking positionality across articulating fields of power*' (Brah 1996: 186, original emphasis). It is racisms (rather than racists) that articulate, racisms (rather than racists) that 'in present-day Europe . . . position various categories of people differentially in relation to one another' (Brah 1996: 19).

I have dwelt at some length on Brah's text because it is representative of the strong Foucauldian programme and the consequences for analysis of conflating culture (racism as ideas or systems of representation and signification) with agency (social practices). Before summarizing the advantages and disadvantages of Foucauldian and postmodern approaches I shall deal with the third category of theories that broadly draw on these: those concerned with developing a notion of race as an axial principle for the organization of the 'lifeworld'.

Race, authenticity and lifeworld

The final strand of contemporary theory applying postmodern ideas to the analysis of race and racism is that which views race categories as descriptive of an authentic 'way of life'. There are two currents within this broad approach. First, there are those who argue that race concepts are simultaneously a means of ordering and defining the social world and expressive of a particular kind of collectivity in that world (for example Outlaw 1996). Second, those who argue this but do not link it to a social ontology, instead attempting to argue that race refers to a key form of social relationship (for example Omi and Winant 1994).

Outlaw's work represents the most ambitious effort in contemporary theory to reinstate the race concept. For him, analysing 'the hows and whys of humans forming themselves into bonding, self-reproducing social collectivities' (Outlaw 1996: 4) requires a:

> philosophical anthropology and social ontology that include an understanding and appreciation of senses of *belonging* and of a shared *destiny* by which individuals are intimately connected to other individuals in ways that make for the constitution of particular kinds of social collectivities, what I term *social-natural kinds*. Races and ethnies [sic] are such 'kinds' of collectivities.
>
> (Outlaw 1996: 7)

The processes – biological, sociocultural, and historical – by which such collectivities are formed and maintained, he describes as raciation and ethnicization. These processes are facts of human evolutionary histories. I mean by this that they are important aspects of the socially contingent, but anthropologically necessary, ways in which we humans, as social animals, organize meaningfully, give order to, and thus define and construct the worlds in which we live, our life worlds, and do so in the process of surviving while subject to the evolutionary forces of social and natural histories.

(Outlaw 1996: 5)

Races, then, are those collectivities who share a relatively permanent place of geographical origin and a relatively distinct gene pool. These factors hold even in diasporic conditions (see Andreasen (1998) for a more sceptical attitude towards the survival of gene pool populations in the contemporary world). In turn the situated practices and experiences of the collectivity influence the gene pool and cultural practices to condition raciation – that is the formation and evolution of the biological and cultural factors collectively characterizing the race. Raciation is an 'important means through which we construct and validate ourselves' and for this and other reasons, 'we should understand races . . . as natural, that is as particular types of bio-social collectivities that develop or evolve, as do all things in the natural world, but in ways that are characteristically human'. (Outlaw 1996: 11–12).

The problem Outlaw faces is one that faces all attempts to mobilize notions of race. As Appiah (1992) notes, the relationship between biology, culture and destiny inescapably issues in some form of undesirable essentialism (undesirable in the sense of being ahistorical, asociological, aphilosophical and, one might add, unworkable). Outlaw is no exception: 'What makes it possible and appropriate initially to group diverse intellectual endeavors of diverse persons under a single heading', he observes,

> is the extent to which the persons share racial-ethnic identities as African and African-descended, thus share socially and culturally conditioned biological attributes, cultural traditions, and historical experiences more or less distinctive of the African race and its ethnies.

(Outlaw 1996: 88)

Ironically, in view of its author's explicit championing of a 'politics of identity', this notion of races as communities of meaning based on shared 'racial-ethnic identities' – groups of people who look roughly alike and who 'share' a body of cultural norms and values (authentic cultural life worlds) – leads to a selective application of the 'difference and diversity principle'. Recognizing that 'Difference has become a significant basis of political mobilization . . . a highly valued preference that many persons and groups would have accommodated and recognized as the basis for their participation in civic, political and economic life,' (Outlaw 1996: 140) does not apparently allow for difference between those sharing a common culture on the basis of their 'racial-ethnic identity'. (And I am drawing a veil over the sociologically dubious notion of sharing a common culture, the problems of empirical demonstration associated with it and the illegitimate way in which it assumes what it purports to discover. For further discussion see Carter, 1998.)

These strains in Outlaw's arguments are very much the consequence of trying to renovate a notion of race as a viable social category with some explanatory purchase. This enterprise has a long history in the USA, from Alexander Crummell and Frederick Douglass through DuBois, Martin Luther King, Malcolm X to Louis Farrakhan, a history to a great extent impelled by the experience of coping with racism and exclusion. It is also a history in which communal resources have been crucial in meliorating the damaging effects of a racist society. It is a moot point, though, how far a notion of race takes us in making sociological (or indeed any other) sort of sense of this. Notions of race always embroil their sponsors in shady deals with disreputable claims about common destinies and traditions, life worlds and genes.

SUMMARY AND CONCLUSION

In this chapter I have considered the impact of postmodern ideas on sociological concepts of race. The work of Foucault, and particularly his notion of discourse and his view of the relationship between power and knowledge, has been a significant influence. I have argued that Foucault's ideas can be fruitfully applied to sociological accounts of racism, but only in their 'weak' form. In their 'strong' form I have suggested that they are less helpful, especially as they have been taken up by various currents of what I have termed, following Rosenau, as affirmative postmodernism. In the next chapter I shall begin to outline a realist view of these matters, but before doing so let me summarize the main features of the 'strong' Foucauldian, discourse – driven perspective.

On the positive side, the focus on identity and difference that is a central preoccupation of this approach has highlighted the role played by race discourses and ideas as interactional and affective resources for social actors. This is an important dimension of social life (as we shall see in Chapter 8), one often either overlooked in studies of racism or reduced to a matter of individual psychology, and postmodern writers are surely correct to draw attention to it. In some cases this has produced some rich empirical descriptions of how some collectivities have pursued political projects (Gilroy's work on the 'Black Atlantic' is an outstanding example). In others it has prompted a reassessment of particular theoretical traditions and urged the formation of new ones as a matter of political necessity (Eze 1997a and b; Outlaw 1996; Pittman 1997a and b).

However, it seems to me that there are some serious reservations to be noted. Many of these have been pointed out already, but I wish to note three more. First, discourse and postmodern theorists continue to employ the term *race* in an under-theorized sense and, in so far as they do this, they continue to reaffirm its common sense connotations within social science. Second, and as a direct consequence of this, they find it difficult to develop a critique of race ideas. This leaves unclear the meaning of the injunction to challenge or contest racist discourses, since the basis on which this may be done is not at all obvious. Third, by bracketing out the content of ideas and propositions in favour of a genealogical account of their situatedness within discourses, postmodernists signal a withdrawal from 'World Three' and the social practices of critique and objectivity that are based upon it. In this sense, they come dangerously close to irrationality (see, for example, Callinicos 1995; Geras 1995; Habermas 1987; Norris 1993).

In this and the previous chapter I have discussed the various ways in which notions of race continue to be used within sociology. I have also identified some of the conceptual and methodological difficulties that arise from this and which, in important ways, are a product of the theoretical perspectives that implicitly or explicitly inform this sociology. In the next three chapters I want to develop an alternative, realist approach to understanding racism and race.

NOTES

1   The extent to which, in Habermas's phrase, Foucault's genealogical method is 'criticism without critique' is a matter of some debate. Recently Owen has argued that 'the immanent relation of genealogy to resistance entails a principle of critique in terms of which forms of constraint may be evaluated' (Owen 1994:162). In other words a genealogical approach, in seeking answers to the question of how we came to be what we are, implicitly identifies not only other possible versions of what we might be but also identifies those social factors that have inhibited the development of autonomous, alternative modes of self. Whether this convinces depends on how far one buys the (Nietzschean) notion of freedom as the continuous accomplishment of personal autonomy. See Dean (1994) for another defence of genealogy as critique, whilst Dews (1987) and Soper (1993) take a less sympathetic view.
2   The implicit targets of Foucault's capillary view of power are, of course, Marx and Weber, who, according to Foucault, both held to the proprietorial notion of power. More particularly, Foucault is deeply sceptical of what he regards as a key Marxist claim that a world without power is possible (Foucault 1982).
3   See below and Layder (1994), Pawson (1989a) and Sayer (1994) for a fuller discussion of structured social relations and their implications for sociological analysis.
4   I am indebted to Andrew Sayer for his trenchant comments on the limitations of Foucault's critique of essentialism (personal communication).
5   Foucault's anti-essentialism needs some refinement here. To claim that there are no 'essential truths' about who we are, in the sense that human subjectivities are not the product of some transhistorical human essence, is one thing (and sociologically unremarkable). However, to claim that human subjects as social beings have no properties whatsoever is another thing entirely (and sociologically unacceptable). For a fuller discussion of the various meanings of essentialism see Sayer (1997).
6   Although the significance Foucault places on discourse varies (Fairclough, for example, has argued that the move from archaeology to genealogy represents a decentering of discourse Fairclough 1992: 49), his definition of discourse remains constant.

3   A realist social science

We have seen in the previous chapter how sociologists encounter difficulties in providing consistent accounts of racism and race and that their lack of clarity over the ontological status of race is a source of many of these difficulties. This lack of clarity, it was also argued, reflects a larger uncertainty over the sociological enterprise as a whole, an uncertainty exacerbated by the rise of postmodernism and the various forms of relativism associated with it (see, for example, Bauman 1987; Harding 1991; Mouzelis 1995).

These relativisms are inimical to the project of a critical social science. Against this, the argument developed here will contend that a modest realism affords the basis for a non-relativist defence of social science. This raises the question of what would constitute a realist social science? How is it to be distinguished and what might be regarded as its central tenets? These questions are the topic of this chapter.

After briefly introducing the notion of realism and identifying the problems attached to applying it naively to the interpretation of the social world, the chapter turns to contemporary forms of realism, beginning with a look at some examples of recent realist research. The dominant forms of contemporary realism within the social sciences are influenced in the main by the work of Roy Bhaskar and his notion of a critical or transcendental realism (Bhaskar 1979, 1989). Bhaskar's claims to lay the foundations for a naturalist social science are assessed and some shortcomings of his case examined. Finally, a modified form of realism is advocated, one which it is argued is more suited to the purposes of social science and is based on the work of Sayer, Layder and Archer (Archer 1989, 1995; Layder 1985, 1990, 1994; Sayer 1994).

WHAT IS 'REALISM'?

Realism has represented a small, although not perhaps insignificant, current within the philosophy of social science over the past decade or so (Archer 1995; Bhaskar 1979, 1989; Collier 1994; Keat and Urry 1982; Layder 1985, 1990; New 1995; Outhwaite 1987; Pawson 1989a and b; Pawson and Tilley 1997; Porpora 1989; Porter 1993; Sayer 1994). The publication in 1979 of Bhaskar's *The Possibility of Naturalism* revived the debates about the possibility of objectivity in social science.

It offered a determined response to the claims of interpretivists that sociology was an essentially hermeneutic discipline whose methods and aims were fundamentally different from those of the natural sciences.

Broadly speaking, realism entails a belief in the existence of a reality independent of individual consciousness; in common sense terms, a belief in 'things out there' that exist even though we may not perceive them directly. Thus few people believe that when they walk out of their house and down the street, the house ceases to 'be', or that because they cannot see (or, possibly, understand) the law of gravity it ceases to operate. This is a sort of practical, everyday realism without which we would rapidly cease to function adequately as social beings. For instance, try persuading the bank manager that you should only pay the mortgage when you are physically in the house since the rest of the time the house does not exist for you, or try leaving the frustrating staff meeting by the fifth floor window. Trivial examples, perhaps, but they do demonstrate the core idea of any sort of realism, that is the notion that there is some sort of reality independent, 'outside', of us as individuals, of our cognizing experience.

However, this assertion begs some important, and difficult, questions. For instance, if reality is independent of us as individuals, how can we ever have knowledge of it and what sort of knowledge would this be? A second question, and one of particular pertinence to social science, is that whilst we may be prepared to go along with the notion of a physical and natural world independent of our cognizing experience – the law of gravity is real in the sense of being unaffected by how I choose to think about it or interpret it – what about phenomena in the social world? Surely whether I choose to see a pile of stones as a source of ammunition, a place of worship or as evidence of past architectural endeavour is crucial in determining the nature of my reality? (And perhaps more crucially, what I am likely to do – pick them up, drop to my knees or consult the guide book?) (See Layder 1990: 60.)

Thus we seem to have arrived at some fundamental issues with regard to a realist view of social as opposed to natural reality (although later I shall argue that this opposing of natural and social reality is itself a false opposition). First, there is the issue of how we can attain knowledge of a reality that is independent of us. This is an epistemological question about what sorts of knowledge we can have. Second, there is the central importance of an interpretive element in the definition of social reality, that is, what is to count as social reality will critically depend on who is doing the counting and what they are doing it for. These are ontological questions about the nature of social reality and the relations of men and women to it. Needless to say, these are not new questions and one way of exploring them is to see what sorts of answers to them have been proposed by those writers who explicitly identify themselves as realists. The difficulty is that there are as yet few examples of realist social research. For this reason I shall concentrate on a study by Porter, a writer who would wish to endorse the claims of realism within sociology (Porter 1993).

IS A SOCIAL SCIENTIFIC REALISM POSSIBLE?

I want to suggest that a social scientific realism requires more in the way of a defence than Porter offers and that the version of realism he elaborates runs into difficulties when applied to the analysis of racism and race. This critique will allow me to identify some of the key elements in a sociological realism and to point to some of their implications for a sociological account of racism.

Porter's article attempts a realist defence of ethnography, arguing that the critical or transcendental realism of Bhaskar (of which more later) provides a viable basis for defending ethnography from the criticisms made by Hammersley (Hammersley 1992). It is particularly pertinent to the present study because Porter tries to develop a realist interpretation of racism. For this reason I want to pay special attention to his article.

Hammersley's critique of ethnography raises a number of issues for the ethnographer, all of which stem from ethnography's bashfulness towards structural theories, and its efforts to preserve the integrity of the culture or community or group being studied. Principally, for Porter, these issues can be summarized as: the need to explicate the representational claims of the study, to decide, in other words, what or whose culture is being represented and by whom; the need to examine the explanatory status of a methodology that explicitly rejects determinism; and the need to make explicit the ontological status ascribed to social structures. It is Porter's claim that critical realism can come to the aid of ethnography and beat off these cavils.

Critical realism can do this, he argues, because it is able to provide ethnography with a theory that recognizes that the way things appear to social actors in their everyday lives and milieux is not the way they really are, or, at least, that is not all they are. According to Porter's critical realism, social phenomena are the result of generative mechanisms, that is are the outcome of the interplay between the properties and powers of social objects.

An example of a generative mechanism would be class relations. Class relations are not observable and cannot be directly apprehended; they exist independently of individuals' consciousness, that is class relations are antecedent to individual consciousness and will continue to generate social phenomena such as class conflict and inequality irrespective of whether individuals acknowledge their existence or not. In fact, such generative mechanisms can only be identified by their effects; the existence of the effects demonstrates the reality of the structures, rather like falling out of the window demonstrates the reality of gravity. Social analysis from this perspective consists of the 'synthetic a priori production of hypotheses about the nature of structures, and the subsequent testing of them through empirical examination of their effects' (Porter 1993: 593).[1]

Such a perspective requires some account of the ontological status of structures. Structures have two core features, according to Porter. First, they are *relational* and this in two senses: structural positions are always and necessarily social and so are always and necessarily defined in relation to other social positions – the notion of worker can only make sense in relation to the position of boss, the notion of slave in relation to the position of master; and for such relational positions to function in this way they must be relatively enduring and stable. The second core feature of structures for Porter is their ontological depth, by which he means that 'their existence lies behind, and affects, manifest phenomena' (Porter 1993: 597).

Applying this to racism, Porter argues for a notion of structural racism. This implies the existence of relatively enduring structures of discrimination (an empirical claim) and the notion that structural racism underlies specific manifestations of racism (an ontological claim which disguises an empirical claim). I shall return to this idea of structural racism presently, for not only is it central to Porter's case for a critical realist ethnography, it also – partly because of this – illustrates some of the key weaknesses and shortcomings in a critical realist approach.

The ethnographic setting for Porter's study was a metropolitan hospital in the north of Ireland. He developed the study in response to an earlier investigation by Hughes (Hughes 1988). One of Hughes' main findings was that nurses' deference towards doctors broke down in interactions with doctors who were immigrants from the Asian subcontinent. Porter did not find this. Instead he identified several inter-actional strategies – the public display of medical knowledge, for example, or the utilization of formal occupational power – adopted by Asian – and African – trained doctors which had the effect of ensuring the professional deference of the nurses. How is this difference in findings to be explained?

Porter considers first the claim that there is an absence of racism in Ireland (Hughes carried out his study in England). He rejects this, citing 'backstage' complaints by nurses about doctors that were often expressed in racist terms. Another possible explanation Porter examines is that in Hughes' study the doctors were unfamiliar with the cultural cues of the host culture and so were more dependent on the nurses for cultural translation, thereby altering the balance of interactional power between them. Further, these doctors sometimes misconstrued events because of cultural mistranslation and so were frequently seen as not competent by many of the nurses.

Thus for Hughes, lack of deference amongst nurses towards black doctors is an example of a status dilemma. This is a situation where a status position is strongly associated with certain characteristics and yet one of those characteristics is absent from the incumbent of that position. Whiteness is identified by Hughes as one of the key auxiliary characteristics of medical doctor status. Therefore the relations between young, relatively inexperienced black doctors and experienced white nurses involve status dilemma. 'In other words, there are two contradictory social mech-anisms at work here. Racism tends to reduce social status, while professional power enhances it' (Porter 1993: 604).

Porter can now address the different findings of his and Hughes' study with the aid of a critical realist vocabulary. The question, reformulated in critical realist terms, becomes why the 'tendency of racism' was exercised unrealized in his study, but realized in Hughes' study. The answer is that the actual outcome of a tendency – in this case structural racism – is generally co-determined by the activity of other mechanisms. (It will be recalled that social phenomena in the critical realist schema are produced by the operations of generative mechanisms.) In the specific case considered by Porter structural racism was not realized in the nurse-doctor professional relationship because the black doctors in his study were culturally literate and could not be construed as incompetent. Blocked off in this way, structural racism seeks another outlet in 'backstage' commentary. In Hughes' study, the black doctors were not as culturally literate and structural racism was able to express itself through a 'rational' veneer. Nurses construed black doctors as professionally incompetent and could be disrespectful on 'professional' grounds. The realization of the tendency of structural racism in each context was partly determined by its interaction with another generative mechanism, that of professional power. Where professional power can be effectively realized, as by the doctors in Porter's study, then the effects of structural racism will remain unrealized or latent; where it cannot be, as in Hughes' study, the effects of structural racism will be realized or manifest.

Does Porter's critical realism revivify ethnography and *inter alia* offer a basis for a realist, sociological account of racism? My short answer would be that it cannot do the first because it is unable to accomplish the second. That is, the account of racism that Porter advances is seriously flawed and the reasons why it is flawed invalidate Porter's claim to be able to defend a critical realist ethnography against Hammersley. I am not so much concerned here with a defence of ethnography, so I shall concentrate on Porter's notion of structural racism and his efforts to develop a critical realist interpretation of racism and professionalism in a medical setting.

My first point is to take issue not with the substantive case study that Porter explores, or with the explanation he proposes, but with the relevance of critical realism to it. Simply, Porter does not need critical realism. His central argument about the expression of racist attitudes being subdued by an ethic of professionalism in certain circumstances, and not being subdued by it in other circumstances, does not require all the ontological hardware about structures and causality; it can be made perfectly well without it. This is a recurrent feature of critical realism: it tends to be strong on the theory end of things, less helpful at supplying the practical tools of social analysis. This means either that critical realists debate at a fairly rarefied level, largely shunned by practising sociologists, or they append critical realism on to their empirical research or case study rather like an optional extra. Furthermore, the effort required to fit the critical realist key into the sociological lock often prompts a forced entry, with all the attendant damage. The tell-tale clues to the break in in Porter's study lie in his concept of structural racism and it is worth paying some attention to this.

Interestingly, Porter does not define his key term 'structural racism', despite its crucial role as the coupling between ontological deep structures and social action. Instead, he defines its two elements separately. First, structures, as we have seen, comprise two elements: they are relational and they have ontological depth. Second, racism is defined as a structural tendency in that it:

> involves enduring relationships between agents in different social positions.
> Being Black in a racist society entails being categorised in numerous

> disadvantageous ways. Racist engendered positions predate any of the indi-
> vidual actors now situated within them, and may well outlast them.
>
> (Porter 1993: 597)

Now structural racism is distinguishable, at least analytically, from racist acts and racist attitudes, since Porter goes on to argue that it is the articulation of all three that is important. Moreover the relations between them are not invariant:

> 'Individuals' attitudes and actions are not predetermined by the social structures
> within which they live . . . individuals will enjoy more or less powerful enabling
> positions in a society which displays structural racism, depending on how they
> are categorised in racist terms.
>
> (Porter 1993: 597)

This can be translated roughly as follows. Goods and resources are distributed unequally. This unequal distribution pre-exists individuals, who are thus differentially placed within these distributions, some in more powerful positions than others. They may reject this placing and do something about it, reject it and not do anything about it, or acquiesce in it or even accept it. If this distribution is racialized, individuals will find 'race-ist' interpretations available to account for these distributions and their place within them and these will influence what they do and how they act. Put this way, we can begin to see some difficulties with the notion of structural racism, difficulties that stem from Porter's need to provide a definition of racism wired with critical realist componentry.

To begin with, what appears to define certain discriminatory distributions of power, prestige and reward, as structural racism is that the distribution takes place on the basis of social categorization. But social categorization requires someone to do the categorizing, requires someone to interpret, to make judgements and, importantly, be in a position to make the categorization stick. This, though, implies agency rather more than structure.

This leaves Porter in something of a quandary. For either structural racism amounts to a *description*, not an explanation, of those instances where structural distributions are interpreted by actors in terms of race, leaving the connection between race and structure a contingent, not a necessary one. Or it refers to relatively stable, relatively enduring systems of social categorization based on race, in which case we are left again with a descriptive rather than an explanatory concept and one that, moreover, assumes what an adequate account of racism would need to consider, namely how do social categorizations based on race emerge in the first place?

In fact, despite (or, as we shall see, partly because of) a critical realist vocabulary, Porter here repeats the reification of race characteristic of those writers considered in Chapter 2. Like them, Porter accomplishes this reification by avoiding discussion of the ontological status of the concept of race, thus allowing it to continue its schizophrenic life as a sociological category, a common sense notion and a structural feature of social relations. So Porter observes that 'racism is entirely premissed upon an ideological category, "race" being nothing more than a reified social construction' (Porter 1993: 598). This does not mean, however, that it can be reduced to the status of superstructural epiphenomenon, for 'Racism, although founded upon ideological assumptions which have little bearing on reality, nevertheless has real effects upon social relations' (Porter 1993: 598).

The oddity of this argument is that it does not define racism at all. It is 'premissed' on 'race', so presumably it rests on ideas about race. So racism may be understood as an ideology, a more or less coherent framework of beliefs and notions held by social actors and organized around concepts of race. Yet racism, Porter points out, although 'founded upon ideological assumptions', nevertheless has 'real effects' and is therefore not reducible to these assumptions. Now in one sense, this is no different from the arguments advanced by interactionists that 'race' is real in its consequences, with all the residual empiricism that we have seen those arguments to carry. In another sense, though, Porter seeks to free race from its agential anchoring in order for it to function as a generative mechanism, a structural form 'underlying' the manifestation of social phenomena. In short he must 'ontologize' it. This now allows for the 'possibility of unintentional racism. Because the social world may be opaque to the actors within it, it is possible for actions to have the effect of maintaining racist structures without actors realising that they are doing so' (Porter 1993: 598).

This seems to me a confused argument. If racism is founded on beliefs about race, then such beliefs cannot be unintentional, they require a conscious cognizance of social reality; one might as well talk of being an unintentional monarchist or an unintentional Buddhist. Of course, individuals and groups may well pursue particular courses of action on the basis of certain ideas, and the outcome of these actions may well include unintended consequences (although these will not always be a consequence of the opacity of the social world and nor will they always be apparent to the actors themselves). But it seems absurd then to view the actors' original intentions and actions as containing the unintended consequences which the actors themselves, by definition, could not have foreseen or anticipated. This is rather like saying that in Weber's study of the Protestant ethic all those Western European seekers after salvation, thriftily accumulating their capital in pursuit of God's grace, were unintentional capitalists. One of the unintended consequences of their religiously motivated behaviour may have been a 'spirit of capitalism', a mode of orientation to the practical, material world that favoured capitalist social relations, but it makes poor sociological sense to describe them as unintentional capitalists. One of the unintended consequences of my actions may be the reproduction, or intensification, of discriminatory structures and practices; that does not make me an unintentional racist (although it might identify me as a racist if the consequences of my actions were convincingly pointed out to me and I persisted in them nevertheless). This leaves to one side the further difficulty of establishing whether, and in what ways, the unintentional consequences of my actions have contributed to the maintenance of particular sorts of structures.

This conflation of the analytical distinction between structure and agency makes it difficult to identify in what senses we are meant to understand racism as a structural phenomenon in the context of Porter's arguments. Are we, for example, meant to assume that structure is given by the fixity of categorizations? That what counts as structural racism (as opposed to 'ordinary', 'unstructured' racism?) is that categorizations on the grounds of race persist over time in a sort of hermeneutic inertia? Curiously, race and racism *are* reduced to epiphenomenal status here. The determinate content of particular racisms – anti-Semitism, anti-Irish racism, Nazism, anti-black racism and so forth – are seen as expressions of a structural racism and denied any autonomy, any sense of having properties emergent from, and so not reducible to, the historical circumstances of their genesis. For example, the ways in which the contours of anti-black racism in Britain after 1945 shifted as a result of political exigencies and changing perceptions of political opportunities amongst elite groups are recalcitrant to an analysis which seeks a structural racism underlying particular manifestations.

Porter's version of critical realism compels him to ontologize race into structural racism. Structural racism can then function as independent of cognizing experience, generating specific manifestations of racism and maintaining itself in the face of actors' contrary intentions. This privileging of ontology avoids the issue of how we come to recognize ontological features of social reality (this is the problem at the root of the notion of structural racism – it is a contested category, as an ontology of the social necessarily has to be). As Layder has noted, 'The question of what we take to be the basic features of social reality is inseparable from questions relating to the procedures we adopt in coming to know this reality' (Layder 1990: 63; see also Pleasants 1999 for a similar point).

In fact, as indicated earlier, Porter's substantive case study does not rely on his critical realism beyond his claim that if racism is suppressed by professional ideologies of medical expertise at the public level, it will most likely be expressed in other social realms. There is nothing particularly realist about this claim, and it seems to me that Porter's efforts to appropriate for realism a residually empiricist method – ethnography – developed within a different theoretical perspective, do not provide a compelling case for the usefulness of critical realism as an approach to sociological research.

BHASKAR'S CRITICAL REALISM

Critical realism has been perhaps the most influential form of realism in the social sciences over recent years. It will be clear from the preceding discussion, however, that in my view the contribution of critical realism to social science, and particularly to the sociological study of racism and race, has been a mixed one. I want now to consider Bhaskar's case for 'the possibility of naturalism' in the social sciences, partly to draw out what I consider to be the positive elements of this case, partly also to identify what I consider to be its shortcomings. After this I will adumbrate an alternative, modified form of realism within social science.

I want first to set out the general features of Bhaskar's approach and then go on to consider its specifically sociological relevance. Bhaskar starts from Marx's claim that all science would be superfluous if the outward appearances and essences of things directly coincided. This discrepancy between the ways in which the (natural and social world) appears to us and how it 'really is' is, if you like, the minimum condition for any sort of social scientific realism. From here we seem to be confronted by an obvious difficulty. If the world as it appears to us is discrepant from the world as it 'really is', how can we have knowledge of the 'real world'?

One answer to this question is that proposed by Kant. Kant, in trying to demonstrate the insufficiency of Humean empiricism, attempted to show that although certain concepts such as cause and substance cannot be found in, and therefore proved by, experience, their applicability is presupposed by our being able to have intelligible experience at all. This applicability must be universal, that is, available to all human consciousness, for intelligible experience of the world to be possible. Kant therefore describes notions such as cause and substance as transcendental.

Like Kant, Bhaskar argues that although it is not possible to compare what reality is like *in itself*, or directly, with the scientific representation of it, we can establish a priori that reality must have certain features in order for scientific activity to be possible. So, for example, causality must operate in the world in order for scientific practice based on it to be effective. If this were not the case and, say, gravity did not cause objects to fall to earth then scientific activity based on a theory of the law of gravity simply would not be effective. This is what Bhaskar means when he claims that 'one assumes at the outset the intelligibility of science . . . and asks explicitly what the world must be like for those activities to be possible' (Bhaskar 1979: 10). Thus Bhaskar's realism starts from this central ontological question: what must the world be like for science to make sense of it? (Note that this is quite a different sort of question from the one posed by Kant.)

The key ontological feature of the world for Bhaskar is that it is governed by generative mechanisms. These are the tendencies of objects to behave in certain typical ways by virtue of their essential structures, so that, although these structures will be necessarily imperceivable, we can know them by their effects. This allows for the notion of ontological depth, the idea that real, causal structures underlie the surface manifestations of phenomena; we merely see the flowers blossom, we cannot see the complex generative structures concealed in the seed. Further, if we adopt a superficial approach we might be misled into thinking that it is the seasons that 'cause' the flower to grow, rather than merely providing some of the conditions under which the generative mechanism of the seed is activated.

This ontology of underlying generative mechanisms allows Bhaskar to develop a series of themes that together comprise a distinctive approach to science. First, he argues for an essential unity of method between the natural and the social sciences since the natural and the social worlds are characterized by similar ontological features, namely underlying generative mechanisms. The essence of both natural and social science 'consists in the movement . . . from manifest phenomena to the structures that generate them' (Bhaskar 1979: 24). The principal concern of science is with the identification of the causal laws that govern such generative structures and their tendencies, rather than with the 'constant conjunctions' of surface appearances. Finally, the social world, like the natural world, is, as an object of enquiry, necessarily theoretical 'in the sense that, like a magnetic field, it is necessarily imperceivable. As such it cannot be identified independently of its effects, so that it can only be known, not shown, to exist' (Bhaskar 1979: 57).

Second, Bhaskar is able to claim, within the social sciences, a repudiation of both empiricism and interpretivism. Empiricism has mistakenly confined knowledge to objects sensuously perceived and so has been unable to grasp the generative causal mechanisms underlying things as they appear to us: empiricists have pursued their constant conjunctions of events in the vain hope of catching a law-like regularity. Interpretivists, on the other hand, in rejecting natural scientific methods on the grounds that they inescapably entailed empiricism with its derogation of meaning and intentionality in human affairs, have forfeited access to scientific objectivity. Realism, in Bhaskar's view, is able to offer a third way, one which preserves the empiricist concern with a unity of method in the sciences, and its correlate emphasis on objectivity, whilst incorporating the interpretivist anxiety about the reification of structures by insisting on the crucial role of human agency in the maintenance and transformation of *social* structures. The role of human agency is a core difference for Bhaskar between natural and social structures.

This last point gives Bhaskar's realism its specifically sociological relevance and allows him to advance a number of claims about the ontology of the social. The central ontological feature for sociology is social relations. Sociology, for Bhaskar, is concerned with 'the persistent relations between individuals (and groups), and with the relations between these relations (and between such relations and nature and the product of such relations)' (Bhaskar 1979: 36). There is perhaps an ambiguity here as to how far relations are relations between actual individuals (and groups) or are relations between structural positions and roles. The disadvantage of defining relations as relations between actual individuals (and groups) is that it makes it difficult to see social relations as historical, as persisting, or stretching in time both backwards as well as forwards, to use Layder's formulation (Layder 1990: 123). In other words, if social relations are to be tied to concrete relationships between actual individuals it becomes difficult to appreciate the force of Comte's observation that the 'majority of actors are the dead' (Archer 1995: 148).

This ambiguity notwithstanding, Bhaskar is adamant that 'In social life only relations endure' (Bhaskar 1979: 52). This brings us to a further ontological feature of the social world. The existence of enduring relations implies the existence of society prior to specific individuals and this in turn implies its existence 'outside' the individual. However, reification is avoided, since it remains true to say that society would not exist without human activity. 'But it is no longer true to say that men create it . . . they reproduce or transform it . . . Society stands to individuals . . . as something they never make, but that exists only in virtue of their activity' (Bhaskar 1979: 42). Additionally, this conception also entails a stratified view of social reality, one divided between the 'parts' and the 'people'. Bhaskar thus introduces an analytical dualism between individuals and societies, such that 'while the properties and powers of individuals and societies are *necessary* for one another, they are *irreducible* to one another' (Bhaskar 1989: 63).

Finally, Bhaskar notes some ontological differences between social and natural structures. He identifies three: social structures, unlike natural structures, do not exist independently of the activities they govern; social structures, unlike natural structures do not exist independently of agents' conceptions of what they are doing in their activity; and social structures, unlike natural structures, may be only relatively enduring (Bhaskar 1979: 48–9).

In summary, Bhaskar proposes an ontological model of social reality which is structured (between 'parts' and 'people', necessarily related but irreducibly distinct); 'open' (that is, experimental controls on social situations are impossible and therefore experimental prediction irrelevant to the social sciences); and whose manifest, surface features are the product of (usually) imperceivable, generative causal mechanisms.

SETTLING WITH THE 'VEXATIOUS FACT OF SOCIETY': BHASKAR AND BEYOND

Social theory, as Archer has reminded us, 'has to be useful and usable: it is not an end in itself' (Archer 1995: 135). There is much that is useful and usable in Bhaskar's naturalism, particularly in his efforts to defend a notion of objectivism in social science. However, in some ways it is too philosophical a tool for more finely grained sociological research. Its prioritizing of the ontological elements of social reality tends to compel its advocates, such as Porter, to engage in unnecessarily programmatic statements bearing often only a nebulous connection with their substantive empirical claims. A distinctively *sociological* realism, therefore, requires some considerable refinement of Bhaskar's *philosophical* naturalism, a scaling down of its universal ontological pretensions and a critical recasting of its conception of the agency-structure dualism. In this way the practical utility of realist sociology might be greatly enhanced.

The first stage in elaborating a useful realist sociology is to bridge the gap between statements about the nature of social reality with the sorts of knowledge that it is possible to have of it. It should then be possible to specify how practically we obtain this knowledge, that is how empirical knowledge of the social world is to be obtained and how its validity and objectivity is to be assessed (Pawson 1989a). This is a central point for the present study – after all, what are we measuring when we measure race? Bhaskar's philosophical naturalism is not wholly suited to this task of evaluating and defending the place of empirical evidence in social research.

Bhaskar rightly takes to task those writers, predominantly within the empiricist and positivist traditions, who regard empirical evidence as an external feature of the world to be garnered through appropriate scientific methods. Against this, Bhaskar argues that evidence is not *given* through method but has to be won, that is scientists have to work to reproduce experimentally those conditions under which the relevant generative mechanisms can be activated and observed. Evidence requires interference; it does not present itself, neatly dressed and ready for inspection, it has to be coaxed and cajoled into making an appearance at all. There is much to be said in favour of this account, but, as Pawson has cogently pointed out, without 'a conception of measurement as a significant and separate stage in empirical inquiry' it is crucially incomplete (Pawson 1989a: 145). Without some notion of how we define what we are measuring, how we measure it and how any results of this measurement are to be evaluated, we are left with evidence as confirmatory – demonstrating that particular generative mechanism(s) are operative – rather than as adjudicatory – enabling us to judge between different theories about which mechanisms are operating, when and where. This is because Bhaskar's version of how evidence is manufactured, whatever its descriptive merits, remains, in Pawson's words, 'entirely driven by theoretical assumptions about the underlying mechanism' (Pawson 1989a: 143).

The second major piece of renovation we need to perform on Bhaskar's naturalism as the basis of a realist sociology is the critique of its formulation of the agency-structure dualism. The agency-structure dualism (or to use Archer's less formal phrase, the relation between 'the parts' and 'the people' of a social system) has long preoccupied social theorists (although not always profitably). This is not the place to recount the history of this debate, but, to oversimplify greatly, socio-logical theories have tended to lean towards explanations that have favoured either 'the parts' (structure) or 'the people' (agency). In the former camp, for example, can be found the structural functionalism of Parsons, the various forms of structuralism itself, deterministic forms of Marxism and so forth. In the latter camp can be found the various phenomenological, hermeneutic and interpretive sociologies, with their stress on the role of intention and meaning in social life. The more definitely an approach has declared its allegiance to one camp, the more vulnerable it has become to the critiques advanced by the other. Unsurprisingly, therefore, there have been several efforts at rapprochement in recent years, most notably perhaps, the structuration theory of Giddens (see also Delanty 1997). Bhaskar also claims to have resolved the conflict but in a realist direction.

Bhaskar begins his proposed resolution by considering the two camps noted above and their characteristic weaknesses, namely reification in the case of the structure camp and voluntarism in the case of the agency camp. He also considers a third camp, that of Berger and Luckmann and their dialectical view. For Berger and Luckmann social structure is the product of human activity, but may come to be seen in an alienated way as standing above such activity and appearing to be independent of it. From this perpective, in Bhaskar's words, 'society is an objec-tivation or externalization of man. And man, for his part, is an internalization or re-appropriation in consciousness of society' (Bhaskar 1979: 41–2).

However, despite its obvious peacemaking appeal (it appears to avoid both the reification of the structure gang and the voluntarism of the agency crew), Bhaskar rejects this model as 'seriously misleading'. His grounds for doing so are that structure and agency, parts and people, 'refer to radically different kinds of thing' (Bhaskar 1979: 42). Far from being 'dialectically connected', structure and agency are ontologically distinct entities.

Most fundamentally, structures are historically antecedent to individuals: ideologies, the banking system, the distribution of property ownership, and many other things besides, existed before I was born. This rather compromises the conciliatory potential of the Berger-Luckmann scheme. First, contra voluntarism, human beings cannot make society, since, in significant ways, it is already given for any actual, historical individuals. The best we can do therefore is modify, sustain or (exceptionally) transform society. Second, concrete and conscious human activity will always occur within, and presuppose, the prior existence of social forms; it must always and necessarily be activity on given objects. Human activity in the abstract is literally inconceivable since 'society is a necessary condition for any intentional human act at all' (Bhaskar 1979: 43). Bhaskar insists, too, that this applies to discursive as well as non-discursive practices: we inherit, for example, not only legal systems and property arrangements, but ideas, paradigms, theories, views of the world and so on.

Bhaskar's realist resolution rests on his claims about the ontological limits to naturalism. Bhaskar specifies several key differences between natural structures and social structures, two of which seem to me to weaken his plausible case for the ontological distinctiveness of structures. Thus, he claims that:

1. Social structures, unlike natural structures, do not exist independently of the activities they govern;
2. Social structures, unlike natural structures, do not exist independently of the agents' conceptions of what they are doing in their activity.

(Bhaskar 1979: 48–9)

These statements are not easily reconciled with Bhaskar's earlier commitment to the notion that structures are *given* to social agents as antecedent conditions within which and upon which they act. As Layder observes, 'How can social structures be the prior conditions of human agency at the same time as being dependent upon this same agency for their very existence?' (Layder 1990: 127). It is one thing to recognize that structures are 'concept- and activity-related', that without human activity nothing in society could happen or come about, quite another to deny structures a relative independence from the activities they govern.

In my view Bhaskar is equivocal on what I would regard as a distinctively realist resolution of the structure-agency conflict. Such a resolution should recognize that structure and agency refer to different things, with different sorts of properties (given and emergent), and are therefore not reducible to each other.

Clearly, then, an adequate realist sociology (one at least adequate to the task of providing a social scientific account of race and racism) requires us to spell out the conceptual and methodological linkages between it and Bhaskar's critical realism. This task has already been undertaken and the basis for an effective and viable realist sociology already exists, in the work of Layder, Sayer, Archer and Pawson (Archer 1979, 1989, 1995; Layder 1985, 1990, 1994; Pawson 1989a; Sayer 1994). The next section sets out five cardinal principles of this realist social science, based on the work of these authors.

A REALIST ALTERNATIVE

Analytical dualism

This is a core principle of a realist approach and insists on an *analytic* separation of structure and agency, or 'the parts' and 'the people'. In seeing both elements as irreducible, it rejects conflationism in its upwards (reducing parts to people), downwards (making people the puppets of parts) or central (structuration, Berger – Luckmann dialectical connection) forms (Archer 1995).

Apart from its rejection of all forms of conflationism, analytical dualism provides a powerful explanatory potential for social science. First it permits a distinction between system integration and social integration, a distinction to which Lockwood drew attention many years ago (Lockwood 1964). Lockwood's distinction is important. It enables us to recognize that a well integrated structural arrangement (well integrated from the structure point of view that is) may not be one that encourages the commitment of the people who make it work. Similarly, a social system that many people regard as commodious may, structurally speaking, be a shambles. Such a distinction also encourages a view of the 'parts' and the 'people' as operating within different temporal modalities or according to distinct or different time scales.

This way of viewing things has obvious benefits for the sociological researcher. For example, governments may pursue a laissez faire policy towards the arrival of migrant workers because this is a cheap and efficacious means of meeting a severe labour shortage. It makes sense in terms of system integration, we might say. However, such a policy may allow migrant workers to be stigmatized by other workers as outsiders and illegitimate competitors for jobs and housing. Violence, discrimination and political disruption may well be a consequence. So system integration and social integration can be 'out of synch'; indeed policies designed to further one may inhibit the other. (In extreme cases they may be pulling in entirely opposite directions.)

Further, whilst the system integration side of things can, in this case, have an immediate impact – workers arrive and fill the job vacancies – the social integration side of things moves to a different rhythm, its political consequences only slowly becoming apparent. And, of course, although some politicians might be willing to pursue alternative policies, particularly in the light of changing system needs such as increasing unemployment leading to a reduced demand for migrant workers, the different tempo of social integration will constrain them too. (The negative political consequences of racism, for example, turn out not to be significantly diminished by the implementation of immigration controls. In fact they may well be aggravated by it.)

The second sense in which analytical dualism offers explanatory potential is that it allows us to view parts and people as not only having distinct properties and temporalities, but also as internally differentiated. Some parts have greater strategic significance than others for system integration and some actors have greater strategic influence than others for social integration. Further, we can distinguish between individual and collective actors, each with correspondingly different potential and ability to effect social change, and each of these may be seen, to use Mouzelis' typology, as macro, meso or micro actors (Mouzelis 1991). This is not, it should be noted, a function of size. Macro actors can be powerful individuals, micro actors can be relatively powerless groups. Nor is it a holistic or complete description – an individual may be powerful in some spheres of social life, her job say, and relatively weak in others, for instance in her ability to influence the movements of global capital.

A stratified social reality

Analytical dualism minimally insists on regarding structure and agency, parts and people as analytically distinct, as irreducible and as possessing distinct, as well as emergent, properties. For a realist programme to be effective in generating research, further differentiation between these two elements is required. In other words, the 'parts' and the 'people' are both stratified entities and recognizing this enables the formulation of the important question 'whose activities are responsible for what and when?' In what sense, though, are parts and people stratified?

The most fundamental distinction is that between individual actors (actual persons) and collective actors (groups and collectivities, organized or inchoate). These two types of actors are characterized by different properties and temporal modes (usefully summarized by Layder (1990: 130)). When examining individual actors, we are dealing with the properties of intentionality, reflexivity, interpretive skills and purposiveness. Further we are dealing with their operation in biographical time, the time in which the individual is an extant social actor. When examining collective actors – social classes, interest groups, political groups – we are dealing with properties of collective decision making, actions and definitions and common interests. Clearly, too, in assessing the development and impact of collective actors a notion of biographical time is less pertinent, whilst a notion of group or organizational time is central. This is true irrespective of whether the collective actor is organized, such as a political party, or inchoate, such as the poor (Layder 1990).

Layder's account can be usefully augmented with a further differentiation of the 'people' introduced by Archer (Archer 1995). This differentiation, perhaps more exactly a further ontological property, is between collective agents and individual (and collective) actors. Since this is a critical distinction, and one which provides important links with the discussion of structures, it requires some elaboration.

Archer defines agents as 'collectivities sharing the same life chances', where the relations between these two elements are necessary and internal ones (Archer 1995: 257). So, when we refer to working class agents or women agents, we are also saying something about the relations between the sorts of life chances available to someone in that position and the nature of the position itself. In other words, being a working class agent of necessity only makes sense in the context of the relationship between a working class and the class(es) that define it as such in terms of the distribution of resources. Thus,

> the major distributions of resources upon which 'life chances' pivot are themselves dependent upon relations between the propertied and the property-less, the powerful and the powerless, the discriminators and the subjects of discrimination: and these, of course, are relationships between collectivities.
>
> (Archer 1995: 257)

Now the point about this notion of persons as agents is that we are agents before we are social actors. Our location within particular social arrangements that distribute certain sorts of life chances according to that location, is involuntary and objective – we are not consulted about whether we want to be born to Jewish parents in an anti-Semitic society, or female in a sexist one. As agents, that is persons born into an already existing sociocultural system, we will be strategically located too. Certain agents (note the term can only be used in the plural, since being an agent means by definition being part of a collectivity) will have a greater say than others in social change and transformation. Recall, additionally, the point made earlier about actors being powerful in some spheres and relatively powerless in others; the same applies to agents who may be effective in some domains, yet relatively ineffective in some others.

Those agents self consciously organized in the pursuit of specific social interests, and who tend to form the object of social and political analysis, Archer terms 'corporate' agents. Those agents not able to make their interests felt, not able to effectively 'have a say' in what goes on, because they are formally excluded, say, or because they have no clear idea what their interests might be, she describes as 'primary' agents (Archer 1995: 258–9).

Like other strata of social reality, agency in this specific sense also has powers and capacities of its own, unrecognized when it is conflated into the unimodal concept of 'people'. The articulation of shared interests, organization for collective action, generation of social movements and the general movement from primary to corporate agency are all capacities of agency.

Besides distinguishing between individual actors and collective actors, we need to further distinguish between persons as agents (involuntary, allocative, objective and collective) and persons as actors (intentional, voluntary, purposive, individual). This also produces a useful distinction noted by Layder between social *relations*, that is the reproduced institutional properties or relations between social agents, and social *relationships*, that is relations between actual individuals or social actors (Layder 1990: 123). I shall return to the significance of this in a moment.

If we turn our attention to the contexts within which people operate as agents and actors, a realist approach would want to discriminate between two types of social context conditioning social activity – situational and structural – both with different capacities and emergent properties. Situations are those contexts where face to face interaction generates emergent 'definitions' of reality, and where, correspondingly, actors have varying degrees of influence over these definitions (Was your plea for an extension to your assignment successful, embarrassing, a waste of time?). Actor determination is at a maximum in situational contexts (it makes a difference whether you ask politely for an extension, if you have completed previous assignments on

time, if you avoid asking the lecturer as they are going to the toilet or are about to
have lunch). Structural contexts, on the other hand, are much more refractory
to actor determination. They involve institutional constraints and enablements that
are themselves partly the product of the distribution and allocation of economic,
political and cultural resources (you cannot refuse to do any assignments at all and
still expect to be awarded a degree). Situational and structural contexts are, perhaps,
best regarded as forming a continuum, with highly malleable situational contexts
at one end (which assignment you want to do and which theorists you propose to
examine in doing it) and highly refractory structural contexts at the other (being born
into a poor family). This is not to imply, of course, that we are aware of, or act as
fully knowledgable actors and agents in, all these contexts.

Let me summarize the distinctions drawn thus far. Starting from the basic
proposition of analytical dualism, that we must hold to an analytical separation
between social and system integration, or 'parts' and 'people', we have seen that
further refinements are possible. Within a concept of the 'people' we can distinguish
between social agents (people allocated to positions within an anterior distribution
of social and cultural resources) and social actors (people as 'making a difference
in the world'). We can further distinguish between individual and collective actors
(both of which can be viewed as more or less significant, micro or macro, within
different contexts). Within a concept of the 'parts' we can distinguish between
situational and structural contexts, which will be more or less refractory to redefinition and renegotiation; and between social relations, the reproduced institutional
properties or relations between social agents, and social relation*ships*, relations
between social actors. We are in a position now to make a little more of this final
point, since it permits a further key distinction identified by Layder, between the
generic and specific senses of structural contexts.

As Layder puts it:

> although any social structure depends upon the existence of situated activity in
> a generic sense (that is, without some human agents reproducing its features
> there would be no structure), they do *not* depend on this or that specific episode
> of situated activity.
>
> (Layder 1990: 132)

Your institution depends on students completing their assignments, but it does
not depend on *you* doing your specific assignment.

The notion of a stratified social reality is seen to entail a significant modification
of the simple proposition that people and social structures have ontologically distinct
properties. Furthermore, an insistence that 'parts' and 'people' are both stratified
entities allows a key sociological question to emerge more fully and sharply, namely
'whose activities are responsible for what and when?' (Archer 1995: 141). The
importance of this question for accounts of racism and race is central and I will
return to it once our summary of realist principles is complete.

Social science and 'common sense'

> It is the resolution of this paradox between formal philosophical concerns and concrete empirical issues of research and social analysis that presents, perhaps, the most formidable challenge to a realism which aspires to anything more than a peripheral relationship with mainstream practitioners of social science.
>
> (Layder 1990: 170)

> 'Science is redundant if it fails to go beyond a common-sense understanding of the world'
>
> (Sayer 1994: 39)

Sayer takes the most combative view of the relation between social scientific and common sense understandings of reality. Common sense descriptions tend to naturalize social relations, and to the extent that they successfully do this, they are plainly inconsistent with social science. On the other hand, social science has common sense as one of its objects. In seeking to understand the everyday world and popular consciousness, social science will draw attention to the structural conditions of action, necessarily antecedent to individuals, which condition such action. It will unavoidably, therefore, point to the limited knowledgeability of social actors and to the partiality of their common sense grasp of social reality. Quoting Ricouer, Sayer notes that the restoration of meaning inevitably slides into the reduction of illusion: 'in order to understand and explain social phenomena, we cannot avoid evaluating and criticizing societies' own self-understanding' (Sayer 1994: 39).

One of the examples he mentions in this context is apartheid. It would be 'factually incorrect', he argues, 'to say that the architects of apartheid were factually correct in their beliefs about race . . . unless we decide whether the actors' own explanations of their actions are right, we cannot decide what explanations to choose ourselves' (Sayer 1994: 40). Although I would like to be convinced by this argument, it seems to me to have several shortcomings.

First, I am not so sure that explanations of our own, sociological explanations that is, are dependent on an assessment of actors' own accounts, which is emphatically not to claim that actors' accounts are irrelevant. This seems to beg the questions of which actors and whose accounts and seems to imply an overly rigid sequential element to research – do we have to assess actors' own accounts before arriving at our own?

Second, and more substantially, it postpones the question of how, sociologically, we determine the right-ness or wrong-ness of actors' accounts, that is the procedures we adopt for assessing common sense notions in the light of social scientific knowledge. Whilst Sayer's case is particularly acute when it comes to sociological explanations of racism, we need to explore more fully the arguments for a realist view of the relation between social science and common sense.

I want to propose an alternative view of the relationship between social science and common sense based on a distinction identified by Layder (1990). He argues that rather than referring to social scientific and lay languages, we should distinguish between two modes of lay language – what he terms the personal and the interactive – and two modes of social scientific language – described as structural and technical.

I think that this effort to distinguish between modes of language is very useful. However, Layder's use of the term 'language' is rather loose. It tends to suggest a typology of discrete languages, and minimizes the intra-linguistic connections between them. Furthermore, it does not distinguish between what Halliday has termed the interpersonal and ideational uses of language (Halliday 1978, 1985). Halliday's distinction recognizes not only that languages can have distinct epistemological orientations (some sorts of languages are designed for analysis), but also that the different purposes to which people can put languages can give rise to different sorts of linguistic practices.

Which practices are used by whom will depend on context and setting and on people's ideas of appropriateness and also their own social and linguistic competence. For example, the solvent amongst us generally regard lecturing the bank manager on Marxist economics as an inappropriate strategy for obtaining a loan. Individuals shift amongst different sorts of language practices, depending on the language's degree of accessibility and the individual's level of competence.

Furthermore, people can use a variety of linguistic practices to accomplish a range of social ends, often simultaneously. Academic texts (such as this one) may serve many purposes – to do with an author's status, career, standing amongst one's peers and not offending potential rivals and referees – which will shape their rhetorical production. Nevertheless, they are still also making certain sorts of claims, still providing theoretical descriptions of something, and to that extent are judged by criteria of evidence, conceptual consistency and rigour, and so on.

Distinguishing between languages in terms of their epistemological orientation and function does not commit us to the position that the knowledge resulting from the practices of science is only available to social scientists or that the relationship between it and lay knowledge is a hierarchical one (Perkmann 1998). A major advantage of the Hallidayan approach is that its emphasis on what people *do* with languages avoids both of these positions. Second, as a social practice, science cannot claim infallibility or incorrigibility (Fuller 1997), although it may claim to provide more adequate knowledge of certain sorts of things. With this considerably refined notion of language in place, let me return to Layder's account.

The two modes of lay language Layder distinguishes are the personal and the interactive and these have distinct authorial origins. The personal is that used by the individual in interpreting their own biography, and in making sense of their own lives. Personal lay language will draw on all sorts of discursive, practical and interpretive skills that we have acquired as accomplished social actors, as well as the deep familiarity with the rules and mores of common sense and the 'mutual knowledge' of our social milieu.

I would suggest that personal lay language, concerned as it is with the everyday exigencies of 'getting on' and the consequent drawing upon of routine ways of thinking and their capacity for making encounters 'run smoothly', will sometimes employ notions of race. Many actors' accounts of themselves and their lives will draw on race ideas to a greater or lesser extent. In so far as the individual's intention in employing such ideas is primarily a practical one, to do with the accomplishment of routine social interaction, perhaps through conforming to peer or reference group expectations, then we may refer to the individual's use of lay linguistic practices.

As Layder explains, the interactive lay language, on the other hand, is employed by social analysts in the *description* of how social actors accomplish their everyday social conduct, how they 'get on' in negotiating the myriad encounters of daily interaction. There is a different epistemological orientation from personal language, since the social analyst is seeking to describe the discursive penetration of the interactional rules of social life, which actors may not formally be able to describe despite having a common sense awareness of them. Interactive language also has a different function, since the analyst is primarily seeking to illuminate the various 'ethno-methods' and interpretative schemas actors use to negotiate and sustain interactional encounters.

There will be an unavoidable use in lay interactive language of concepts and ideas employed by actors in the personal mode. Thus in explicating how actors use race ideas, analysts will employ these as *descriptive elements* in any account (see, for example, the work of (Back 1996; Cohen 1992) on interpreting the use of race ideas as elements of working class and masculine identities or biographies). However, to recognize the role of race ideas as interactional resources is not to endorse a concept of race. Race ideas are only activated by actors' use of them as interactional resources. The use of these ideas by people may carry all sorts of consequences, but such consequences are a property of social action, of people doing things (stereotyping, discriminating, using violence). They are not caused by *race*.

It is in the relationship between the two modes of lay language – the personal and the interactive – that the partial truth of the arguments considered in Chapters 1 and 2 may be found. The use of race ideas, and their symbolic forms, by individuals is plainly part of the social reality sociologists may want to describe and analyse. The subsidiary claim – that therefore these analyses should be accountable, or translatable, to actors' accounts and should accord the latter existential and hermeneutic authenticity – is also persuasive when made about the interface between these registers. This is separate, however, from any claims about the truth or falsity of these accounts or propositions, or about whether these ideas are likely to lead to the realization of actor goals or interests.

So in both modes of lay language, race ideas may be prominent. Explaining how actors employ such ideas discursively, to locate themselves and others, to form identities and boundaries is, of course, a legitimate and productive exercise, but we need to be aware of the sociological limits of accounts fixed at this level. Such accounts run into difficulties in depicting the structural conditions of action, since these are, to varying degrees, opaque to actors (individual and collective) and agents.

Thus terms and concepts that may be appropriate to the description of such structural conditions – terms such as class relations, rationalization, global economies of scale – are not routinely available to individuals drawing on mutual knowledge and common sense for their ways of 'getting on'. Other languages –

social scientific ones – utilizing such terms and concepts have to be engaged in to describe, interpret and analyse these conditions.

This brings us to Layder's two social scientific languages: the structural and the technical. The crucial distinction between these and lay languages is that whereas the latter 'reach into networks of common sense and mutual knowledge for the retrieval of their referential sense', the former 'reach into formal conceptual networks for theirs' (Layder 1990:149–50). Although there may be a sharing of terms between lay and social scientific descriptions – class is an obvious example – the content and meaning of these will differ. What a sociologist means by class may not (and need not have) much to do with common sense understandings of class. The sociologist will look towards conceptual networks such as structural function-alism, Marxism, rational choice theory or some such to give their notion of class a social scientific meaning. (Again, and to repeat, this does not mean that they disregard, or are indifferent to, the meanings social actors may attach to notions of class; it is merely to assert that a sociological definition of class will not look to actors' definitions of class as its *referential* source).

In my view, this distinction is even more marked when it comes to the term *race*. I have already argued for the notion of race ideas, literally ideas about race, as elements of the cultural systems of many societies and as forming the basis of existentially valid interpretative schema. Explaining sociologically why people adopt such ideas, in which contexts and for what purposes, requires theoretical descriptions. The objectivity of these is ensured partly by the fact that they are *descriptions* of postulated or observable entities (in this case, people's use of ideas of race), and partly by their embedded-ness in auxiliary networks of social scientific theory. Exploring Layder's distinction between the two modes of social scientific language will amplify the relevance of theoretical language.

Layder terms the first of his social scientific mode of language the structural. This language attempts to capture analytically the structural features of social life, using concepts such as bureaucracy, social class, racism, discrimination, inequality. Again some of these terms may well share a common linguistic referent with terms in lay language, but again they look towards formal conceptual networks for their referential sense and the different ends they seek to accomplish give rise to a different sort of linguistic practice.

Sociological concepts should be derived from, sedimented in, the second mode of social scientific language, the technical. This refers to the theoretical and analytical presuppositions, the ontological and epistemological claims upon which the terms and concepts of the structural mode draw. There are two key distinguishing features of the technical mode. First, there is its 'holistic, organic nature which marks out a domain of questions and answers (problematics) about the nature of social reality as a whole' (Layder 1990: 151). Second, 'The holistic nature of these languages requires not only support from allied concepts which represent other contiguous features of social reality, but also support is required from epistemological premises as foundational elements' (Layder 1990: 152).

A concept of race, I would argue, does not have this theoretical and conceptual backup. Race as a social scientific concept is unsupported by allied concepts – as we have seen in earlier chapters, sociologists tend to 'ontologize' it and counterpose it as an independent variable to other concepts such as class or gender – and its epistemological premises are threadbare. Indeed most sociologists employing the notion justify it by a theoretical realpolitik, pointing to its experiential, phenomenological empirical frequency as the basis for its inclusion in a social scientific vocabulary. This is to confuse an interpretive claim about how social actors 'get on' in everyday interaction, and the forms of practical and discursive consciousness they employ in doing so, with social scientific claims about the conditions of social activity. These conditions, to quote Layder again,

> are to be understood in relation to the different orders of social reality that structural and technical languages [registers] depict . . . Beyond the interpretations of actors' interpretations, their reasons, meanings, accounts and so forth, social theorists are in the business of making theoretical decisions as to the relevance of such things in relation to a much wider theoretical universe of *social objects*.
>
> (Layder 1990: 152–3)

Much of the language of social science is therefore 'an attempt to conceptually model the elements constitutive of the conditions of social activity' (Layder 1990: 156).

This is also to argue that the languages of social science generate different sorts of linguistic practices from the lay modes of language. The primary function of the technical and structural modes is to depict and describe with as much accuracy as possible the objective, independent features of social reality. This purpose drives particular sorts of linguistic practices to do with intelligibility, commensurability, argument and evidence. These practices are, in turn, embedded in the various (no doubt, imperfectly realized) institutions and arrangements of scholarly accountability.

A concept of race does not qualify for social scientific status because, as we have seen, it is derived from, and remains bound to, the experiential world of everyday social activity and its consequent partiality therefore makes it unsuitable for analysing *social scientifically* the contextual conditions of action. Notions of race make it impossible to explore the structure – agency dualism identified as an earlier cardinal point of our realist programme because of the interactionist assumptions on which the concept is based. Objectivist accounts of something called *race* therefore are not possible (although this does not apply to an objectivist account of race ideas or racism). Developing such an account requires us to connect the structural and technical languages of social science with a model of empirical research.

Models, capacities and empirical research

It is a central feature of realist accounts in social science that research cannot be confined to the empirically given. Nevertheless, the realist views empirical data and research as essential elements in the growth of social scientific knowledge. Further,

I want to set this claim within a strong case for social scientific knowledge as cognitively valid knowledge. Having set out my decidedly unfashionable stall I now want to make my sales pitch for the benefits of a realist view of the relation between empirical research and sociological knowledge.

Perhaps the first thing to note about realist approaches to empirical research is their claim that societies are 'open' systems. This suggests that the sorts of experimental controls that are possible in laboratory conditions (although the extent of such controls can be exaggerated) cannot be applied to the analysis of social reality. This is not simply because people are reflexive, interpretative beings, or that social reality has a limitless number of 'variables' interacting upon and influencing each other. It is also because a key idea of realist social science is that of emergent properties or powers. These, it will be recalled, arise from particular combinations of elements and have a causal influence on those elements as well as a reciprocal influence on other emergent properties and powers. Social reality, in other words, tends to resemble a 'structured mess' and 'structured messes' prove notoriously recalcitrant to dissection into variables (see, for example, Byrne 1998).

How, then, is empirical research possible in social sciences? Pawson's notion of a generative model has considerable potential here. A generative model utilizes a social ontology of generative mechanisms and emergent powers to examine how the system under investigation is constituted. Only after the model is developed are research hypotheses advanced 'explicit enough to have direct consequences for empirical research and measurement practice' (Pawson 1989a: 171). Empirical data (though not empirical reality), according to this view, is constructed from theory or, as Pawson elsewhere puts it, all measurement is primarily an act of translation (Pawson 1989a: 287).

Models tell us what we need to know and how to go about measuring it. In order to do this our models, because they are concerned to grasp generative relations and emergent properties, must draw upon the structural and technical registers of the social sciences since they attempt to encompass the contextual conditions of action. Again the provenance of the race concept in lay registers tends to ensure that models based on it treat it as an independent variable ('race' and social policy, 'race' and politics), but its very incoherence, a product of its lay origins, generates confusion. If what is being explained by a concept of race is not made explicit (and it rarely is), how are we to determine its conceptual parameters? If we cannot define what race is, neither can we define what it is not – and how are we to decide on a basis of measurement for empirical inquiry? For example, what are we examining when we look at, say, race and educational performance? Discriminatory patterns? Discriminatory behaviour? Or the mobilization of race ideas in pursuit of, and resistance to, these ends?

Empiricist sociology (whether phenomenological, experiential or material) deals with variables like race as discrete. This has been a 'recipe for arbitrary and contested operationalization since measures are based erratically on everyday connotations of the concept in question' (Pawson 1989a: 186). Social scientific concepts are by contrast developed as part of a generative model in which key measurement parameters are known independently of any operation devised to measure them.

This is a considerable distance from an approach that adopts as its chief criterion the empirical incidence of a belief amongst a population.

A further advantage of this formalist strategy of concept formation is the possibility it affords for adjudication between theories. In a formal system the meanings of terms and concepts are established by their place in a formal network of postulates, themselves derived from the structural and technical languages of social science. Within this account race theories do not possess the requisite structure and coherence to act as the foundation for a measurement language. Pawson again: 'Ordinary language reasoning cannot sustain the development of a logically consistent network of concepts' (Pawson 1989a: 243). Interestingly, sociologists, with very few exceptions, do not attempt to defend at the theoretical level a formal theory of race, the favoured option being to point to its putative empirical use by social actors. This indicates the impossibility of grounding a theory of race in social scientific analysis.

One major consequence of the relationship between theory and measurement outlined above is that it recasts empirical testing as adjudicatory rather than verificatory. That is, empirical evidence is constructed so that it relates to rival theories and is not a measure of the 'real world' directly.

The argument I am proposing here entails a particular view of the nature of sociological knowledge and its relations to social reality. Contrary to empiricism I am contending that observation is not an independent appropriation of the ontological and real features of the social world. Rather, how one gains knowledge of structures will affect to some extent the ontological and explanatory status of those structures. 'Operationally and existentially independent of our cognizing experience they may be', notes Layder, 'but the elementary structures of the world never escape the net of language and knowledge, as *our* knowledge' (Layder 1990: 53). We can never know the world in its pristine or pure state because it would imply some notion of a pre-linguistic, intuitive 'knowledge'. So, too, we cannot get knowledge of generative structures via unsullied observation. Instead we must look at the theoretical context being used to understand the world – hence the importance of generative models.

It is difficult to examine the theoretical context in which concepts of race are employed since its theoretical context is lay usage. Because it is an element of actors' practical and discursive consciousness and so a 'social object', it is given ontological status, yet it is its location within the registers of lay reasoning that necessarily renders the concept inconsistent and incoherent. This is why, as an under theorized lay concept, race should not be imported into social scientific analyses. When it is, its absence of theoretical underpinning leads to competing and confusing notions of what is to count as observational evidence capable of assessing models based on it. The debates about race and educational performance are instructive in this respect (see, for example, Carter and Williams 1987).

The question of adjudication is not a matter of invoking observation neutral criteria – since there are not any – but depends on two things: invoking epistemological criteria of validity such as coherence, explanatory scope and adequacy; and a notion of formal conceptual networks that feed into adjudication between competing claims. Objectivity flows, not from empirical corroboration, but from seeking entrenchment within a pre-established system of theoretical models and empirical regularities (Pawson 1989a: 148).

History and a morphogenetic approach

The final element in this outline of key realist principles is Archer's morphogenetic approach (Archer 1989, 1995). In its uncompromising insistence on the historical nature of sociological understanding (both as itself historically shaped and as having an inescapably historical dimension), it is especially fruitful in its application to an account of racism and race ideas.

Analytical dualism for Archer 'accords time a central place in social theory' (Archer 1995: 89). More specifically, it allows a purchase on the *structuring* of social systems over time. Morphogenesis indeed 'refers to the complex interchanges that produce change in a System's given form, structure or state ("morphostasis" is the reverse)' (Archer 1989: xxii).

The morphogenetic analysis works in terms of three part cycles composed of a) structural conditioning, a given structure that conditions but does not determine b) social interaction. Social interaction arises from actions oriented towards the realization of interests and needs emanating from current agents and leads to c) structural elaboration or modification, that is a change in the relations between the parts of the social system.

> What is crucial, then, is that the morphogenetic perspective maintains that structure and agency operate over different time periods – an assertion which is based on its two simple propositions: that structure necessarily predates the actions which transform it; and that structural elaboration necessarily post-dates those actions.
>
> (Archer 1995: 90)

Archer sets out the basic propositions entailed in the practical application of the morphogenetic/morphostasis analysis. These are:

i   that there are internal and necessary relations within and between social structures;
ii   that causal influences are exerted by social structure(s) on social interaction;
iii that there are causal relationships between groups and individuals at the level of social interaction;
iv   that social interaction elaborates upon the composition of social structure(s) by modifying current internal and necessary structural relationships and introducing new ones where morphogenesis is concerned. Alternatively, social interaction reproduces existing internal and necessary structural relations when morphostasis applies.

> (Archer 1995: 168–169)

Analytically Archer distinguishes three cycles of morphogenetic analysis, those of structure, culture and agency. In each case, the above four propositions apply and the same analytical cycle of conditioning, interaction and elaboration occurs. Clearly a morphogenetic approach emphasizing the analytical distinctiveness of structure, culture and agency, seeing each as relatively autonomous, relatively enduring and as irreducible each to the other, and which stresses the antecedence of structure and culture to agency, cannot be other than profoundly historical. This is the methodological approach that will be employed in the account of Cabinet responses to colonial and Commonwealth migration in postwar Britain in Chapters 6 and 7.

SUMMARY AND CONCLUSION

This chapter has set out a number of key principles fundamental to a realist social science. The first of these is analytical dualism, that is the viewing of agency and structure as analytically distinct. In allowing for the exploration of their interplay, analytical dualism also provides other bonuses for the social researcher, namely the distinction between social and system integration (the 'people' and the 'parts' of society) and the recognition of the different properties and temporal modalities of structure and agency.

Our second principle, the stratified nature of social reality, follows from the commitment to analytical dualism. Together, it was argued, these two principles facilitate the emergence of a key sociological question 'whose activities are responsible for what and when?' The complex view of the social world implied by the ontological and analytical independence of structured social relations gives rise to the third principle of realist research, the distinction between social science and 'common sense'. Social science requires the development of theoretical languages for its descriptions of the nested, stratified character of social life. This requirement imposes conditions on the sorts of terms and concepts employed by social researchers. The most significant of these is that social science languages look towards formal theoretical networks for their referential sense, precisely because their primary purpose is the generation of theoretical descriptions.

It was also argued that this had implications for a realist approach to empirical measurement and research. For the realist, empirical research provides 'traces' of the causal relations operating in a social world structured in complex ways. All measurement is, then, primarily an act of translation. This is why, when we draw up our models of empirical research, we should do so using terms and concepts from the structural and technical languages of social science.

Finally, the chapter pointed to the profoundly historical nature of a sociology based on analytical dualism and argued that Archer's three stage morphogenetic model, our fifth principle, provides an appropriate methodological tool. The next chapter will apply a realism grounded in these principles to the analysis of race and racism, setting out its broad implications for both conceptual vocabulary and empirical historical research. These will then be explored substantively in Chapters 5, 6 and 7.

NOTES

1 Several writers have argued that the Kantian language is no accident. Bhaskar's critical realism, Rose has argued, continues Kant's quest for the a priori justification of objective validity (Rose 1995: 212). As we shall see it encounters the very same hazard that plagued Kant, namely that 'the object of knowledge can only be subsumed under, or subordinated to, those (a priori) forms . . . In the name of a neutral method which seeks solely to justify knowledge, transcendental philosophy justifies infinite ignorance not finite knowledge' (Rose 1995: 44–5). Pleasants (1999) also advances some objections to Bhaskar's 'transcendentalist' approach, but from a Wittgensteinian perspective.

4 Realism, race and racism

In the previous chapter the key principles of a realist social science were set out. I now want to assess the explanatory potential offered by this realist programme by considering the ways in which realism offers a critical perspective on the thorny tangle of terminological chaos that has characterized sociological debates about concepts of race.

My central argument is that the absence of a viable notion of structure has led to a conflation of race ideas with notions of racism and discrimination. Using Archer's morphogenetic scheme and a modified version of Miles' concept of racialization, the chapter explores how a realist social science might be employed in the analysis of specific historical instances of racism. This provides the conceptual foundations for the illustrative examples considered in the following three chapters.

RACE IDEAS AND THE CULTURAL SYSTEM

The basic proposition I wish to begin with is that race is a concept in a formal theoretical sense, a term devised to describe accurately certain features of human populations. However, if the common claim that races are socially constructed is to have any sociological meaning, then it is surely that, whatever the descriptive, biological value the term has, people act on the basis of assumptions, propositions and notions of race. In this sense, race is simply a concept or, to use Anderson's well-known formulation, races are 'imagined communities' (Anderson 1983). Race ideas are those ideas, or imaginings, that draw upon a concept of race (the question of whether we can talk of race ideas when a concept of race is not employed explicitly is something I shall leave aside for the moment, but will return to).

Within this ambit are a vast range of phenomena, from Nazi Aryan fantasies, through apartheid notions of separate race-ial development to liberal notions of 'thresholds of tolerance' and radical notions of 'separate but equal' policies. How any particular individual or group is making use of race ideas (and their associated symbolic forms) in a particular context is a matter of empirical investigation but the key claim here is that race *is* a concept.

As an idea, race is an element in the cultural system. The definition of cultural system I am employing here is Archer's. She takes culture as a whole 'to refer to all

race — Darwin
culture   culture-ethnicity
she

intelligibilia, that is to any item which has the dispositional capacity of being understood by someone' (Archer 1989: xvi). The cultural system is the 'sub set of items to which the law of contradiction can be applied', namely propositions about the nature of the world which assert truth or falsity. Archer thus also describes the cultural system as 'the propositional register of society' (Archer 1989: xvi). Whilst the cultural system at any given time is the product of previous sociocultural interaction, that is of what previous social actors have accomplished, intentionally or otherwise, its elements will at any specific historical moment share two essential qualities. They will have a relative independence or autonomy from social actors 'in the sense that these are independent of anyone's claims to know, to believe, to assert or to assent to any of them' (Archer 1989: 107). And second, they will have a relative autonomy from each other (or, strictly speaking, from the propositional forms of each other). A further claim follows from these two ontological properties of the cultural system, that objective relations of logical contradiction and compatibility will often link its components.

Race ideas may be linked to all sorts of other ideas within the cultural system, such as ideas about civil rights, about national identity, or about whom it is appropriate for your offspring to have relationships with. There are also many ideas with which it has little or no connection at all, such as your preferred make of car or the shrubs you choose to plant in your garden. Ideas can have two sorts of logical relation to other ideas: contradiction or compatibility. Again, examples are more efficacious than bald abstraction. If individual A, or political group B, believes that certain groups of people are inferior, this will be a view compatible with all sorts of other ideas about colour, about culture, about inequality and all sorts of political arrangements. (We will leave aside for the time being what these ideas entail about the sorts of actions likely to be undertaken by individual A or group B as a consequence of holding these ideas.) There will thus be an incentive for A or B to preserve the compatible ideas, since they are mutually reinforcing, by seeking out further evidence for these beliefs. On the other hand, if A or B believes in a hierarchy of races with different degrees of assimilability to a national 'way of life', but also are committed to the idea that discriminatory behaviour is unacceptable, there will be an incentive for them to rectify the extent to which these ideas are contradictory. We will return to these different 'situational logics' in due course when we turn to consider the effects on social action of holding ideas related in different ways.

In this way, race ideas have an objective existence, in books, pamphlets, and the various symbols of 'banal nationalism' (Billig 1995). The existence of race ideas is therefore not reducible to the individuals or collectivities that may claim to 'know, believe, assert or assent' to them. As with the cultural system generally, race ideas are at any given time the product of how previous social actors have employed them. Once they have emerged, they develop properties of their own, wriggling free of the grip of their progenitors and assuming an independent status within the cultural system. What sorts of properties are these?

Race ideas contain constraints, such as making sense only within particular sorts of discourses. The discussions among senior Cabinet ministers about the desirability and practicability of immigration controls of black citizens in postwar Britain, for example, drew on race ideas about assimilation that compelled an analysis based on restriction and exclusion. Race ideas also embody new possibilities, such as opportunities for political advantage, or new applications, such as the defence of particular systems of inequality, discrimination or exclusion. Finally, they introduce new problems: first through the relationships between the emerging entities themselves (for instance the shift from ideas of race to ideas about culture as an exclusionary motif in late twentieth century politics – see, for example, Furedi 1998) and second, between these and human actors (who is exempt from immigration control and who is not, who is 'British' and who is not) and the physical environment (the creation of so called 'ghettoes' and *bidonvilles*). And, of course, these conflicts and contradictions exist independently of people noticing them or caring about them (they may even be unaware of them).

So far we have identified race as an idea, sharing an active social life in the cultural system with all sorts of other ideas. We have identified the cultural system, following Archer, to be constituted of 'nothing but objective items, "texts" and the logical relations between them' (Archer 1989: 134). Note again, that this is an *analytical* distinction between the cultural system and sociocultural interaction, between what people say, that is the claims they make, and what people mean, that is how they employ ideas discursively to make practical sense of their social milieu.

We have also established the significance of intellectual histories of race ideas, the importance of tracing the emergence of race ideas as discourses, drawing out the significance of their shifting forms and their utilization of a wide range of cultural elements. This makes possible an account of race ideas *in their own terms*. In other words, exactly what people believe in when they believe in race ideas (or routinely employ their symbolic forms) comes to have some significance. (Ironically, this is what tends to get lost in the interactionist approach of seeing race as merely socially constructed, since it smothers consideration of the relatively autonomous, emergent properties of race ideas and the complex and sophisticated strategic orientations individuals and groups can take towards them.)

Analytical dualism allows us to go further though. The claim that races exist is a proposition. The claim is therefore an element in what we might call the cultural system domain, with specific ontological features (irreducibility to individuals, partial independence from those who elaborate it) and emergent properties. Race ideas, for example, were originally espoused as a means of signifying subordinate sections of European capitalist societies (see, for example, Callinicos 1993; Malik 1996; Miles 1993, 1994). Later, though, race ideas come also to be used as a means of justifying colonial domination, and later still as a basis for affirmative action proposals or as the bases for 'race relations' legislation and equal opportunities policies. As part of the cultural system domain, race ideas are also subject to the invariance of contradiction – the logical claim that nothing can be both p and not-p (races cannot both exist and not exist); and the possibility of adjudication – we can make a considered, logical argument for the proposition *qua* proposition.

These advantages arise from our dualist approach and are denied to those of an interactionist, social constructionist bent who conflate the cultural system and socio-cultural domains. The interactionist account runs together, or does not distinguish between, what race ideas *say* as elements in the cultural system (such as that certain collectivities, somatically defined, are unchangeably inferior to other collectivities) with what people take them to *mean*. As we have noted before, this is a difficulty that is unavoidable if 'sayings' and 'meanings' are held to be mutually constitutive.

We can also now apply the distinction, elaborated in the previous chapter, between social scientific and lay discourses to our dualist conception. At the level of everyday life, we find race ideas and symbolic forms employed as resources by individuals, both at a personal, biographical level, where race ideas are used to identify a particular sense of self as a member, say, of this or that race (see, for example, Back 1996; Billig 1995; Cohen 1992); and, more generally, as elements in the cultural 'ways of going on' where race ideas form part of the stock of mutual knowledges actors draw upon in their negotiation of everyday encounters. In this way, as writers such as Thompson and Smaje have pointed out, symbolic forms of race ideas – national anthems, routine discursive depictions of 'them' and 'us' and the daily rituals of what Billig has described as 'banal nationalism' (Billig 1995) – are continuously and creatively implicated in the constitution of social relations (Smaje 1997; Thompson 1990). A consistent realism will, however, circumscribe the extent of this constitution, since important aspects of structured social relations, such as those to do with the location of agents within distributions of material and cultural resources, are involuntaristic and anterior.

As an item of intelligibilia in the cultural system, race ideas can also be taken up by people with social scientific purposes, and within such discourses, and for these purposes, they can be the object of critique. Thus we have analysts' accounts of actors' accounts. Analysts' accounts must recognize the existential, hermeneutic validity of actors' accounts, so the employment of race ideas and symbolic forms by social actors in the formulation of interactional rules for 'getting on' is not a consequence of 'cultural doping or duping'. This should not prevent the analyst of actors' accounts from recognizing the limited and partial character of these accounts or from framing their own accounts in terms and concepts more suited to social scientific purposes. Further, these terms and concepts will often occupy an implicitly critical position towards the notions employed by actors themselves, partly because they are more explicitly the objects of logical and theoretical scrutiny.

We can separate race ideas from something called 'race'. Race ideas are ideas about race, the division of human populations into groups designated as races. As cultural system items, race ideas are cultural resources available for mobilization by individuals and groups for all sorts of purposes. Furthermore, the relations between ideas are logical. Ideas cannot cause anything; they are inert until taken up by social actors. These logical relations are a proper object of sociological knowledge and can be examined as such. As we saw earlier, social scientific concepts have to take their place within, assimilate with, already existing networks of formally defined concepts, themselves the product of more all-embracing theoretical discourses such as Marxism, functionalism, interactionism and so forth. In social scientific accounts, then, the proposition that there are races in any socially significant sense of genetically fixed, biologically determined groups within the human population is demonstrably false.

Race ideas make this claim, and in so far as they make it, are plainly illusory. Note that this is a claim about what race ideas *say* as logical propositions; it makes no statements about what social actors *mean* when they employ race ideas for their own purposes. Certainly the fact that an idea is illogical or contradictory does not disqualify it from being used by people, nor does it imply that they are misinformed or irrational in using it. They may not be aware of its contradictory or illogical nature, perhaps because this is not apparent until the idea is considered in a different discourse and placed in relation to other ideas; perhaps because the contradiction is contestable; or perhaps because the contradiction or illogicality is not regarded as significant or worth doing anything about. The meat eater may well love animals and the car driver may well care about the levels of air pollution but it does not make their positions any the less contradictory or inconsistent as *logical propositions*. Whether they want to do anything about the inconsistency will depend on the balance of social forces as it were: eating a vegetarian diet may be too expensive and inconvenient, for instance, or the reliability of public transport too poor.

The illogicality of race ideas, however, does disqualify them as *social scientific* concepts, since they have no material referent and are therefore a misidentification, at the level of common sense lay discourse, of social processes, relations and relationships. Again this does not mean that in providing sociological accounts of actors' accounts, we cannot recognize the role of race ideas in such accounts, but it does mean that in social scientific accounts race ideas cannot figure as *explanatory* concepts.

Let me add a final rider to this discussion. Whilst race ideas are illusory, it is essential to note that this illusoriness can only be demonstrated *within scientific discourse*, that is where race ideas make claims about the genotypical and phenotypical characteristics of human populations on the basis of concepts that overlap with common conceptual networks within such discourse. Precisely because of this overlap, as we have noted before, the validity of race ideas can be assessed within scientific discourses, and *within these discourses*, we can assert race ideas to be false and illusory. This is an entirely separate question from how actors employ such ideas and for what purposes. It is to this that we now turn.

Having established some ontological properties of race ideas at the cultural system level, a realist analytical dualism requires that we analyse its two-fold relationship to human agency. This relationship can best be expressed in the following questions. How do consistencies and contradictions at the cultural system level affect people, by, for example, compelling various sorts of cognitive modification? And how do our actions affect consistencies and contradictions at the cultural system level, that is, how do people form and transform its logical properties?

Let us begin the task by summarizing first of all what analytical dualism implies about race ideas:

1   Race ideas are elements in the cultural system and like all such elements they originate from sociocultural interaction and are generated therefore by social actors.

2   Over time, race ideas escape the clutches, as it were, of their originators and

acquire autonomy as denizens of the cultural system, after which time we can examine how they act back upon subsequent generations.

3. Since people go on making culture we can investigate how new items enter the cultural system and older ones get displaced, for example, the displacement of race ideas by notion of cultural difference as a basis for dividing human populations.

This three stage, temporal cycle of analysis is Archer's morphogenetic cycle (Archer 1989, 1995). The cycle begins at stage one (T_1), where we specify the cultural conditions that are necessarily antecedent to the cultural interaction that takes place at stage two (T_2), and which in turn eventually issues in some form of cultural elaboration at stage three (T_3).

Returning to the logical relations between elements within the cultural system, we can now reintroduce the notion of situational logics. My argument is that in mobilizing various elements of the cultural system for their particular purposes people enmesh themselves in certain situational logics which derive from the logical relations between those elements.

For example, two central notions in the cultural system of postwar Britain were a belief in a hierarchy of races with different degrees of assimilability to a putative British 'way of life' (belief A) and a belief in the non-legitimacy of colour discrimination (belief B). The arrival of colonial subjects seeking work in the UK after 1947 prompted some senior politicians to mobilize these beliefs in their efforts to secure legislative control of immigration from the colonies. The logically contradictory nature of the propositions themselves compelled a particular situational logic for these politicians. The conflicting elements of belief A and belief B had to be reconciled by, for example, seeking criteria for legislative control which would conceal its colour discriminatory intent or restricting colonial immigration by covert administrative means (Carter, Green and Halpern 1996; Carter, Harris and Joshi 1993). In other words, we have a situational logic in which certain social actors are constrained by the logical relations between ideas and wrestle to minimize or otherwise reconcile these.

The specific ways in which different individuals and groups grapple with the situational constraints generated by logically contradictory cultural system elements is a matter for empirical investigation. Yet, the result is always cultural elaboration in which both belief A and belief B come to be modified by social actors in the pursuit of their particular interests. Such a situational logic is, of course, conditional not determining, and allows a variety of means for its resolution, as we shall see in detail in the next two chapters. Nevertheless, we can discern here a causally influential relationship between cultural system items and sociocultural interaction which points again to the importance of being attentive to the forms and content of race ideas.

So far I have made a series of claims about the ontological features of race ideas as cultural system elements. I have further suggested they can be assessed as logical propositions within social scientific discourses, where they can be found to be incoherent, inconsistent and false. This does not compromise their existential vitality as ideas accessible to lay actors as a means of ordering the rules of the everyday world and as constitutive of personal and interactive discourses. Finally I have repeatedly stressed the significance of social scientific accounts of the forms and content of race ideas. This is important first because the concrete forms of actors' beliefs are sociologically significant. So, although they may all use versions of race ideas, there are crucial distinctions to be drawn between the member of the Ku Klux Klan, the working class supporter of Jean Marie Le Pen and the Cabinet minister arguing for immigration controls of 'coloured colonial workers'. Second, the logical relations that exist between race ideas and other items within the cultural system, and the situational logics that flow from these, can only be adequately identified if the propositional forms of these ideas are given ideational integrity.

RACISM AND RACIALIZATION

So far in this discussion we have not had to identify an ambiguous notion of race by clamping it securely in a collar of inverted commas. Instead we have talked of race ideas, in much the same way as we might talk of Enlightenment ideas or conservative ideas or ideas about sexuality. Race ideas are items available for use by the average person seeking to pursue their common or garden interests as well as by the more fastidious social scientist seeking a way of making sociological sense of those interests (as well as of their own).

Unsurprisingly, perhaps, since it is consistent with the analysis offered above, I wish to regard racism as a particular form of race ideas. Following Miles (1989), I suggest that racism is characterized by the following features: first, the signification, in terms of a notion of race, of some biological characteristic as the criterion by which a collectivity may be identified and 'marked out'; second, the group identified in this way must be attributed with additional characteristics that are evaluated negatively. Third, these group characteristics are often seen to carry damaging consequences if allowed to proliferate or intermingle with those outside the group, a theme usually expressed in images of contamination or pollution.

Racism, as a particular form of race ideas, is also an item in the cultural system. This means that its logical relations with other cultural items can be assessed and that its propositional claims – that there are races, that these are biologically grounded and their boundaries unalterable, that races should not commingle – can be evaluated. Social science has much to say about racism, then, beyond the endless description of its various phenomenological forms. Second, the status of racism as an element in the cultural system is analytically distinct from its status as a factor in social and cultural interaction.

This allows us to make two further, important claims about racism:

1   that it is practically adequate, in the sense that social actors and agents take up
     cultural system resources in so far as they can provide a working account of their
     social world and its rules and regularities. Few individuals will persist with a view
     of the world that persistently disables the pursuit of their interests and does not
     allow them to function as social actors within their particular milieu;

2   that it is analytically distinct from exclusionary practices – Miles (1989: 78) again: 'the concept of exclusionary practice refers to both intentional actions and unintended consequences which create patterns of inequality'. From our dualist perspective it is clear why racism should be regarded as analytically distinct in this way, since racism is a configuration of ideational elements whilst exclusionary practices are the products of sociocultural interaction. Thus, as Miles observes, 'the concept of exclusionary practice refers only to a concrete act or process and does not presuppose the nature of the determination' (1989: 78). In other words, patterns of inequality are not *straightforwardly* the product of human intention – class inequalities are not the simple outcome of class discriminatory intentions, for instance, as I have argued elsewhere (Carter and Williams 1907). Rather, it is the *links* between culture and agency that are crucial, links that can only be demonstrated on the basis of concrete, historical analysis and which are accessible only to accounts that recognize their analytical distinctiveness.

However, it is partly because of the commitment to the analytical distinctiveness of culture and agency noted above that I wish to register some reservations about the concept of racialization as employed by Miles. The realist argument advanced here does point to some difficulties and ambiguities with the term. I wish to propose a more specific use of the racialization concept, one that I shall adopt in the analysis of postwar immigration policy in the UK.

Miles uses the concept of racialization:

> to refer to those instances where social relations between people have been structured by the signification of human biological characteristics in such a way as to define and construct differentiated social collectivities . . . The concept therefore refers to a process of categorisation, a representational process of defining an Other . . . Racialisation is a dialectical process of signification.
>
> (Miles 1989: 75)

Racialization has a specific temporal relation with race ideas, since it also refers 'to the historical emergence of the idea of "race" and to its subsequent reproduction and application. Furthermore, the racialization of human beings entails the racialization of the processes in which they participate and the structures and institutions that result' (Miles 1989: 76).

Now the term 'entails' seems to have very broad shoulders. It is required to carry a claim about ideas – the emergence of the idea of race and its subsequent reproduction and application as a signifying process, or in our terms its development as an item within the cultural system – over to the domain of structural conditions and processes. What seems to be missing is the mediating dimension of agency: it is not racialization as a signifying practice *itself* that structures social relations but those who employ this practice. Of course, subsequent social actors will encounter these signifying practices as structural givens, which they may modify or reproduce, but their provenance in previous sociocultural interaction must not be overlooked.

So, it remains the case that if racialization refers to a 'process of categorisation', then it must be a product of agency (only persons can categorize on the basis of ideas), and the structuring element remains ambiguous.

The conflation of structure and agency that seems implicit in Miles' formulation has some important consequences. First of all it gives rise to an ambiguity of meaning about the racialization process itself. Is it an ideational phenomenon, describing a historical shift in which groups and individuals draw more and more widely on race ideas in their interpretations of the social world and as a basis for their interaction within it? Or is it a structural phenomenon in which social institutions and practices increasingly operate on principles derived from race ideas. Or is it about both of these things?

This raises a further difficulty, namely the sense to be given to the claim that racialization refers to 'those instances where social relations between people have been structured by the signification of human biological characteristics in such a way as to define and construct differentiated social collectivities'. It is unclear here whether the structuring of social relations in terms of race ideas means that exclusionary practices are based on race ideas, that is organized on the basis of, or justified in terms of, race ideas; or that social relations are understood by social actors in terms of race ideas; or that race ideas have become the dominant mode of understanding social relations. As noted above, one might wonder whether to what extent it may be claimed that social relations are structured by a signifying process. This lack of clarity is reflected in the inconsistent ways in which the racialization concept has been employed by practitioners (see, for example, Law 1996; Malik 1996; Small 1994), often so loosely as to mean anything understood by social actors in race terms.

A second consequence of Miles' formulation is that it has a latent empiricism at its heart (this is itself a product of the conflation of agency and structure noted earlier). If racialization is a representational process of defining an Other which 'entails the racialisation of the processes in which they participate and the structures and institutions that result' then we are back to the experiential empiricism that dogged the interactionist accounts examined in Chapter 1. Here, it will be recalled, it is what social actors believe, how they represent the world, that structures social relations. Miles' formulation carries a strong implication that structures and institutions are the product of racialization, that is of the ideas people have about race. This in turn appears to sit awkwardly with his argument that exclusionary practices must be analytically separable from their determinations. If structures and institutions 'result from' a racialization process, a process of signification where collectivities get constructed as 'races', then surely such structures and institutions, along with the exclusionary practices which they enforce, do carry their own determinations. How can we know whether social relations have been racialized unless their determinations are given in the relations themselves, that is unless we take racialized social relations to be those relations understood and interpreted by actors in terms of race ideas – a point which Miles uses to impressive effect in his own critiques of 'race relations'? (See Anthias and Yuval-Davis 1993 for a similar point.)

Finally, if racialization is taken as a description of the incidence of race ideas amongst groups and individuals and their use in the pursuit of interests, then it must be a contemporary process; dead actors cannot think. And if it is a contemporary process, then the ways in which action always occurs within, and is conditioned by, antecedent structural and cultural relations with their own emergent properties, are obscured. Once again the temporal dimension is sunk without trace.

A concept of racialization is undoubtedly useful, and analytical dualism allows a rescue operation (although not one that Miles himself might be grateful for). Consistent with the position I have advocated here, racialization as a process must be restricted to a description of the take-up of race ideas. However, regarding race ideas as partially autonomous cultural system items allows us to explore the links between their take-up by current actors and their status as the outcome of earlier social and cultural interaction, that is as the outcome of historical agency, of what previous social actors have done. Racialization, in this modified version, rests on race ideas, is posterior to them and is a description of their popularity as items within the cultural system. Its effects on social structures and social relations is a matter of the analysis of social interaction and it is unhelpful to argue that structures and relations too can be racialized, except in the sense of coming to be interpreted by social actors in terms of race ideas. Racialization is not a causal process that will out no matter what actual discourses or ideas actors employ. Using this modified notion of racialization, the next section outlines a realist account of the relations between racism and inequality drawing on the morphogenetic model of Archer.

EXCLUSIONARY PRACTICES, INEQUALITY AND RACISM: A MORPHOGENETIC APPROACH

Archer's morphogenetic model rests squarely on analytical dualism, the analytical separability of structure and agency and of culture and agency. Analysis itself proceeds in the form of three stage cycles. It begins from the structural (and cultural) conditions at T_1. These are antecedent and so partially autonomous from the social (and cultural interaction) occurring at T_2, where social actors (collective and individual) pursue interests under the conditions given by T_1. This culminates in structural (and cultural) elaboration at T_3, where in pursuing their interests social actors and agents, both consciously and unintentionally, modify or reproduce the conditions at T_1. This brings us to the start of another morphogenetic cycle with a new T_1.

So our morphogenetic account must begin with the structural and cultural conditions of action at T_1. The specific systemic configuration identified will be an emergent feature of the relations between component parts or structures. For example, amongst the component structures of the post-1945 British nation state were capitalist relations of production, colonial and imperialist relations with a large overseas empire, structures of governance and political power, as well as various ideological notions about women and domestic labour, about social democracy and the postwar world and so on. The contingent combination of these social structural relations in turn generates further emergent systemic properties. The decision of the Labour government in the immediate postwar period to police a vast empire, itself a decision conditioned by other component structures to do with the global distribution of economic and political power following the defeat of Nazism, led to conflict between the demands of indigenous capital for an expanded source of labour and the government's political commitment to raising the school leaving age and to reducing the number of women in paid employment outside the home. One significant emergent property of this particular, conflicting combination of parts was the creation of a postwar labour shortage.

We need to pay some attention to the notion of an emergent property (EP). An EP is quite different from the overt and relatively enduring regularities in social life such as the patterns of income distribution or educational attainment by social class or voting preferences. In each of these examples the attributes identified – respectively level of income, level of educational attainment and voting behaviour – have no necessary relation to the pattern itself; the pattern is merely a summative description. For instance, the lottery winner and the director of the privatized water company will tend to get placed in similar categories of income distribution but this will not reveal anything about the connection between their class position and their sources of income (and crucially their ability to renew their income). Emergent properties, on the other hand, are defined by the necessary and internal relations between their components: what the entity is, and its very existence, depend on these (Sayer 1994). Thus parenting is an emergent property of the relations between an adult and a child. Without either of these components, parenting simply cannot emerge (a child cannot parent itself, any more than an adult can be its own child).

Because they are irreducible to their component parts, EPs suggest certain ontological features of the world. First, they point to the fact of stratification, rather than mere differentiation: the powers of parenting exist at a different stratum from the powers of the adult or the child. Second, and most importantly, their irreducibility to their component elements gives EPs partial autonomy and thus generative causal powers producing certain social effects. Parenting, for instance, sets in train a complex network of causal influences producing a whole range of social effects, psychological, cultural and political.

Furthermore, such causal powers may be unexercised (a parent may have their child adopted or may take a radically libertarian view of parenting or may be absent for other reasons) or exercised but obscured at the level of events (parenting may have a customary range of effects, such as respect for parental authority, say, or a deep sense of emotional security, but these may be overridden by some trauma, such as war, famine, or political persecution). Although I have deliberately chosen this example because of its vividness, it is also possible to argue, as I shall be doing, that class relations, as structural elements, and race ideas, as cultural elements, are emergent properties possessing generative causal powers and producing certain social effects.

As we have noted, the powers inhering in social structures may exist unexercised or unrecognized. This means that there must be a disjunction between them and the everyday phenomenal experiences of people so that structural EPs and the actual experiences of actors are not synchronized. This is why at T_1 we need three levels of analysis: one to disengage the properties of social structure so that we can properly identify their EPs and their causal powers; a second to conceptualize the experiential so that we can properly identify its EPs and their causal powers; and a third which links them by explaining how structure actually does impinge on agency (the who and where questions) and how agents in turn react back to reproduce or transform structure.

In terms of the morphogenetic model we can see that the three levels or domains of structure, culture and agency will all have EPs, all, in turn, relatively autonomous, relatively enduring and each irreducible to the other (features which, of course, make their identification at T_1 possible). Structural EPs are distinguished by their primary dependence on material resources (physical and human); they are the outcome of resource-to-resource relations. Thus children, who command few material resources because of their formal prohibition from the labour market, usually find themselves dependent on the adult who happens to be their parent. Cultural EPs, on the other hand, are dependent on cultural and ideational resources; they are the outcome of rule to rule relations. There are fairly clear, if often inconsistent, ideas about how children should be and what childhood is, in relation to what parents should be and what parenting is, which are the outcome of earlier cultural and political conflicts.

The key feature of structural EPs and cultural EPs is that they are defined independently of their incumbents and of the social interaction taking place between these. Again a consistent realism requires this since EPs are anterior – the individual child or parent encounters an already given set of material and cultural resources, themselves the product of previous social interaction – and because the relevant context for the identification of CEPs and SEPs are respectively, cultural and social structures. As we have argued before, the level of social interaction only yields the fallible, partial appreciation which people have of their structural context.

What does this model offer to our analysis of racism? First of all, we can suggest that class relations are a structural emergent property and that these relations are *primarily* responsible for distributions of wealth and income within capitalist societies. Now the relationship between class relations and income distribution is, in terms of our earlier discussion, a necessary and internal one, whilst the relationship of both with exclusionary practices or mechanisms of discrimination based on race ideas is contingent. This is the case in two senses: discrimination on the grounds of race ideas does not have a necessary and internal relation to class relations and when such ideas do figure in, say, defining the parameters of the working population, this is itself contingent.

Second, structural relationships account for why people find themselves in particular positions – their locations as 'social agents' in Archer's vocabulary. Structural relationships thus condition those with whom they are or are not objectively predisposed to collaborate. Second, structural relationships account for why people find themselves in particular positions – their locations as 'social agents' in Archer's vocabulary. Structural relationships may thus condition those with whom they are or are not objectively predisposed to collaborate. How and why people come to occupy particular locations may tell us whether the social relations operating to place them there are congruent or incongruent. Some will be there primarily because of class relations, others because of the ways in which exclusionary practices, such as discrimination or immigration policy, have operated within the context of class relations. How these structural relations have combined with contingencies to place people in similar positions of poverty or powerlessness will affect those with whom one will feel a shared or common interest. Will the pursuit of class-based politics, for instance, benefit those who consider their poverty to be a result of discrimination or other exclusionary practices?

So, the first practical step in providing an account of racism and exclusionary practices is to identify at which historical instance we wish to 'slice' social reality. At whichever point we choose, there will necessarily be structural and cultural conditions antecedent to the interaction we wish to examine. The delineation of these conditions forms our particular T_1 in the morphogenetic cycle. Our T_1 conditions then refer to the objective, involuntaristic distribution of cultural and material goods and resources. We can be the victims or the beneficiaries of exclusionary practices prior to, and irrespective of, our ability either to recognize this or to do anything about it.

However, the realist, observes Archer, is 'committed to maintaining that the causal power of social forms is mediated through agency' (Archer 1995: 195). The very fact that structures are antecedent means that they can be identified and described and that they can have autonomy from agency. They can therefore exert a causal influence upon it by providing actors (collective and individual) with strategic objectives and interests and by providing contextual conditions for social action. The term 'conditions' needs careful attention.

From the realist point of view, structures can only condition and not determine agency because people also possess emergent powers. This has some important implications. First, any form of social or cultural conditioning can exert its effects only on people and is efficacious only through people and so is always subject to reflexivity and interpretation – structures cannot operate too far 'behind the backs' of actors lest they leave the theatre altogether. Second, the social relational positions to which agents are allocated – the working class, for instance – themselves represent emergent powers with their two defining features. They modify the capacities of their component members (working class forms of recreation rarely include a day out at Ascot or dining at the Dorchester); and they exert causal powers proper to their relations themselves vis-à-vis other agents and their groupings (working class organizations, such as trades unions, tend to pursue objectives that are antagonistic to the objectives pursued by employers' associations). Thus the interplay between structure and agency is not an account of the impact of structures on an undifferentiated, inert mass of people, but is 'a question of the confluence between two sets of emergent powers – those of the "parts" and those of the "people"' (Archer 1995: 184). And these two sets of powers may be synchronized with one another or they may not (Lockwood 1964).

Stage 2 of our morphogenetic account will consider the interplay of 'parts' and 'people'. Having detailed the cultural and structural conditions in which agents are objectively located, our T_2 examines the efforts of actors (individual and collective) and agents to alter or maintain these conditions. This entails a steady focus on the question: specifically whose activities are responsible for what and when? In turn, this requires an account of how agents, allocated to positions within a structured distribution of resources, deal with the interests arising from these and in the context of their conditioning influence. In particular, in discussing racism and exclusionary practices, this means specifying the conditions under which agents become collectively effectual (Archer's distinction is between primary agents – a pre-grouped human resource – and corporate agents – groups promoting, pursuing and articulating their collective interests.) Amongst whom, and to what extent, the promotion and pursuit of collective interests is possible will depend jointly on the conditional influences of structural emergent properties – identified at T_1 – and the extent to which these mesh with social factors affecting the cohesion possible within collectivities. For example, the notion of a 'black community' depends on a continuing shared position of exclusion and under-privilege as well as common cultural meanings about colour and about what it is to be 'black'. Although the implications of this conjoining of structural conditions and cultural meanings is discussed more fully elsewhere in this text, an important point to remember is that the potential for various forms of identity is, in a significant respect, structurally conditioned.

Here, the realist notion of a stratified social reality allows a further subtlety in the interplay between 'parts' and 'people'. Following Archer's schema (Archer 1995: 190) we can explore this interplay at four levels:

1   the positional level, where the interplay is between the structured distribution of resources (parts) and primary and collective agents (people). At this level, we can examine how, and in what ways, resources are distributed through, for example, class relations and exclusionary practices, and how these pre-structure actors' contexts and interests and condition and enable actors in various ways.

2   the level of roles, where the interplay between the structured patterning of role expectations (parts) and role performance (people) can tell us much about how racism and racialized role expectations (what it is to be a patriot, or a nationalist, or British, or French) are negotiated and modified by social actors;

3   the institutional level, where the interplay between institutional structures (parts) and organized groups (people) can be used to consider how, for example, immigration and nationality legislation has been the outcome of intense political conflict and debate or to assess the influence and responsibility of different actors (individual and collective) in the transformation or maintenance of particular institutional structures;

4   the systemic level, where the interplay is between the relations between institutional structures themselves (parts) and human populations (people). Thus the links between, say, immigration legislation, welfare policy and the maintenance of a 'reserve army of labour' and the constitution of an 'immigrant population' can be explored here.

This brings us to the final phase of Archer's morphogenetic cycle, the phase of social elaboration T_3. Stage 3 will consist of two tasks: setting out the conditions under which morphostasis versus morphogenesis occurs (whether things stay the same or whether we get change); and accounting for the form which social elaboration takes. 'Since what eventually transpires at the level of events is a combination of the tendential and the contingent,' (Archer 1995: 294) we are not in the business of providing predictive formulas but rather analytical histories of emergence. In other words, the particular ways in which the parts and the people interact in any specific historical conjuncture eventuates in equally particular forms of social elaboration. So our example of postwar Cabinet responses to colonial and Commonwealth immigration will consider the consequences of the middle phase of the cycle – sociocultural interaction – for social and political change in the context of racism and exclusionary practices. Analytical dualism again provides the compass here, with our magnetic north provided by the insight that structure, culture and agency are analytically separable. It thus becomes possible to specify which is more influential for the other, when, where and under what conditions.

SUMMARY AND CONCLUSION

This chapter has drawn out some of the possibilities made available by a sociological realist approach to the study of race ideas and racism. I have argued that race ideas, racism and racialization are all temporally distinct ideational elements, which, as cultural system items, have their own emergent properties and causal powers. Along with Miles, I have suggested that these be regarded as analytically distinct from exclusionary practices. The remainder of the chapter has elaborated a practical research programme based on Archer's morphogenetic cycle, which I have also argued provides an appropriate methodology for a realist social science. The morphogenetic cycle, with its temporally distinct stages of social conditioning, social interaction and social elaboration, grounds analytical dualism by allowing a full and proper exploration of the relations between structure and agency, or parts and people.

The account of postwar UK immigration policy considered in Chapters 5, 6 and 7 will thus begin by identifying the structural and cultural conditions relevant to analysing racism and exclusionary practices at the beginning of a specific historical period. Particular attention will be paid here to the delineation of emergent properties and to sociocultural interaction within the context of these structural and cultural conditions. Three key themes will be explored: the racialization process, that is the development and reproduction of race ideas; the relationship between immigration and nationality laws and notions of citizenship; and the social and political struggles that have developed around these issues.

5 Race concepts and the cultural system

Porpora has identified two major tasks for the realist sociological study of social structure:

> The first task is simply to describe the nature of various social structures as generating mechanisms, paying particular attention to the ways in which they generate their causal properties . . . The second task is to explain particular historical events in terms of conjunctures of structural mechanisms. Partly because each conjuncture is unique and partly because human behaviour is intrinsically non-lawlike, such explanations must take the form of a historical narrative.
>
> (Porpora 1987: 133)

It is the purpose of this and the next two chapters to accomplish these tasks by developing a historical narrative of the introduction of restrictive immigration legislation in the UK between 1945 and 1981. Three themes will be explored: the development of race ideas (the race making process); the employment of these by social actors in the pursuit of immigration restriction and struggles over definitions of citizenship and national identity; and how these struggles have shaped the politics of racism and antiracism.

The account will follow the methodological procedure of the morphogenetic scheme, with its three-stage cycle of conditioning, interaction and elaboration. The key concern of our analysis will be to explain the introduction of restrictive immigration legislation in Britain. This is a concrete sociological concern with who does what to whom, under what circumstances and why. In other words, it attempts to explain social change: how, through social interaction, people modify the world in which they live (not always intentionally, of course, and rarely in the ways they intended). Since this is, in effect, the middle stage of the cycle, it also provides us with a guide to the temporal limits of our examples. Going backwards first, as it were, our account needs to start before efforts to implement restrictive immigration legislation were undertaken since we need to know what it was that people were trying to change. Stage one of a morphogenetic approach then begins with an examination of the context prior to legislation and restriction.

1945 is an appropriate starting point (only for stage one of *this* study, since it is itself the product of previous cycles of social elaboration). At the close of the Second World War the British nation state found itself in a radically changed economic and political climate. More pertinently, and partly as a result of this changed climate, several structural and cultural emergent properties became causally influential in shaping actors' responses to restriction. Necessarily, the choice of 1945 is arbitrary to some degree. Social interaction, social relations and cultural items and properties cannot be confined to temporal brackets in this way. But as I have argued earlier, sociological analysis has to set limits on which sequence of social interaction is to be interpreted and this entails practical judgements about where these limits are to be drawn.

Stage one of the morphogenetic sequence identifies the structural and cultural conditions which shape the projects of social actors (individual and collective) and which facilitate or obstruct them in various ways. Stage three considers the effects of actors' efforts to introduce or resist or counter the introduction of restrictive legislation. 1981, the year in which the British Nationality Act was passed, forms an obvious terminating point for our narrative. The Act brought formal definitions of citizenship into line with the restrictive, informal definitions that had been applied through a series of immigration Acts. In effect, it made further restrictive immigration legislation unnecessary by endorsing a narrow notion of citizenship based on notions of 'belonging' and declaring all non-citizens immigrants, with no rights of entry and settlement (Juss 1993). In so far as this may be regarded as the end of the restrictionist project begun in the late 1940s, it may also serve as the end of our morphogenetic cycle.

STAGE 1: STRUCTURAL AND CULTURAL CONDITIONS

The first stage of analysis is concerned with the delineation of structural and cultural conditions which were influential at the point at which our account 'slices' social reality and with tracing the ways in which they shape the situations in which people find themselves (their contextual conditions of action). Principally, this means first describing the ideational environment and how this objectively limits that which can be reproduced, reformulated, rejected or transformed, a process Archer terms 'logging the cultural register' (Archer 1995); and second describing anterior material structures, the distribution of material resources and the disposition of material relations, that are historically prior to social actors (as indeed they have to be if actors are to engage in practices aimed at modifying or sustaining them).

The notion of structural and cultural conditioning does not entail a commitment to the idea that structural and cultural forces operate entirely autonomously, with 'a mind of their own', pressing on actors with an inescapable hydraulic inevitability. Reminding ourselves of the key tenets of analytical dualism will show us why this is so, since these rest on the idea of emergence and its corollary, the recognition of the (partially) independent powers of parts and people.

The task, then, is to provide an account of how sociocultural structures condition, not determine, what actors can and cannot do. It is still, though, actors that *do* things, have aspirations, political projects, want to accomplish tasks, to change things or keep them the same. Nevertheless, the situations people find themselves in, involuntaristically, will shape what it is people want to do and have some influence on their chances of being able to do it. So we begin our identification of structural and cultural conditions by starting from the actors themselves and what they want. By assessing actors' projects and tracing empirically their efforts to accomplish them we can pick out retroductively the relevant structural and cultural conditions, those structured features of social reality that frustrate or further peoples' efforts either to keep things as they are or to change them in some way or another.

The period between 1945 and 1981 is a key one in the sociological discussion of racism in Britain. It was the period when 'the Empire struck back' and migration from the colonies to the UK became an increasingly prominent feature of political and public debate. Although there were significant numbers of migrants from other nation states, especially Europe and Ireland (Carter, Harris and Joshi 1993; Holmes 1988, 1991; Kay and Miles 1992; Miles and Phizacklea 1984; Moore and Wallace 1975), the salience of colonial immigration had much to do with the fact that it was perceived by some politicians and by significant sections of the public as 'coloured immigration'. Although this migratory movement began in 1947 and 1948 (Carter, Harris and Joshi 1993; Lunn 1989), the ending of the Second World War in 1945 remains an appropriate starting point since some of the structural conditions influencing postwar developments emerge from it.

The passing of the 1981 British Nationality Act (it came into legislative effect in 1983) marks the 'end slice' of the period. The Act effectively redefined British nationality in terms consonant with those established *de facto* by the Immigration Acts of 1962, 1968 and 1971, a redefinition which rested squarely on the notion that 'Britishness' was something that could only be acquired over generations. Immigrants whose British citizenship was the result of imperial largesse rather than birth on British soil, or of a 'kith and kin' connection to it, were therefore ineligible. They could not be British. This marks the end of the political struggle to reverse the imperial commitment to a common subject status in order to prevent the further immigration of 'coloured colonials' to the UK.

Who were the key social actors in this period in terms of the three themes outlined above? First, there was the Cabinet. Ministers of both parties throughout this period saw the restriction of 'coloured immigration' as an important objective. As legislators they were macro actors exerting a major political influence on the passage of immigration and nationality laws. A second influential social group or agent was employers. Confronted with a shortage of labour in the postwar period, their demand for workers both exerted considerable pressure on governments to provide alternative sources of labour and acted as an incentive for direct recruitment from outside the boundaries of the nation state. The availability of employment also indirectly reassured those migrants seeking work in the UK that there were definite advantages attached to doing so.

A third key actor was the migrants themselves, seeking to realize the benefits of moving to an expanding economy and finding that they are subject to discrimination and prejudice. Other significant social actors were politicians, trades unions and the electorate.

This account will take as its primary focus senior politicians in government. There are several reasons for this. First, from a practical point of view it would be beyond the scope and aims of the present book to provide a richly textured history of the postwar period. Second, such a project is not necessary to illustrate the potential of the realist approach proposed here. Theoretical themes and their empirical demonstration can be more readily aligned by concentrating steadily on the actions of senior politicians. Finally, it is a leading point of my account that social change comes about as a result of what social actors do, and senior politicians played a major role in the introduction of immigration and nationality laws in Britain. For these reasons, our example will examine how senior politicians struggled with the issues of controlling who was to be allowed to enter the country and the redefinition of who was properly British that these entailed, although this will at various points involve exploring their interactions with the other social actors identified earlier. The question now is: how were the various projects pursued by these social actors shaped by the anterior structural and cultural conditions in which they found themselves?

Postwar Britain was a capitalist society whose key features were private ownership of the means of production and an associated division of social classes (although the significance of nationalization should not be overlooked; private ownership of the profitable means of production is perhaps a more accurate description). In this sense Britain after 1945 was very much the same society as it had been before 1940. The war, though, had generated a host of structural and cultural features that in many respects ensured that it would be markedly different. Materially, Britain was now a country 'cut to the bone', in Attlee's words. There were shortages of coal, transport, food and raw materials, and the country 'did not have the resources to pay the bills which would be necessary to meet her obligations, to feed the people and bring the troops back home' (Harris 1984: 271). The abrupt termination by President Truman of the wartime Lend-Lease arrangement exacerbated this desperate situation and necessitated the negotiation of a loan from the US government, the conditions of which, many experts felt, were impossible to fulfil (Childs 1992: 24). The restoration, expansion and modernization of industrial production thus became a major priority for the new Labour government of Clement Attlee (Tiratsoo and Tomlinson 1993: 19–20).

However, the government's vested interest in striving as quickly as possible for a more efficient capitalism, especially in conditions of postwar austerity, had to be balanced against other vested interests generated by the experience of the war. Four social actors were especially significant in this context: private industry, the trade union leadership, trade union members and the electorate.

The government swiftly reassured private industry that its interests were not likely to be jeopardized, despite an ambitious nationalization programme and an overwhelming popular mandate for reform. This was because there were clear costs to be paid for ignoring the managerial and technical skills of private industry in meeting the economic crisis; also the government felt that needlessly antagonizing private industry would make the crisis a good deal worse. Further, as Morgan notes, it had doctrinaire reasons for not extending its programme of nationalization, insisting instead on 'democratic forms of planning' that ruled out compulsion and 'respected the rights of the individual' (Morgan 1984: 130–1).

In the matter of recovery, the interests of private industry and the government were largely congruent, generating a situational logic in which both shared the objective of industrial expansion. Put more formally, the relations between the Labour government and private industry were second order relations between emergent properties which were necessarily complementary: what private industry wanted, so too did the Labour government, and the satisfaction of both rested crucially on what the other did (which is not to say, of course, that industrialists always appreciated the efforts of government to intervene in this area). This situational logic entails at the cultural level a process of ideational systematization, whereby the ideas of the mixed economy and 'democratic forms of planning' logically endorse ideas about welfare capitalism and the private ownership of the means of production. Advocating one invokes the other in a constant logical process of protection and correction that causally conditions what the actors consider possible and desirable and the sorts of ideas they can draw upon in order to accomplish these.

Relationships with the trade union leadership were of a different complexity. The union leadership had emerged from the war with increased influence within the Labour Party, a fact reflected in the union-based political careers of men like Ernest Bevin, Attlee's Foreign Secretary, Aneurin Bevan, the Minister of Health and George Isaacs, the Minister of Labour. Furthermore, the trade union leadership had demonstrated during the war its effectiveness as a 'responsible fourth estate' not least in its readiness to discipline recalcitrant members. After 1945 men such as Tom Williamson of the General and Municipal Workers' Union, Arthur Deakin of the Transport and General Workers' Union and Jack Tanner of the Amalgamated Engineering Union enjoyed ready access to the Labour government. In return they discharged their role as the 'labour lieutenants of capital', to use Wright Mills' phrase, with exemplary expedition, ensuring union support for the wage freeze imposed by the government in 1949, vehemently denouncing the striking London dockers in the same year and striking market workers and London busworkers in 1950.

This 'intimate symbiosis between the unions and the Labour Party' (Morgan 1984: 79) was again a consequence of the necessary complementarity of vested interests between them. For the union leadership a Labour government meant not only enhanced political influence and status, with its attendant bonuses of political rewards; it was also widely seen as the political arm of the trade union movement. What was good for Labour must be good for the union leaders, since the unions and the Labour Party together represented the interests of the working class. Again, at the ideational level this generated a logic of ideational systematization, the mutual reinforcement and embellishment of ideas, producing, as

Morgan notes, a 'community of outlook between the ideas and instincts of the Labour Party and the TUC at every stage, from 1945 onwards' (Morgan 1984: 79). We have here another set of second order relations between emergent properties, as a result of which the roles occupied by union leaders came to have an enlarged scope after 1945 whilst the capacities of the government to discipline and constrain the working population were correspondingly widened.

Whereas the second order relations between the Labour government and private industry, and between the Labour government and the trade union leadership, were ones of necessary complementarity, this was not the case with the other two social actors to be considered, namely the trade union rank and file and the electorate. Organized labour has a vested interest in improving or defending its standard of living. The evaluation of the costs and benefits accruing to particular ways of doing this is difficult. It may be the case, for instance, that people are convinced that accepting a pay freeze under a Labour government is a necessary measure if the economy is to recover and if a government fundamentally committed to representing their interests is to remain in power. On the other hand, they may be prepared to go along with this temporarily, reasoning that a permanent pay freeze hardly amounts to adequate representation of their interests.

The predicament of capitalism in Britain in 1945 was obviously likely to render the relations between organized labour and government fragile, although this was subdued to an extent by the widespread belief that the newly elected Attlee government was a 'people's government'. Initially at least, the organized working class seemed prepared to wait and see. Ministers anxious to legitimate measures that hit working class living standards especially hard did so by appealing to a common purpose based on this forbearance. The programmes of nationalization and the introduction of a National Health Service also suppressed the incompatibilities between the interests of a government aiming to restore the productiveness of a private enterprise economy and the interests of the working class.

However the situational logic of necessary incompatibilities is compromise, because the advancement of vested interests always carries the risk of counter actualizing the contrary interests and so threatening the relation itself. Efforts to improve the productiveness of British capitalism were conditioned by the unwillingness of sections of the labouring population to accept the consequences for their own living standards. Between 1947 and 1951, the Attlee government faced strikes by miners, dockers, London busworkers, gas workers, power workers, Smithfield market drivers and railway workers. System integration and social integration were thus liable to go 'out of synch'.

The final social actor considered here is the electorate. Obviously this group overlaps with the previous ones (members of trade unions, for instance, are also part of the electorate) and the situational logic is similar too, namely compromise. Governments cannot afford to push policies that threaten to actualize oppositional interests (the struggle to implement a National Health Service in the teeth of opposition from the medical profession is a case in point). There is little doubt that the new Labour Government enjoyed a great deal of popular support in 1945 (Childs 1992; Harris 1984; Morgan 1984) and this gave it considerable room to manoeuvre, but already by 1947 the balancing of capitalist regeneration with the policing of a colonial empire and a programme of social reform was undermining the government's popularity.

Having sketched in broad strokes some of the general structural and cultural conditions of Britain in the immediate postwar period, let me now focus more sharply on the three themes central to this account: the development of race ideas; the expression and embodiment of these in immigration and nationality legislation; and the political consequences of this.

RACE IDEAS AND CULTURAL CONDITIONS IN STAGE ONE

A number of writers have testified to the vigour and importance of race ideas in postwar Britain (Banton and Harwood 1975; Barkan 1991; Carter, Green and Halpern 1996; Foot 1965; Gilroy 1987; Hall *et al.* 1978; Hiro 1971; Humphry and Ward 1971; Kohn 1996; Malik 1996; Miles and Phizacklea 1984; Phizacklea and Miles 1980; Rattansi 1992; Rex and Tomlinson 1979; Richmond 1961; Robbins 1997; Smith 1987; Solomos and Back 1995; Stepan 1982). The concern in this section is with a key cultural emergent property that powerfully shapes the use of race ideas during the 1945–81 period: the growing contradiction between the ideas of science and the ideas of race.

It is beyond the scope of the present work to delineate the development of race ideas in Britain from the seventeenth century onwards, but as Malik and others have shown, ideas about race and ideas about science were initially mutually reinforcing (Barkan 1991; Kohn 1996; Malik 1996; Stepan 1982). This relation was captured in the term commonly used to describe the race ideas of the Victorian period, 'scientific racism'. 'Scientific racism' itself emerged from an earlier period of sociocultural interaction and it powerfully wedded a positivistic commitment to scientific principles and progress, principally realized through the discovery of objective laws, with a belief in the reality of races.

It is important to note that for 'scientific racism', and certainly for many Victorians, race ideas were 'a description of social distinctions not colour differences' (Bolt 1971; Lorimer 1978; Malik 1996: 91). Race ideas were drawn upon to interpret not only colonialism and imperialism, but also the inequalities of European societies. The key propositions of 'scientific racism' were that humanity could be divided into discrete groups called races; that these divisions were immutable because of their provenance in scientifically established biological categories; and that these divisions entailed social and political consequences (Malik 1996; Stepan 1982). This made 'scientific racism' sufficiently flexible for a variety of political projects.

For as long as race ideas depended heavily on scientific rationality for their credibility they remained vulnerable to any divergence between race thinking and science. Such a divergence emerged in the 1930s as scientists applied scientific rationality to race ideas themselves, a process prompted by changes in the political attitudes to race ideas. Barkan has provided an excellent account of these developments. 'If science legitimized racism', he observes, 'it also made it vulnerable to changes in scientific outlook. To the degree that science was subject to its own internal dynamics, scientific developments served eventually to discredit racist claims' (Barkan 1991: 19).

This shift in the logical relation between cultural system items – race ideas and scientific rationality – from one of complementarity to one of contradiction carries consequences for those who wish to employ race ideas. Again Barkan sums it up nicely: 'once a theory was categorically proved wrong, no political commitment in an open society could sustain it' (Barkan 1991: 5). This is an important cultural condition applying in the postwar period in Britain. The notion that there are races, biologically grounded and scientifically demonstrable, could no longer be publicly sustained. Those who wish to employ the notion face a limited number of options. They may abandon the concept altogether, for instance. Alternatively, they may dispute the scientific critique. Finally, they may adopt some sort of compromise, either by modifying the critique (it may be the case that races do not exist in the narrow biological sense but the term still has a general social utility as a description of different human groups) or by seeking a defence of immutable difference in a domain invulnerable to scientific critique (such as culture). Each choice carries penalties and rewards.

In 1948 the Attlee government found itself confronted with the contingent prospect of migration from the colonies to the UK as colonial workers found the appeal of work in the 'mother country' stronger than the appeal of likely unemployment in a British colony. Colonial workers, as British subjects, had unrestricted rights of entry and settlement into the UK, a right that in 1948 the government had reaffirmed in the British Nationality Act. Under the Act, British subjects became 'Citizens of the UK and Colonies', a designation that continued to carry the right of unrestricted entry and settlement.

However, senior politicians and some MPs regarded the migration of colonial workers in terms that drew on race ideas. Two days after the arrival of the passenger liner *Empire Windrush* at Tilbury, carrying 492 Jamaicans coming to England to search for work, Clement Attlee received a letter signed by 11 MPs from his own party. The letter called for the control of colonial immigration, arguing that 'An influx of coloured people domiciled here is likely to impair the harmony, strength and cohesion of our public and social life and to cause discord and unhappiness among all concerned' (HO 213/244, J. Murray *et al.* to Prime Minister 22 June 1948).

In succinctly linking a phenotypical attribute – skin colour – to assimilability, the MPs actualized an emergent feature of colonial relations, namely the encoding of subordination and inferiority in terms of colour, a process of signification largely accomplished through the use of a notion of race. In the postwar period the mobilization of these forms of race ideas faced actors with a tangle of logical difficulties.

First of all the notion of race itself was scientifically disreputable: any claims that races existed as a matter of scientific fact would have been artless and indefensible. Furthermore, the genocidal mania of the Nazi regime, and the sustenance it drew from race ideas, made any explicit use of such ideas politically perilous. This may be why the Labour MPs avoided any reference to races in their letter to Attlee.

Additionally, there was a powerful second order emergent property (a product of the relations between relations) operating in the context of postwar Britain that provided a further cultural condition within which politicians had to operate. The pre-war conviction among Labour politicians that Britain must remain a great power (Darwin 1988; Louis 1977) persisted after 1945. In practical terms, to compete with the USA and the USSR meant the retention of an empire. Retaining an empire in the changed context of the postwar world could not be justified on the basis of race ideas, however. Rather, the Attlee government emphasized the 'multi-racial' character of the British Empire, or Commonwealth as it was increasingly referred to, and its role as a democratic model. 'British leaders', Darwin has noted, 'saw Britain as offering a distinctive ideology to the world, a practical, democratic middle way' (Darwin 1988: 73). One of the key features of this 'distinctive ideology' was the commitment to a shared subject status amongst members of the Commonwealth, a commitment embodied in the 1948 Nationality Act.

The Act will be dealt with in more detail presently, but in introducing a 'Citizenship of the UK and Colonies', it emphasized the equality of all Commonwealth peoples. Colonial migrants and British politicians exploited this notion in different ways. Nevertheless, once in circulation as an item within the cultural system, the notion becomes common property and so cannot be eradicated easily. It comes to possess autonomy as a cultural system item, and has logical relations with other items. Hence the inconvenience of the backbenchers' letter: you cannot publicly espouse the equality of all Commonwealth citizens whilst simultaneously proposing that those who are 'coloured' are unsuited, because of an arbitrary phenotypical quality, to live and work in the UK. The claim that skin colour renders a person unassimilable to life in Britain logically contradicts a belief in the 'multiracial' equality of the Commonwealth, a contradiction US policy makers were quick to seize upon (Louis 1977).

Perhaps even more to the point, it made the practice of colour discrimination at the point of entry to the UK difficult to pursue openly. In 1948, with the prospect of significant colonial migration seemingly unthinkable, this did not seem to Labour Ministers to be much of an issue. It rapidly became one, however, and in seeking to deal with it Ministers found their courses of action constrained by the necessary incompatibility between the belief in equality and the belief that people of colour could not assimilate to life in Britain.

A relation of necessary incompatibility between ideas is an emergent cultural property that gives rise to a situational logic of constraining contradiction (Archer 1995). Within such a logic, efforts to realize idea A are invariably constrained by the fact that to do so would encourage the realization of its opposite, idea B. Thus, the readiness of politicians to pursue the Commonwealth ideal of equality, embedded in the equal right of all UK and colonies citizens to freely enter and reside in the UK, was conditioned by their awareness that this must unavoidably include 'coloured' citizens who were, because of their 'colour', held to be unsuitable for settlement in the UK. Necessary incompatibilities between items in the cultural system are therefore sites of cultural tension, as actors seek to address the contradiction and subdue it by reinterpreting the component elements.

In the case of postwar Britain, corrective action required the reinterpretation of the meanings of nationality and citizenship. This allowed the issue of 'coloured colonial' immigration to be recast as a social problem whose resolution in the form of discriminatory immigration controls was held to benefit all parties: immigration controls 'were necessary to good race relations'.

Adding a further complication to this was a third order emergent property: the asynchrony between an acute labour shortage (a structural emergent property) and the emergent cultural property of necessary incompatibility discussed above. Whilst the prospect of finding work drew UK and colonies citizens from the colonies and India and Pakistan to the UK, government policy sought vainly to curb it. Yet in order to do so it had to provide a case for restricting the movement of Commonwealth citizens while continuing to meet its labour shortage by recruiting non-UK and colonies citizens from Europe. All the while it had to take pains to ensure that the counter notion – that colour made a difference to one's entitlements as a citizen of the UK and colonies – was not actualized.

SUMMARY AND CONCLUSION

This chapter has sketched out the salient features of structural and cultural conditioning applicable to our chosen T_1 – postwar Britain in 1945 – and relevant to the particular themes of this book. Britain in 1945 was a capitalist society. This entailed that its revival in the postwar period crucially depended on expanded production that in turn required an adequate supply of labour. This became a crucial structural condition within which British policy makers had to operate and which constrained them in particular ways by making certain courses of action advantageous and, conversely, others disadvantageous.

Moreover, this emergent feature of the postwar world interacted with another: the promise of reform expressed in the comprehensive electoral victory of the Labour Party. Labour leaders thus found themselves constrained by political commitments to a national health service, the raising of the school leaving age and the nationalization of major industries.

These commitments had to be reconciled with a desire to retain an empire. Even in its Commonwealth version this still required policing, and so entailed the continuation of conscription. An additional burden was the cost involved in Attlee's decision to develop an independent nuclear deterrent. Emerging from the relations between these emergent relations (a second order emergence) is the central structural condition of labour shortage. That is, the size of the working population is itself an emergent product of political decisions about who is to count as a member of the working population (Harris 1987). So, for example, the Labour government's decision to raise the school leaving age to 15 immediately removed a cohort of 14–15 year olds from the working population by reassigning them to the school population. Making it difficult for women to work outside the home similarly made their regular participation in the formal working population problematic.

It will be clear from this summary outline that rapid economic growth represented the government's best chance of being able to resolve the pressures of these conflicting structural conditions. Such growth required an increase in the size of the working population but such an increase could not readily be sourced from within the indigenous population for the above reasons. Inexorably the government was driven towards the only other option: the recruitment of labour from outside the boundaries of the nation state.

However, a contingent consequence of the labour shortage in Britain was the attraction which migration to the 'mother country' came to have for British subjects in the colonies. Once here they encountered an ill assorted and frequently logically contradictory set of ideas and values. Two of these form significant cultural conditions at the beginning of our morphogenetic cycle: the use of race ideas in connection with notions of colour and the deployment of both in the designation of colonial status; and the formal public commitment by politicians to the notion of a 'multiracial' Commonwealth whose democratic credentials and moral leadership were captured in the equal rights of all British subjects. These two sets of ideas are not easily reconcilable, as we shall see presently.

Structures do not, of course, force people to do anything. However, they do provide the context within which interaction takes place and, by generating vested interests and situational logics, provide good reasons for doing things. It is up to actors to reflect on these and to make judgements about what is worth pursuing and the means by which it may be pursued (and these, in turn, will of course be shaped by an anterior distribution of material and cultural resources). As we have noted before, analytical dualism requires an active notion of agency. Further, this notion of agency is an emergent one, since agency is itself transformed in the process of transforming social and cultural conditions: in changing the world, people change themselves. Actors are not puppets, since their interaction generates irreducible emergent features and properties so that agency, like culture and structure, develops a partial autonomy which enables it to modify structure and culture. On the other hand, this does not commit us to a notion of fully knowledgeable social actors consciously creating the social world, as in some forms of interactionism. By emphasizing the key role of 'contextual conditions of action' (Layder 1981, 1990), realism points to the fact that interaction cannot produce its own conditions of existence. With these prefatory remarks in mind, let us now move to stage 2 of our account, the stage of social interaction.

6 Culture, structure and agency (1): 1945–51

INTRODUCTION: HISTORICAL NARRATIVE AS A RESEARCH METHOD

Stage 2, the middle stage of the morphogenetic cycle, is concerned with interaction. This raises the problem of an appropriate research method. Following Porpora (Porpora 1987), I want to suggest historical narrative as the most suitable approach, one sufficiently sensitive to the shifting and contextually specific allegiances of agency and yet capable of depicting the more obdurate influences of structural relations. There are a number of compelling reasons why historical narrative should be particularly well suited to a sociological realism.

The first of these has to do with the nature of realist explanation itself. In accounting for particular events – in this case the shift from a position of no controls on colonial and Commonwealth migration to the UK to a position of control – the realist explanation seeks a model in which a particular conjuncture of generative forces and relations, through their interaction, produces a historically unique sequence of events. This will necessarily involve a narrative description, because such a causal process will always involve a temporal sequence.

Furthermore, realist explanations accord a central place to agency. They therefore have to acknowledge methodologically the place of reflexivity and consciousness. As Porpora has noted,

> What is distinctive about consciousness as a generative mechanism is that even when it is operating in isolation, it produces behavior in a manner that is neither deterministic nor, strictly speaking, stochastic . . . Human actors grow in experience and understanding and that experience and understanding provide a necessary historical context for the explanation of action.
>
> (Porpora 1987: 93, 99)

Additionally, the effects of reflexivity and consciousness (and of what social actors and agents do) occur within the causally open system of the real world. The narrative form is most appropriate for exploring these ontological features of agency.

Porpora has summarized the general features of historical narrative as follows. First, narrative, by placing social actions in contexts that make them recognizable as representative products of the way human actors characteristically behave, can make such actions understandable (Porpora 1987: 100). Second, narrative can be couched in the conceptual vocabulary of social theory: 'if the vocabulary adopted represents a conceptual apparatus that illuminates causal connections, then the adoption of that vocabulary does provide explanation' (Porpora 1987: 101).

Third, not only can a narrative be couched in a theoretical vocabulary, but also the entire narrative can be shaped and informed by the general principles of that theory. This is especially important given the resonance that the notion of narrative has in the human sciences, particularly those influenced by postmodern notions of relativism and rhetoric. (See, for example, Billig 1993; Burke 1992; Callinicos 1995; Evans 1997; Geras 1995; Jenkins 1995; Lipstadt 1993; Rorty 1989.) For the realist, historical narratives are informed and shaped by theory, but theory understood in the specific, cognitive sense discussed in Chapter 3. Historical narratives thus need not be arbitrary stories in which empirical research and historical fact are simply insignificant minor characters.

Finally, Porpora notes, narrative is uniquely suited to capturing the stratified nature of social reality because 'It can weave together several different story lines, some involving the actions of significant individuals or groups of individuals and some involving impersonal social forces'. The narrative form is thus 'capable of integrating the structural and agential features of social life' (Porpora 1987: 103).

This is the objective of the present chapter. Utilizing a narrative form, it will seek to trace out the second stage of the morphogenetic cycle, using an empirical exposition to explain a specific sequence of events in terms of a realist account of structure and agency. Before beginning this narrative, however, we need briefly to return to the issue of empirical evidence.

Since the realist narrative seeks to move backwards and forwards across the various social domains or levels of social reality it perforce must draw on a wide range of evidential sources. The discussion of government responses to colonial and Commonwealth migration to the UK after 1945 is based on primary source material located at the Public Records Office. This provides an invaluable resource for investigating the deliberations of senior government officials, but it is not without its limitations, as Scott, for example, has pointed out (Scott 1990).

He identifies four criteria for assessing the quality of documentary evidence, all of which derive from the recognition that texts are socially situated products: authenticity (is the evidence genuine and of unquestionable origin?); credibility (is the evidence free from error and distortion?); representativeness (is the evidence typical of its kind and, if not, is the extent of its untypicality known?); and meaning (is the evidence clear and comprehensible?) (Scott 1990: 6). In addition, Scott notes, the investigator using Cabinet papers 'would have to know whether the papers he or she is able to consult are a complete or at least representative collection of all Cabinet papers produced in the relevant period' (Scott 1990: 24). Denscombe has also pointed to the fact that documents often owe more to the interpretation of those who produce them than to an objective picture of reality (Denscombe 1998).

Subject to Scott's caveats, PRO documents are used here to explore the stratified dimension of agency, that is the different powers and capacities accruing to actors and agents from their various social locations. Methodological procedures work here more as a 'counsel of prudence', to use Dunn's apt expression (Dunn 1978: 175): not as a demonstration that some accounts are wholly true (or wholly false) but as a means of guiding our recognition that human matters are matters about which descriptions can be true or false (or partly true and partly false). In view of the above, there are several points to bear in mind when considering the narrative that follows.

First, the example worked through here is an illustrative one, meant to suggest both the explanatory possibilities offered by a sociological realism and the suitability of narrative as a research method for such a realism. Second, to use Scott's distinction, I am using documentary sources as *resources* rather than as *topics*. Scott's use of these terms captures a difference in emphasis between an interest in what documents denote about the world (documents as resources) and an interest in explaining documents themselves (documents as topics) (Scott 1990: 36). Third, it follows from the realist insistence on the role of the theoretical-technical register of social science that all empirical evidence involves an act of translation or, to use Scott's formulation, 'Facts are not raw perceptions but are theoretically constructed observations' (Scott 1990: 54).

This means that the choice of concepts in social research is crucial (and this is why race as a sociological concept does not appear in the narrative account that follows). It also implies two further checks on the arbitrariness of narratives. Their embeddedness within the technical register of social science places them in the public domain within which such languages are cognitively scrutinized and assessed; and the nature of the evidence adduced is itself available for examination in terms of those technical languages. With these qualifications in mind, let us now turn to developing our narrative of stage 2 (T_2) of the morphogenetic cycle.

A STRATIFIED VIEW OF SOCIAL ACTION: ACTORS AND AGENTS

So far, we have used the terms actor and agency fairly interchangeably. When dealing with stage 2, however, greater precision is needed. Analytically, human beings may be viewed at three different levels. Human beings first are biological organisms, particular individuals with specific organismic arrangements – neurological, chemical, genotypical and so on. They may also be said to have a particular psychology or individual 'make-up' and a personal identity ('This is what I am'). Using Archer's terminology, we may refer to human beings here as persons (Archer 1995). At the level of understanding human beings as persons, social science may have only a limited usefulness (Craib 1997).

We may also regard human beings as the occupants of social roles: as parents, as students, as politicians, as working class, as immigrants. Here human beings are more properly understood as social actors, interpreting, reflexively monitoring and, depending on the context, more or less modifying the various roles they encounter. (The distribution of roles, and their malleability for different actors, will be partly determined by the anterior distribution of cultural and material resources that actors encounter at stage 1). From now on, the term social actor will be used in this specific sense. Note that the term is relational, in the sense that all social roles are relational.

There is a third level at which we may examine people and that is as agents. Agents are collectivities sharing the same life chances, where internal and necessary relations exist between these elements, namely belonging to a collectivity and sharing similar life chances. Thus in contemporary capitalist societies, being working class entails a likely distribution of cultural and material resources: more likely than the middle class to experience unemployment and poor wages, less likely to go to public school or university, shorter life expectancy and so on. Colour and sex, amongst other things, can be the basis for material and cultural distributions, although, in so far as this is the case, it is hard to see how these are internal and necessary features of capitalist societies, as opposed to contingent discriminatory features. Put another way, they are not necessary for system integration in capitalist societies. Whether, and to what extent, they are necessary for social integration is another matter (one considered further in Chapter 8).

At the level of agency (and agents are always considered in the plural, since their properties as agents derive from their membership of collectivities) we need one further distinction before being able to apply this schema at stage 2. Again following Archer's vocabulary, we can distinguish between primary and corporate agency. Primary agents are those collectivities who are unorganized, and whose effects are merely aggregate ones (the homeless, visibly sleeping in doorways, compel changes in policing). They are, to adapt Marx, agents-in-themselves, the product of anterior and involuntaristic distributions; the poor, for example, or the unemployed may be regarded as primary agents. Corporate agents are organized collectivities, conscious of shared interests and organized to pursue them. These are agents-for-themselves, players with a punch; political parties and trade unions fall into this category.

It will be clear from this account that the shift from primary agency to corporate agency is central in stage 2 of the morphogenetic cycle. Agency is not only influenced by the structural and cultural conditions obtaining at the end of stage 1, but also by the emergent properties appropriate to the agential level. These include the capacity for articulating shared interests (In what ways, and to what extent, can 'black and white unite and fight'?); for organizing collective action; for generating social movements (is antiracism an adequate political objective?); and for exercising corporate influence on decision making. In order to effect the transition from primary to corporate agency, a collectivity requires ideational alternatives (such as civil rights, black power, or antiracism) to dispute the legitimacy of the currently dominant ideas and to secure an autonomous definition of interests (equal treatment, an end to discrimination and so on). In addition collectivities require organization, that is a means of bringing together other significant interest groups in order to challenge the dominant group. As we shall now see, throughout the interactional sequence, the restructuring of immigration and nationality law and the redefinition of political agents go hand in hand.

STAGE 2: FROM UNRESTRICTED ENTRY TO CONTROLS

The movement of non-British citizens (known as aliens in British immigration law) into the UK had already been restricted by the 1905 Aliens' Act. Originally intended as a temporary measure, the Act had been renewed in 1914 and 1919, and its scope extended by the Alien (Coloured Seamen) Act of 1925 (Bolt 1971; Cohen 1984; Foot 1965; Holmes 1988; Miles and Phizacklea 1984). There were no controls on the rights of entry into, and settlement in, the UK of British subjects.

As we have seen at the end of stage 1 of our cycle in 1945, there were several groups with a vested interest in maintaining the 'no controls' position. There was the Labour Cabinet, heading a government facing daunting obstacles to reconstruction and capital accumulation. The Empire was central to the government's strategy for overcoming these, especially in the light of the government's commitment to welfare reform based on a policy of full employment. This was partly why the government introduced the 1948 Nationality Act, with its public reaffirmation of the unity of the Empire/Commonwealth embodied in the United Kingdom and colonies category of citizenship.

A second group with a vested interest in a 'no controls' position was employers, for whom labour shortages in the immediate postwar period were a pressing priority. A third group was the migrants themselves, for whom the absence of controls made material improvement through migration a practical possibility. We can now begin to refine this analysis by identifying how primary and corporate agents in stage 2 mediate the structural and cultural conditions encountered from stage 1.

Stage 2 (T_2), change in the structural and cultural conditions obtaining at stage 1(T_1), effectively begins in 1949, when the Cabinet comes to consider the possibility of restricting the movement of colonial British subjects into the UK. As a powerful interest group possessing ideas and organization, the Cabinet may be regarded as one of the key actors in our morphogenetic cycle. This is not to imply that the Cabinet, formed from whichever party, acted as a collective actor on all the issues confronting it, merely that it did so over the matter of colonial immigration. Its capacity to do so, and the manner in which it pursued the introduction of restrictive legislation, was influenced by the contextual conditions of action inherited from stage 1.

World war had exacted a harsh price on the British economy and enforced a burdensome indebtedness to the United States. The termination of the wartime Lend-Lease arrangements forced the Labour government to negotiate a £3,700 million loan from the US, as a condition of which the government was compelled to accept the Bretton Woods proposals setting up the International Monetary Fund and the International Bank. These institutions effectively established the dollar as the main reserve and trading currency in Europe. A further condition of the loan was that sterling should be made convertible with the dollar within a year. This produced a run on sterling, so ensuring that much of the loan was unavailable for industrial investment and compelling a devaluation of sterling in 1949.

Victory had also unleashed a train of expectations. For many of those who voted Labour in the 1945 general election, this was to be the government that would ensure a 'people's peace' with full employment, decent housing, a national health service and an improved standard of living. For many of those from the colonies who had fought for the allied cause and had suspended their struggles for national independence for the duration of the war, this was to be the government that would look favourably upon their demands for an end to colonial status. A flourishing and efficient capitalism was a necessary condition for satisfying any of these hopes.

The prosperity of British capitalism before 1940 had rested on a system of imperial exploitation and it quickly became clear that the postwar Labour government also saw the role of the colonies as principally one of supporting the ailing metropolitan economy (Fieldhouse 1984). There were other political advantages to being 'great friends of the jolly old empire', as Herbert Morrison, a key figure in the new Labour Cabinet, sentimentally expressed it (Palme Dutt 1954: 334). In 1945, the British Empire was still the largest colonial empire in the world. Its global status provided credibility for the Labour government's claims for an independent political role for Britain in an international setting increasingly dominated by the cold war rivalry of the USA and the USSR. Emphasizing its uniqueness as a political institution and as a source of moral leadership in the post-Nazi world also proved a useful means of holding at arm's length the imperial designs of the US government, who were only too anxious to espouse the cause of national liberation for colonial territories and so create fresh markets for US capital (Darwin 1988; Goldsworthy 1971; Louis 1977).

There were, of course, divisions within the Labour government, as well as between government departments such as the Foreign Office and the Colonial Office, about the role and future of the Empire. For example, MPs such as Fenner Brockway and Tom Driberg frequently raised in the House of Commons issues about the colour bar and discrimination in the colonial territories as well as Britain. It is not so much that these represented the views of a minority, easily brushed aside in the face of the political and economic challenges of postwar recovery, but that the Cabinet had a vested interest in retaining the Empire as a vital source of political authority and economic wealth. Thus, as Hennessey has pointed out, 'the appetite for Empire, albeit a modified one with less stress on firepower and more on welfare-cum-economic development, continued to excite "the official mind", especially when it turned to Africa' (Hennessey 1992: 224).

Defending this interest in turn generated further consequences. In its determination to ensure that colonial independence was granted only on terms favourable to what the Cabinet saw as Britain's interests, the Labour government found itself facing challenges to its rule in many parts of the Empire. Yet policing the Empire required resources and personnel, thereby increasing the strain on an already beleagured domestic economy. On top of this, the Attlee government's support for the US confrontation with the USSR and Eastern Europe through the North Atlantic Treaty Organization (NATO), set up in 1949, entailed an expensive military presence in Europe.

So, at the beginning of stage 2 we find a powerful (because organized and occupying a central position for systemic change) collective actor – the Labour Cabinet – facing a major difficulty: how to carry through a programme of domestic reform whilst simultaneously meeting the demands generated by its commitment to NATO, to a world power role based on the leadership of an increasingly rebellious Empire, and to electoral promises to raise the school leaving age – in short, how to expand domestic production whilst pursuing policies which have the effect of reducing the indigenous working population. The strain on military resources was partly met by the development, in secret, of atomic weapons and by the continued conscription of colonial troops. The labour shortage that was an emergent property of those earlier decisions was met by the recruitment of foreign labour. Before considering this in more detail, we need briefly to return to the structural constraints placed on the Cabinet by the social relations of British capitalism and the degree of discretionary judgement, or interpretative freedom, these allowed.

The other key element, besides an expanded labour supply, in securing a prosperous and efficient capitalism was the regulation of capital itself, its subordination to national economic objectives. This was the central idea of Keynesianism. When aggregate demand was too low to attract private investment, the government would intervene to increase demand through borrowing and public expenditure; when it was too high, then the government would reduce demand through increased taxation or expenditure cuts. In this way, capitalism could be managed more efficiently, securing full employment without incurring the socially dis-integrative consequences of 'boom and slump' cycles. The problem with this strategy was that it encountered an inflexible systemic imperative: in capitalist societies capitalists cannot be regulated.

Certainly the Labour government attempted to direct capital investment in various ways consonant with its policy objectives. It nationalized unprofitable sectors of the economy such as coal mining and railways, whilst legislation such as the 1947 Industrial Organization and Development Act sought to attract industry to regions, like the North East, that had experienced the mass unemployment of the 1930s. Another, long term, option was to 'modernize' capitalism by compelling the adoption of modern technology. Even had these designs not run counter to the capitalist social relations of postwar Britain, they formed a long term strategy based on cajolery and inducement. The Labour government needed a much more urgent remedy. It thus turned from policies aimed at compelling capital to move and improve productivity, to policies that would compel the labour force to move and increase productivity.

Here, though, the government found itself constrained by other cultural and structural factors. First, there were limits to the extent to which labour could be directed within a 'liberal-democratic' capitalist system where the 'freedom' of workers to choose where and when they worked was an important legitimating principle. Second, an emergent feature of the postwar world was the Labour government's close relationship with the trade unions, who were adamant that changes in the working conditions of their members should not be the price to be paid for a more efficient capitalism.

Third, the Labour government's commitment to a Keynesian reform of British capitalism further limited their options. In claiming to found a welfare state based on full employment and a minimum wage, the government undermined the key elements of capitalist discipline: free from the twin threats of unemployment and poverty, workers did not need to work in ill-paid or unpleasant jobs or move long distances to get them. It was this complex combination of structural and cultural constraints that compelled the government towards its particular resolution of the problem of how to find workers who could be directed to where capital required. This was to recruit migrant workers who could both be directed and have conditions of work imposed upon them.

Arthur Greenwood, Lord Privy Seal in the Labour Cabinet, suggested in 1946 some possible sources of migrant labour:

> we should first turn our attention to the possibility of utilising the services of bodies of foreign labour which are already in this country . . . secondly we should consider the desirability of increasing further our resources of manpower by permitting and if necessary encouraging the entry of special categories of workers. Our primary need is no doubt for unskilled workers for the unattractive industries, but there may also be a case to be made for a certain intake of skilled labour.
>
> (PRO/CAB 124/872, Memorandum to the Cabinet Foreign Labour Committee (CFLC) by A. Greenwood 1 March 1946)

Greenwood's suggestion was put into practice in the European Volunteer Workers (EVW) Scheme. By January 1947, the scheme was recruiting labour from several sources: the Polish Resettlement Corps living in camps in Britain; 'displaced persons' camps throughout Europe; and the unemployed of various European countries. Within a year, the scheme had recruited 80,000 EVWs, as well as 80,000 members of the Polish Resettlement Corps and 23,000 Ukrainian and German prisoners of war. The industries into which women EVWs were directed were principally cotton and wool manufacture and the new National Health Service (NHS). For men, the major industries were agriculture and coal mining (Kay and Miles 1992).

The benefits of the migrant worker solution for the government were succinctly put by the inter-departmental working party set up in 1948 to review the possibility of using colonial workers, who were, of course, UK and colonies citizens, as a means of meeting the labour shortage. In rejecting this latter strategy, the working party identified the key advantages for the government of migrant labour:

> Besides being kept out of the 'inessential' industries, European Volunteer Workers who have been brought into this country could not for any length of time remain unemployed and live at the public expense . . . Unlike British citizens, European Volunteer Workers must not only accept whatever job is selected for them, but approved employment. If their employment record in this country is unsatisfactory in any respect, the sanction of deportation lies at hand.
>
> (PRO/CO 866/6 Working Party on the Employment in the United Kingdom of Surplus Colonial Manpower, Report: The Possibilities of Employing Colonial Labour Power in the UK October 1948)

Not only did the sanction of deportation enable the government to direct and discipline migrant workers, but it ensured that they did not compete with indigenous workers. 'There is no danger for years to come that foreign labour will rob British workers of their jobs,' the Ministry of Labour assured the unions in 1947. 'The government is prepared to ensure that foreign labour will not be introduced into specific employment while British labour is available' (PRO/LAB 37/17 Economic Survey for 1947 cmd. 7046). The social integration difficulties thus emerging from the use of migrant labour to meet system integration needs could in this way be minimized.

For similar reasons the government also arranged skill and language training for EVWs and made a point of defending their democratic credentials and their similarities with the people of Britain. The Ministry of Labour report *Workers From Abroad*, published in 1948, noted that

> Poland was possessed of many ancient Universities and cultural institutions revered not only in their own country but throughout the world of culture and science . . . in fact they are in this way equivalent to any cross section of our own ex-service men and women.
>
> (Ministry of Labour 1948: 4)

In framing the issue of importation of foreign labour in terms of 'like-ness' between national populations, politicians drew on well-established discourses about assimilation, about people's ability to 'fit in' and 'get on with each other'. Such discourses operate with a variety of criteria for deciding which groups will 'get on' with each other. In this case, as we have seen, the Labour government found itself driven ineluctably towards the employment of workers from outside the boundaries of the nation state and was thus compelled to mute those 'anti-foreigner' discourses likely to be activated by those opposed to this policy. It moved to reassure trade unions that migrant labour would not be competing for their members' jobs and sought to highlight the adaptive capacities of North Europeans. These capacities were derived from their being 'just like us' and having, in the words of James Chuter-Ede, the Home Secretary, 'traditions and social background . . . more nearly equal to our own' (Joshi and Carter 1984: 56).

The felicitous easing of the dilemmas posed by the need for economic growth, the expansion of public spending and an acute labour shortage which the use of migrant workers seemed to promise was, though, to be checked by an entirely contingent factor: the arrival of colonial citizens hoping to better themselves and help the 'mother country' in its time of need. This activated a constraining contradiction between ideas about 'free entry' to UK and colonies citizens and notions of who was 'British' based on notions of race and colour and prompted a new round of interaction aimed at reconciling this contradiction. This in turn provoked a series of further emergent, unintended consequences.

Colonial governors had approached the Colonial Office as early as 1947 to see whether colonial British subjects in the Caribbean could be engaged under schemes similar to those being used to recruit European workers. High levels of unemployment in the colonies, and the accompanying prospect of political unrest, persuaded the Colonial Office to approach the Ministry of Labour who declared themselves unenthusiastic. The reasons for this response were spelt out by a senior civil servant. Suggesting that a distinction needed to be drawn between the temporary importation of labour and the permanent importation of British subjects with a view to their ultimate assimilation, Sir Harold Wiles noted that

> Unlike ex-prisoners of war or other aliens, I assume there could be no authority for deporting coloured British subjects if they felt they wished to stay here and take their chance. If there were any assurance that these people could in fact be sent away when they had served their purpose, this proposition might be less unacceptable . . . Whatever may be the policy about British citizenship, I do not think that any scheme for the importation of coloured colonials for permanent settlement should be embarked upon without full understanding that this means that a coloured element will be brought in for permanent absorption into our own population.
>
> (PRO/CAB 134/510 Letter H Wiles to MA Bevan 8 March 1948)

This is the point at which stage 2 proper begins. Confronted by the prospect of 'the importation of coloured colonials for permanent settlement', the Labour Cabinet decided that action had to be taken. It found itself facing an array of structural and cultural conditions that limited its options. The judgement that the labour shortage could be best met by the organized recruitment of foreign workers, for example, was a response to the necessary incompatibility between reducing the size of the indigenous working population and increasing the efficiency of capitalism in Britain.

However, the arrival of colonial workers brought to the fore a host of other emergent properties that further constrained the options available to the Cabinet. Specifically, the members of the Labour Cabinet viewed 'the importation of coloured colonials for permanent settlement' as an undesirable development. It did so on the grounds that their 'colour' rendered such workers unassimilable.

This view was not peculiar to Labour ministers; it was shared not only by their Conservative counterparts, but also by many MPs and civil servants. Sometimes it drew on race ideas explicitly; at other times it rested on discourses about colour as a signifier or indicator of difference. In either case it utilized anterior cultural resources about colour, colonial status and capacity to 'fit in' to life in Britain whilst mixing them in a novel blend more suited to the project of restriction. In so far as ministers made sense of colonial immigration in these terms they found themselves having to navigate some particularly sharp dilemmas such as: how to impose restrictions on the movement of British subjects whilst recruiting foreign workers, i.e. non-British subjects; how to avoid charges of colour discrimination; how to restrict a ready source of labour when employers were complaining of labour shortages; how to retain a viable notion of Commonwealth when discriminating between its members in respect of their rights to enter Britain.

The efforts of successive Labour and Conservative Cabinets to deal with these dilemmas initiates a period of interaction marked, on the Cabinet's part, by a situational logic of compromise. Initially, this took the form of a public policy of indifference towards colonial immigration in the hope that such immigration would remain insignificant.

Thus the docking of the *Empire Windrush* in June 1948 found the Colonial Office and the Ministry of Labour wrangling over their respective responsibilities for the new arrivals. Taking the line that colonial immigration was a Colonial Office affair, the Ministry of Labour refused to make any efforts to place the passengers in employment. Defending this position, Ness Edwards, Parliamentary Under-Secretary to the Minister of Labour George Isaacs, put it plainly enough: 'we do not want to take any action with this ship load of Jamaicans which will encourage others' (CO 876/88 Ness Edwards to the Earl of Listowel 9 June 1948).

In the Cabinet post mortem that followed the arrival of the *Empire Windrush*, the Colonial Secretary, Arthur Creech-Jones, found himself being blamed for not preventing the migration in the first place. Attlee, the Prime Minister, after enquiring whether the Windrush party could not perhaps be persuaded to work on ground-nut projects in East Africa, pressed Creech-Jones to 'ensure that further similar movements either from Jamaica or elsewhere in the Colonial Empire are detected and checked before they can reach such an embarrassing stage' (CO 876/88 Privy Council Office to Colonial Office 15 June 1948).

Attlee's anxiety to 'check' further migration of British subjects from the colonies was unlikely to have been assuaged by the letter he received several days later. Sent to him from eleven of his backbenchers, it urged the government to control immigration from the colonies, by legislation if necessary. The key claim made in support of this proposal was that 'coloured colonial workers' presented insuperable problems of assimilation:

> The British people fortunately enjoy a profound unity without uniformity in their way of life, and are blest by the absence of a colour racial problem. An influx of coloured people domiciled here is likely to impair the harmony, strength and cohesion of our public and social life and to create discord and unhappiness among all concerned.
>
> (HO 213/244 J. Murray *et al.* to Prime Minister 22 June 1948)

This marks the emergence of a new player in stage 2 interaction: politicians concerned about the 'colour racial problem'. This group changes the environment within which the Cabinet operates, expressing the political disquietude likely to follow if the Cabinet does not move to restrict colonial immigration. This is both a benefit, pointing to a course of action that would cut the knot of irresolution surrounding the Cabinet's own attitudes, and a cost, reminding ministers of the penalties of appearing indifferent to the 'colour racial problem'.

Such penalties appeared to be underlined by several incidents that took place during 1948–9. In June 1948 a fight outside an Indian restaurant in Liverpool resulted in scores of arrests. The following summer, in 1949, colonial immigrants were attacked in a men's hostel in Deptford by a white mob. In August Jamaican workers were attacked by Polish workers at a hostel in Birmingham (Glass and Pollins 1960; Richmond 1961).

These sorts of incidents seemed to strengthen the view of some commentators that colonial immigration inevitably brought difficulties. 'There are bound to be difficulties', commented the *Spectator*, 'possibly with the trade unions, possibly with housewives prejudiced against West Indian lodgers.' But, it went on to add, numbers were crucial to the prospects for assimilation, since the difficulties 'can probably be surmounted as far as the 500 [*Empire Windrush* passengers] are concerned. If the 500 became 5,000 it would be a very different matter' (*Spectator* 25 June 1948).

Despite sharing the discourses of assimilation, colour and race evinced by its own backbenchers and sections of the media, and the solution of restriction which such discourses commonly advocated, the Cabinet did not introduce legislation to control colonial immigration. This was because there were severe costs involved in doing so, costs that in 1948 the government did not deem worth paying. A key feature on their balance sheet was the 1948 Nationality Act.

We have already noted the importance of the Empire/Commonwealth to the postwar Labour government, both as a source of economic wealth and of political status. This was threatened in 1947 when the Canadian government decided to introduce a specifically national citizenship. Henceforth people born in Canada would be Canadian citizens, not British subjects. This had obvious implications for any feasible notion of imperial unity, with other 'white' dominions (self-governing states within the Commonwealth) threatening to follow suit, and India set to gain independence in 1948. A replacement for the old imperial notion of British subjecthood was required.

An Inter-Departmental Committee was set up to consider the issue. Its discussion of the several options available illustrates plainly the struggle to find a compromise and the difficulties of doing so. For instance, the idea of a separate UK citizenship accompanied by separate citizenships for each colony, though favoured by the Home Office, was opposed vigorously by the Colonial Office on the grounds that

> The . . . proposals . . . would interrupt the direct link by interposing a new status of local citizenship, which is unknown in the Colonies and for which there is no demand . . . They would obscure what is common and throw into relief what is individual and separate.
>
> (HO 213/202 Colonial Office, Memorandum, British Nationality Law: Proposals for change in the law)

In other words, by emphasizing the separateness of the colonies from the 'mother country' it would offer a hostage to fortune for would-be national liberation movements. A separate UK citizenship might also be seen as a 'hedged in wall of privilege . . . which . . . must be avoided at all costs' (HO 213/202, Fifth Meeting of Committee 10 July 1946).

A second option was to create a single common colonial citizenship separate from that of the UK. Again the Colonial Office was unenthusiastic: it was artificial, impractical, and as with the first option, likely to mark out colonial status as inferior.

This left a third option, the creation of a common citizenship of the UK and colonies. Here the Colonial Office response was less tepid. UK and colonies citizenship would emphasize those ties that were 'common to all irrespective of race, colour or creed. It is much more than a mere vehicle for conferring privileges or imposing obligations. It is a symbol of common loyalty and equal status' (HO 213/202 Colonial Office Memorandum British Nationality Law: Proposals for change in the law). Unsurprisingly perhaps, the Home Office disagreed, noting that conferring citizenship 'upon the inhabitants of a remote island thousands of miles away from the UK seemed to be a violation of geography and common sense' (HO 213/200 Meeting of Inter Departmental Committee 17 May 1946).

Nevertheless, it was the third option that was selected by the committee after strong direction from their chair, Sir Alexander Maxwell. He reminded them that the guiding principle of their decision should be to 'strengthen the ties between the Colonies and the UK'; the political and economic benefits of the Empire/Commonwealth were not to be threatened by misgivings about the boundaries of 'British-ness'. The intervention of the key social actor, the Cabinet, was sufficient to ensure the outcome that most accorded with their political project of establishing a Commonwealth.

Securing a policy outcome is one thing; suppressing the ideational resources activated by doing so is another thing entirely. The Conservative opposition placed much weight on the 'disastrous consequences' of a UK and colonies citizenship 'upon the relations with the natives in our colonial territories, who will think that citizenship assures them of equal political rights with the white settlers' (DO 35/3533 British Nationality Bill, Note of a meeting between Lord Chancellor, Lord Addison, Lord Salisbury, Lord Altrincham, Lord Simon and Lord Tweedsmuir 27 May 1948). The implications of such a citizenship, warned one senior civil servant, was that if colonial subjects chose to come to the UK they would be entitled to and would expect to have the same rights and access to jobs, housing and welfare as those citizens born in England (CO 1032/106 Note, Reflections on the British Nationality Bill, J.S. Bennett 13 July 1948). This was precisely the constraining contradiction the Cabinet did not want realized.

Thus the docking of the *Empire Windrush* just before the bill received its second reading prompted Attlee to warn his backbenchers not to introduce 'extraneous elements', such as the arrival of the 'Jamaica party', into the discussion of the bill (HO 213/244 draft minute prepared by Secretary of State for PM July 1948). This permitted the Home Secretary, Chuter-Ede, to present the bill to the Commons as an expression of a unique moral and political vision:

> The maintenance of the British Commonwealth of Nations as a great, loyal confederation of people enjoying in each individual part self-government and liberty unexampled in the history of the Empires of the world . . . This is a living organism, and we must expect that, from time to time, its growth will entail our having to consider very considerable changes in the structure and relationship of this magnificent political edifice.
>
> (Hansard Commons vol.453 , c.397, 13 July 1948)

So, in its initial efforts to consider the issue of colonial immigration, the Cabinet found itself striving to reconcile conflicting, even incompatible, material and cultural factors, each of which generated particular effects across the different domains of social reality. At the level of contextual resources it needed to recruit foreign labour if the British economy was to recover and expand and provide the basis for a Keynesian style reform programme relying on increased public expenditure. To this end the EVW schemes were set up.

However an adventitious consequence of the labour shortage was the migration of (small numbers) of colonial workers to the UK. As 'coloured colonials' their presence was regarded with trepidation: they could not be deported, nor directed to specific employment and their colour was held to signify race-ial characteristics that rendered them permanently unassimilable to life in Britain. Furthermore their place as UK and colonies citizens in the 'magnificent political edifice' of the Commonwealth had just been reaffirmed. Together, these factors left only a limited range of policy options open to the Cabinet.

The option they eventually came to pursue, by the late 1940s, was a form of covert control of colonial immigration. This in turn gave rise to a cleavage between the private pursuit of restriction on the movements of some UK and colonies citizens on the grounds of their colour, and the public affirmation of the unity of the Commonwealth accompanied by condemnations of colour discrimination. Such a policy always carries the potential to be exposed, leaving its adherents in a difficult position, and this emergent factor becomes more prominent in Cabinet deliberations during the 1950s.

What were the gains and losses of the policy of covert control? The principal gain for the Cabinet was that it could continue to meet a labour shortage through the recruitment of European and Irish workers without provoking adverse comment from the colonies or the Commonwealth. A potentially damaging political confrontation could thus be avoided and the Cabinet could continue to represent Britain to the world as a tolerant, plural society. There were, however, some serious drawbacks to a policy of covert control.

First, because it was covert, the Cabinet always ran a risk of exposure in Parliament by MPs attentive to the difficulties facing Colonial arrivals. Tom Driberg, for example, the Labour MP for Maldon, had raised in the Commons several cases of Jamaicans being refused leave to land by immigration officers. Such instances reminded Ministers of the fragile balance of forces surrounding the covert approach (CO 537/6700 minute A.R. Thomas 8 January 1951). More seriously, the secrecy of the approach imposed a sharp limit on the numbers that could be controlled; if, as one civil servant put it, the 'trickle' were to become 'a powerful stream', then administrative measures might prove insufficient and the need for a more public form of control would have to be faced (CO 537/5219 minute, J. Williams 27 June 1950).

In the meantime, the covert policy was necessarily only partially effective. It relied mainly on discouragement of would-be migrants through leaflets and various propaganda campaigns that portrayed Britain as an undesirable place to migrate, and on making it difficult for such migrants to prove their status as British subjects and citizens, allowing immigration officers to refuse them entry. This would clearly not work with migrants who had the appropriate documents and were determined to migrate. Those who were anxious about an 'influx of coloured people domiciled here', like Attlee's parliamentary correspondents mentioned earlier, were unlikely to be satisfied with such an inefficient compromise.

By 1950, the government itself had begun to realize this. It set up a working party to review 'the further means which might be adopted to check the immigration into this country of coloured people from the British Colonial Territories' (Joshi and Carter 1984). Its discussions revealed keenly the dilemmas facing the Cabinet in its efforts to prevent what it viewed as the development of a 'race problem', by restricting the movement of 'coloured' UKCs into Britain. Essentially, as the working party saw it, the government had three options available.

The first of these was the extension of aliens' control to British subjects from overseas (the provision to control the entry of aliens had existed since the 1905 Aliens Act), but this was rejected on the grounds that it would be difficult to justify the exemption of the Irish. Including them would involve a good deal of administrative inconvenience, and besides it would be 'particularly unrewarding as there would be few, if any, Irish workers whom we should wish to exclude' (Joshi and Carter 1984: 62). A second option was legislation to deport UKCs if they had been in Britain for less than two years and were in receipt of National Assistance, if they were convicted of a serious criminal offence, or if they attempted to create industrial unrest. Finally, the government could consider measures to exclude and deport stowaways (Joshi and Carter 1984).

None of these could get the Cabinet off the hook of maintaining free entry to 'white' UKCs whilst simultaneously denying it to 'coloured' ones. The working party expressed it succinctly in its final report in 1951. Any solution, it noted, 'depending on an apparent or concealed colour test would be so invidious as to make it impossible for adoption'. Yet 'the use of any powers taken to restrict the free entry of British subjects to this country would, as a general rule, be more or less confined to coloured persons' (CAB 129/44 CP (51) 12 February 1951.). Unsurprisingly, the working party favoured a continuation of the compromise solution, arguing that current levels of 'coloured colonial immigration' did not justify legislation at the present time. If such immigration should increase then the Cabinet should reconsider the legislative option (Joshi and Carter 1984).

SUMMARY AND CONCLUSION

At the end of this early period in stage 2 of sociocultural interaction we have seen how the decision of the Labour government to recruit foreign workers to meet a labour shortage was the outcome of a complex interaction between structural and cultural relations and emergent properties. This decision changed the environment for other agents, activating ideational resources and modifying the conditions within which other actors and agents pursue their own purposes and projects. Thus Cabinet discussions about who was entitled to be a British citizen and the related status of colonial workers led to a widening arena of debate about colour, race and English/Britishness involving MPs, civil servants and the mass media. In this process other groups began to organize to promote their interests within this arena, whose significance had been realigned by the Cabinet's deliberations. The effects of the Cabinet's efforts to alter the distribution of international political power and restore the national economy (efforts directed principally at the level of system integration) generated all sorts of consequences at the level of social integration. Particular groups found themselves the object of discussions about who was 'properly British' and UKC migrants found it more difficult to obtain entry. The next chapter examines the continuing efforts of governments to consolidate a restrictive definition of 'Britishness'.

7 Culture, structure and agency (2): 1951–83

Many of the senior politicians in the Conservative government elected in 1951 drew just as strongly on the discursive field of race notions as did their Labour predecessors; for them, too, the prospect of unrestricted colonial immigration gave rise to concern about a permanent, and unassimilable, 'coloured' presence in Britain. Of course, a similar situational logic prevailed, but a solution based on what a Colonial Office official described as 'devious little devices' (CO 537/5219 minute J. Williams 27 June 1950) could only be temporary. Apart from the dubious legality of many of these 'devices', it was clear that they were having little impact on colonial immigration (roughly two thousand migrants per year had arrived from the Caribbean between 1950–3, but this was to increase to ten thousand in 1954). Since it could not alter significantly the demand for labour – partly because this was in the hands either of private employers or autonomous public bodies such as London Transport or the NHS, partly because the shortage of labour remained acute – the Cabinet soon found itself edging towards the legislative option raised by the Attlee government's working party.

Enacting this option, however, required modification of an important cultural condition: public perceptions of colonial immigration. If the public generally were to realize the problems that would surely follow if an established 'coloured' population were settled in Britain, so the argument went, then it would equally surely recognize the need for legislation. The case for control required empirical demonstration:

> This meant gathering information about unemployment and National assistance, 'numbers', housing, health, criminality and miscegenation, which it was hoped would confirm that black immigrants posed insoluble problems of social, economic and political assimilation.
>
> (Carter, Harris and Joshi 1993: 58)

We see here the beginnings of a particular discourse of assimilability in which Cabinet ministers rework and reconfigure earlier discourses about colour and about race in their pursuit of an exit from the dilemma of control. This process was not without its inconsistencies and setbacks. Most importantly, the Cabinet found it hard to come up with the empirical evidence it required to support its 'strong case'.

For example, an early focus of the working party on 'The Employment of Coloured People in the UK', set up in 1953 to provide the Cabinet with current information, was on numbers. How many UKCs from the West Indies were coming to Britain and what was the size of the 'coloured colonial' population? Neither of these questions could be answered in ways satisfactory for the Cabinet's purposes. Since colour was not a census category, and was in any case meant to be irrelevant to the status of UKCs, it proved impossible to assess with any accuracy the size of the 'coloured' population, although even the Cabinet's exaggerated estimate of 60,000 to 70,000 (in a population of 51 million) was hardly likely to present a compelling case for a reversal of Imperial policy. The discovery that roughly 36,000 UKCs had migrated from the Caribbean between 1950 and 1955 was insignificant when set alongside the hundreds of thousands of Europeans recruited under the EVW schemes. It was also a two edged sword, for how could ministers defend an 'inordinate interest in the 36,000 black immigrants . . . when nothing whatsoever was being done about the 250,000 Southern Irish workers who arrived in the same period'? (Carter, Harris and Joshi 1993: 59. See also Hickman, 1998 for a discussion of postwar political responses to Irish migration.)

The working party fared little better in assembling evidence around housing, health and criminality, where it was unable to find convincing data to support the claim that UKCs migrating from the Caribbean were creating problems or otherwise demonstrating their putative lack of assimilability. 'Colonial immigration,' the Cabinet conceded in 1955, 'was not an acute problem at the moment' (Carter, Harris and Joshi 1993: 59).

Thwarted in its efforts to build its 'strong case' on evidence that colonial UKCs were a problem, the Cabinet turned to less direct methods. First a committee of inquiry was proposed in 1954. Its purpose, the Cabinet Secretary, Norman Brook, explained to the Prime Minister, 'would be, not to find a solution (for it is evident what form control must take), but to enlist a sufficient body of public support for the legislation that would be needed' (Carter, Harris and Joshi 1993: 66). The committee idea was abandoned in 1955, however, when it was realized that it would be difficult to select representatives from the opposition and from the trades unions who could be relied upon to support the idea of legislation restricting the movement of 'coloured colonial' UKCs.

A second line of attack was to publish a white paper, intended to provide an authoritative account of the social and economic problems that, in the Cabinet's view, were likely to arise from unrestricted colonial immigration. A major drawback to this, as we have seen, was the absence of any firm evidence to support the Cabinet prognosis; without this, a white paper 'would not have the effect of guiding public opinion in any definite direction' (Carter, Harris and Joshi 1993: 67). Despite having drafted a bill to restrict colonial immigration in November 1954, the Cabinet still found itself unsure about the political consequences of introducing it in Parliament. The audit of costs and benefits had not yet shifted sufficiently in favour of the latter: public opinion had not 'matured sufficiently' and, as the Cabinet noted, 'On economic grounds, immigration, including colonial immigration, was a welcome means of augmenting our labour resources' (Carter, Harris and Joshi 1993: 68). An impending general election did little to harden Cabinet resolve.

Once the election was over the Cabinet returned to the task. In November 1955, a ministerial committee was set up, chaired by the Lord Chancellor, Lord Kilmuir. Its job was to examine the obstacles to legislation and how these might be overcome. By July 1956, though, the committee was reporting to the Cabinet that colonial workers continued to make a significant contribution to the economy and that the public seemed little interested in the matter of their migration.

Frustrated once more in their efforts to resolve the incompatibility between a commitment to equal rights for all citizens and the desire to restrict the movements of colonial citizens, the Cabinet turned again to covert manoeuvring. However, the immigration figures for early 1958 showed a small, but unexpected, increase in the number of migrants from India and Pakistan, and the Home Office now decided to press the matter of legislation. In so doing it precipitated a real threat of counter actualization from the Commonwealth Relations Office, more firmly wedded to older notions of Britain's obligations to the colonies. The CRO sought to minimize the significance of the figures and urged Commonwealth governments to apply their own controls with greater rigour in order to forestall action by the British government.

The announcement from the Ministry of Labour in August 1958 of a 70 per cent increase in unemployment over the past year seemed to strengthen decisively the Home Office position. Not only did the announcement coincide with an increase in Indian and Pakistani migration, it was part of a report that offered a gloomy forecast of labour needs. It claimed that the demand for unskilled labour had virtually exhausted itself and pointed to the expected increase in the numbers of young adults entering the labour force by 1962. The forthcoming abolition of National Service was likely to release another 200,000 young men into the labour market in 1962. Furthermore, the report suggested, Irish migrants could easily meet any residual demand for unskilled labour. Before the significance of the report for the Cabinet's 'strong case' could be assessed, though, events in Notting Hill and Nottingham altered the balance sheet of prices and premiums attached to the Cabinet's decisions about legislative controls.

There are many accounts of the 1958 'riots' in Notting Hill and Nottingham (see, for example Foot 1965; Freeman 1979; Fryer 1993; Hiro 1971; Katznelson 1976; Miles and Phizacklea 1984; Pilkington 1988). My concern here is with the impact the events had on the Cabinet's project of introducing restrictive immigration controls on colonial UKCs and, in this respect, there were penalties and bonuses. Perhaps the major dividend was the powerful boost given by the press coverage of the events to the 'race relations' discourse that had governed the Cabinet's own private deliberations since 1947 (Miles and Phizacklea 1984). Whilst some papers looked to working class hooliganism as a possible explanation (*The Times* 3 September 1958 for instance) and others hinted at fascist manipulation (*The New Statesman* 6 September 1958), most came to regard the events as to do with the presence of 'coloured immigrants'. This presence was signified variously by terms such as 'race riots', 'race relations' or simply 'race' (Pilkington 1988). The Home Secretary, R.A.B. Butler, announced that the source of the disturbances was clear: they were due to competition for jobs, housing and women. 'We are dealing with some of the deepest emotions and oldest problems of mankind', he informed the Cabinet (CO 1032/196 Brief for the Secretary of State for Cabinet 8 September 1958). These views were echoed by the Labour MP for North Kensington, George Rogers, who claimed that the events were the 'reaction of people sorely tried by some sections of the coloured population' (Ramdin 1987: 210).

Paradoxically, the events in Notting Hill and Nottingham made a straightforward advance of the 'strong case' more difficult:

> It is difficult to see how we could maintain our position of moral leadership of a multi-racial Commonwealth if we were to take steps which showed that we are unable to tolerate non-white faces in any numbers in our own midst. And whatever form might be taken by legislation to control entry into the UK, it would be quite obvious that colour prejudice was at the bottom of it. This would be particularly the case if we were now to legislate *after* the racial disturbances.
> (DO 335/7981 Brief for Secretary of State, A.W. Snelling, *Race Riots* 8 September 1958)

Thus, whilst discourses of 'race' and 'race relations' had now made a powerful appearance in the public arena, the events themselves had circumscribed the Cabinet's options because to legislate now would risk counter-actualizing the other incompatible element of their dilemma, namely the charge of colour discrimination. Compromise continued to be the order of the day: when faced with a motion at the Conservative Party conference in October calling for more restrictive controls on 'undesirable immigrants', Butler promised that the Home Office would explore the possibility of deportation powers.

By the beginning of 1959, then, the problems of legislative control appeared to the Cabinet to be as intractable as ever. It had so far failed to effect the compromise compelled by a situational logic of necessary incompatibility, although it remained acutely sensitive to every shift in the political wind, subtly registering possibilities and constantly pressing in particular directions in order to reconcile 'matters of principle' with the need to discriminate on the grounds of colour. Nevertheless, it appeared that the 'strong case' had once more ground to a halt, unable to command unequivocal support from the Cabinet, Parliament or the public. A political imperative for control, even by so powerful a social actor as the Cabinet, was not of itself sufficent to secure its legislative implementation. A shift in the alignment of the 'parts' – that is, in our realist terms, structural and cultural conditions – was required if the Cabinet's project was to be enabled rather than constrained.

We have noted already that a key emergent feature of the British nation state's postwar role in the international order was a labour shortage. Encasing this was a larger, more durable, emergent feature that arose from Britain's peculiar position as the first nation in the modern world to industrialize. The legacy of the Industrial Revolution and its subsequent impact on the development of British political culture and economic development has been much debated (see, for example, Gamble 1985; Nairn 1981; Weiner 1981). One of the chief consequences of being the first industrial nation was the dependence of the British economy on the less developed economies that it generated. Simply, the contingent fact of being the first economy in the world to industrialize gave British capitalism unprecedented advantages over its economic rivals. This was, of course, a major factor in British imperial dominance, but it had other, partly unintended consequences.

In particular, Gamble has argued, the international orientation of the British state and economy led to weak institutional organization, compared to other Western economies, of the principal classes and interests in their relation to the state (Gamble 1985: 99). British industry and finance, according to Gamble, were more concerned with international operations than with the expansion of the domestic economy. The close links that developed between the 'gentlemanly capitalists' of the City (Cain and Hopkins 1993) and the political decision-making process favoured the pursuit of these cosmopolitan interests. (For a fuller discussion of the disproportionate political influence of financial and commercial interests see Cain and Hopkins 1993; Ingham 1984; Newton and Porter 1988; Rubinstein 1993: 35.) The concern of these interests with domestic matters extended often only to the point where domestic policy threatened or jeopardized the pursuit of overseas profitability.

The combination of this international orientation with Britain's postwar role as a social democratic world power at the head of a powerful Empire/Commonwealth resulted in a further systemic tension between 'the new and often combined international operations of British finance, and the requirements of domestic expansion' (Gamble 1985: 110). Important sections of business found it easier to accumulate capital by expanding abroad rather than investing in the domestic economy. Since the Labour and Conservative governments of the postwar period remained firmly wedded to the liberal economic tradition, no controls were contemplated on where business invested or what it invested in. This meant that, as far as the politics of legislative controls on UKCs were concerned, significant sections of the industrial and business classes were neutral, that is, they had little or no direct vested interest in one outcome or the other.

The importance of this elite neutrality is perhaps best grasped by comparing it to the responses to nineteenth-century immigration to Britain from Ireland. Here, as a number of writers have pointed out (Foot 1965; Holmes 1988; Miles 1982), overseas industrial and commercial expansion still rested firmly on the basis of a growing domestic capitalism. This required an extensive 'reserve army of labour', largely supplied by Irish migrants. Thus, despite considerable popular hostility to Irish workers that sometimes involved serious civil disorder, the dominant political and economic elites were uninterested in legislative restriction of Irish migration. (There were other factors involved in this congruence of interest between politicians and industrialists, such as the struggle for Irish Home Rule, but my point is merely that popular animosity towards Irish migrants was insufficently compelling when confronted with the interests of the socially more powerful). Contrastingly, by the end of the 1950s, the most influential sections (though by no means all; see Duffield

1989) of the financial and industrial elites were indifferent to the control of colonial immigration. The room for manoeuvre for the Cabinet was correspondingly enlarged as the arguments for the economic benefits of colonial immigration became less audible.

Besides these larger contextual features, the systemic results of relations between relations, there were also a number of factors more directly connected to the circumstances of the late 1950s and early 1960s that influenced the Cabinet's judgements about whether it should take the political risk of legislative control. To begin with, the significance of the Commonwealth for British policy makers was waning. Efforts to reorganize colonial administrations, such as the West Indian Federation and the Central African Federation, had been frustrated. The West Indian Federation collapsed in 1961, and it quickly became obvious to the Cabinet that the Central African Federation was equally doomed; both had been seen as presenting further opportunities for control of migration at source. Elsewhere the process of decolonization proceeded apace – the Sudan had achieved independence in 1956, the Gold Coast (as Ghana) and Malaya in 1957. The 'retreat from Empire' encouraged the decline in influence of the two departments most closely responsible for administering the Empire/Commonwealth, namely the Colonial Office and the Commonwealth Office. Partly because of their imperial connections, they were also the departments most associated with opposition within the government to controls on UKCs. By the early 1960s their authority within Cabinet discussions on controls was diminishing.

A major element in this 'turning away from the older intimacy with the Commonwealth', (Childs 1992: 135), was the growing importance of the European Community. Negotiations for entry, led by Edward Heath, had begun in October 1961. In some ways the overtures towards the EC made the matter of restrictions on Commonwealth citizens more delicate. The topic of control was kept off the Conservative Party conference in 1960 by the Home Secretary, R.A.B. Butler, because he felt that any action that would necessarily be seen as further discriminating against the Commonwealth would be 'unduly provocative' (Dean 1993: 281).

Dean identifies a number of other factors that contributed to the Cabinet's reassessment of the prospects for control. There was rising constituency pressure from Conservative voters, perhaps intensified by the impact of events in the USA, where the emerging Civil Rights movement was beginning seriously to challenge discrimination and racism. Attitudes within the Labour Party were also shifting. Despite the principled opposition to controls by its leader, Hugh Gaitskell, there was some evidence that the parliamentary rank-and-file were uneasily eyeing their constituencies and pondering their parliamentary futures (Dean 1993). The demand for a 'reserve army' of migrant workers was also likely to ease with the ending of National Service in 1962.

So far, we have considered what we might term structural conditions, examining their modification, partly as a result of Cabinet decisions, and decisions by other groups, and partly as a result of the effects of systemic social relations upon other systemic social relations. However, the Cabinet's equivocations about controlling 'coloured' immigration generated a further emergent outcome: the growth of a parliamentary lobby which saw political advantage in linking the issue of control with larger anxieties about national identity. This is an example of what Archer has termed a situational logic of opportunism (Archer 1995). Here the exploitation of a contingent compatibility – in this case Cabinet vacillation about legislative controls and a conservative politics concerned with defending notions of national identity based on colour – brings only gains to those willing to do the exploiting.

The otherwise obscure parliamentary career of Sir Cyril Osborne, Conservative MP for Louth, was thus revivified in the mid 1950s as he became associated with the campaign for immigration control legislation. (This is not to suggest that Osborne's 'playing of the race card', as Foot (1965) expresses it, was an entirely cynical manoeuvre; he in fact campaigned for controls as early as 1950, when it was not a popular position. A situational logic of opportunism simply recognizes that contingent compatibilities allow for the uninhibited promotion of all the interests associated with, or able to attach themselves to, the compatibilities.)

After 1955, Osborne was joined by Norman Pannell, the Conservative MP for Liverpool Kirkdale, Harold Gurden, Conservative MP for Selly Oak, Birmingham and Martin Lindsay, Conservative MP for Solihull. Throughout the later 1950s, they steadily barraged the Home Secretary with questions linking 'coloured' immigrants with housing shortages, criminality, prostitution, disease and unemployment. Vexatious though these questions undoubtedly were to a Cabinet that wanted to keep a lid on things until it had decided when it thought it would be timely to introduce legislation, they could possibly have been ignored but for the events in Notting Hill and Nottingham. After these, the Cabinet had an interest in Osborne's project.

Significantly, in December 1958, Osborne found himself allowed to move a Private Member's motion demanding immigration control of the 'unfit, idle or criminal'. A Cabinet anxious to test the waters for its own immigration Bill closely monitored the debate over the motion. In presenting the motion, Osborne expressed publicly the private anxieties that had driven the Cabinet's deliberations since 1949, claiming that 'opinion in the country is most exercised by the coloured immigrant . . . and we have a duty to look after our own people' (Hansard 5 December 1958. Vol 596 col.1563). The motion was defeated, but Osborne's position had attracted some parliamentary and public credibility and had drawn some additional supporters from the Labour benches.

By July 1960, Osborne and his supporters felt sufficiently confident to abandon their earlier, limited proposals for health checks and clean criminal records for prospective immigrants and move to a bolder position altogether. Pointing to the government's recent efforts to urge West Indian governments to restrict immigration to the UK (noted earlier), Osborne asked Butler bluntly:

> in view of the mounting disquiet and deep anxiety by great numbers of the general public at the flood of West Indian immigrants into this country, does not he think that this Government ought to . . . control and restrict immigration into this country?
>
> (Hansard 7 July 1960. Vol. 626 cols. 688–90)

In February 1961, Osborne gave notice of another motion, calling explicitly for immigration control on immigrants from the West Indies, India, Pakistan and Africa. 'Britain is a white man's country', Osborne had declared in the *Daily Mail*, 'and I want it to remain so' (*Daily Mail* 7 February 1961).

The parliamentary campaign waged by Osborne and his colleagues had repercussions at the constituency level. At the 1961 Conservative Party conference in October, the issue of controls on 'coloured immigrants' was a major one and delegates gave Butler an uncharacteristically rough ride (Howard 1988). Just twenty days after Butler had faced the Conservative conference, the Queen's Speech opening the new parliamentary session announced that:

> 'legislation will be introduced to control the immigration to the United Kingdom of British Subjects from other parts of the Commonwealth and to give powers for the expulsion of immigrants convicted of criminal offences.'
>
> (Foot 1965: 138)

The bill was fiercely opposed in Parliament. Those opposed to it mobilized precisely those ideas – about Britain's ties to the Commonwealth, about colour discrimination and citizenship, about the anomalous role of Irish migration – that successive Cabinets had feared any overt move to control might activate. These will be considered more fully in the next section. Opposition also came from outside the House. There were regular protests against the bill held by the Movement for Colonial Freedom, various church organizations and by the newly formed Afro-Asian-Caribbean Association. A number of daily papers called for a 'fresh start' to the 'immigration problem'.

Butler sought to pacify his own backbenchers by saying that the bill would be operated benignly and in any case would come before the House for renewal at the end of 1963. Even so, the government felt compelled to introduce a guillotine on the bill, which received its third reading on 27 and 28 February 1962. Despite the abstention of several prominent Conservatives – evidence of continuing unease within the party – and Liberal support for the opposition, there was a very poor opposition vote: 170 against 277 for the government. Royal assent was given to the bill on 12 of April; on 20 April, the Home Secretary announced that the control of Commonwealth immigration would begin on 1 July.

This point effectively marks the end of stage 2 of our morphogenetic cycle. Stage 2 began with the attempt to introduce controls, a social intervention in which specific agents seek to bring about a change in political arrangements. Such intervention is powerfully conditioned by the structural and cultural conditions obtaining at stage 1 and which are the outcomes of previous social interaction. Nevertheless, the introduction of immigration controls on 'coloured' UKCs represents an example of successful agency, of social actors and agents engaging in interaction in order to change or modify the social world. This brings us to stage 3 of the cycle, the stage of structural and cultural elaboration. Since agency always involves working on anterior structural and cultural conditions, and within anterior contextual resources, as well as interaction with other actors and agents, even successful agency is never successful *unconditionally*. No actors or agents ever get what they want, only what they want and exactly as they want it.

Further, the key tenet of analytical dualism, namely the distinctiveness of the two elements of structure/culture and agency, allows for a partial autonomy of each element from the other. This in turn enables a notion of emergence, that is for outcomes not reducible to either element precisely because they are products of the interrelations between structure/culture and agency. It is these products, amongst other things, that are addressed in stage 3 where the consequences of the Cabinet's efforts to change the law controlling the movement of British citizens into the UK are considered.

STAGE 3: SOCIAL AND CULTURAL ELABORATION – THE EFFECTS OF INTRODUCING CONTROLS

For ease of exposition I shall set out the account of the consequences of the Cabinet's successful intervention by considering in turn its effects in the structural and cultural domains before looking at its consequences for actors and agents (Archer's 'double morphogenesis'). I repeat, this is for expository purposes only, since clearly effects in the structural and cultural domains are effects *for* social actors.

Stage 2 has provided a detailed account of how successive Cabinets sought to bring about a significant change in the law governing immigration of UKCs into Britain. In seeking to do this, the Cabinet undertook to reinterpret issues of nationality and citizenship as social problems rather than as matters of economic necessity or moral and political responsibility. In pursuing this corrective action, the Cabinet also changed the structural and cultural conditions for other actors. Stage 3 of the morphogenetic cycle considers these changes (which, of course, also form the starting structural and cultural conditions for subsequent actors and agents). The issue of elaboration does bear directly on how we evaluate the success or failure of agency. In this case, how are we to assess the outcome of the Cabinet's efforts?

In one sense, we are dealing with an example of successful agency. The Labour Cabinet in 1948–9 identified what it saw as the 'problem of coloured colonial immigration' and decided that legislative restriction would eventually have to be introduced if numbers rose. Conservative Cabinets throughout the 1950s shared this perception and by 1954 had already drafted an immigration bill. By 1962 the first Commonwealth Immigration Act was in force. However a morphogenetic perspective which sees social change as emerging from the interplay between structure and agency allows for a more subtle assessment. Even where agency appears to have been completely successful in maintaining or, as in our case, altering, a particular state of affairs, it rarely does so without cost or qualification.

The immigration legislation enacted by governments after 1962 did not halt 'coloured immigration' entirely. More to the point it compromised the reputation of 'fair play' and tolerance enjoyed by British governments internationally and created a draconian bureaucracy of immigration officers and detention camps to ensure that the door now slammed would remain firmly shut. Furthermore, a host of new interests, groupings and relations emerged from this shift in policy (the 'race relations' industry, issues of racism and discrimination, education, the rise of right wing, neo-fascist political parties such as the National Front and so on).

The 1962 Commonwealth Immigration Act placed restrictions on the movement of UKCs for the first time. It sought to regulate immigration through a system of vouchers which classified Comonwealth citizens wishing to enter the country into three categories: those with a specific job with a specific employer; those with skills or qualifications considered to be in short demand; unskilled workers with no specific job (Juss 1993:49). The number of vouchers issued each year was left to the discretion of the Home Office, allowing control to be tightened without recourse to Parliament.

The Act exempted from control those passport holders who had acquired their passports either from being born in the United Kingdom or by being issued with one by the United Kingdom (and not by the government of a colony). It thus introduced the notion of a tangible tie with the United Kingdom as the basis for entry: not surprisingly, those most likely to have such a 'tie' were white.

Further, by connecting suitability for entry with potential for employment through the voucher arrangement, the Act modified the universalist assumptions of the postwar welfare state, adjusting the universe of obligation on which it rested (Bauman 1989). Only the skilled and qualified were welcomed because they could usefully contribute; the rest, by implication, were, if not freeloaders and scroungers, then certainly not uncontestably entitled to the benefits of welfare Britain.

In distinguishing between British citizens in terms of who was, and was not, allowed to enter the country free of restriction, the 1962 Act had the effect of imposing conditions on certain groups of workers, largely defined by skin colour, that constrained their free disposal of labour power in significant ways. In particular, the Act enabled the courts to recommend deportation of Commonwealth immigrants and extended the period of residence before which they could be registered as a British citizen from one year to five. This constituted a disciplinary form specific to Commonwealth immigrant labour with far reaching effects for the conditions under which such workers participated in the labour market (Duffield 1989). The unwillingness of governments to consider anti-discrimination legislation heightened these impediments, allowing discrimination and racism to continue to operate 'according to market forces' (Sivanandan 1981) and effectively constituting black workers as a form of unfree wage labour.

An immediate shift brought about by the introduction of the 1962 Act was the collapse of parliamentary opposition to controls. The Cabinet campaign to correct the incompatibility between a public adherence to equality of all citizens and the need to implement a colour bar had resulted in the virtual elimination of rival ideologies within Parliament. Denis Healey had pledged in 1962, to a meeting in Birmingham of all the principal Commonwealth immigrants associations, that Labour would repeal the Commonwealth Immigrants Act. When Labour were returned to power in 1964, however, they opted for a much more circumspect position.

In a 1965 white paper the Labour government abolished category C vouchers, thereby barring those defined as unskilled migrants from entering Britain. Only those Commonwealth immigrants who could obtain an A voucher (available only to those with a specific job with a specific employer) or a B voucher (available only to those with skills deemed by the Cabinet to be in short supply) were allowed unrestricted entry into the country (Juss 1993; Miles and Phizacklea 1984; Moore and Wallace 1975).

By 1968, when the Labour government decided it could not allow UKCs threatened with expulsion from Kenya to come to Britain, it did not face the opposition that the Conservatives had faced in 1962. Indeed, the 1968 Commonwealth Immigration Act took barely three days to pass from bill to Act. By exempting from controls those who had a 'close and substantial connection' with the UK, the Act drew upon and amplified the idea implicit in the 1962 Act that authentic Britishness was in some sense ancestral and had to do with one's contiguity to a national culture. The ideational labour involved in this refinement was not immense, given the trafficking in ideas of belonging and national identity engaged in by the Cabinet and others during the 1950s. These had created effective, alternative ideational resources for subsequent agents and actors: the equation of immigration controls with 'good race relations' was now a legitimate claim, as its repeated invocation by successive Home Secretaries testifies.

The utility of this proposition was realized fully in the 1971 Commonwealth Immigration Act. Replacing the earlier pieces of legislation, the 1971 Act embodied the most explicit reworking of ideas about identity, belonging and ancestry and gave them a firm conceptual basis in the notion of patriality. Briefly, patrial citizens were those UKCs who had a parent or a grandparent born in Britain; only these passport holders were exempt from immigration control. Non-patrials now found themselves occupying an immigration status similar to that of so-called aliens. They had no right of entry into the UK, were subject to deportation for criminal offences and were initially admitted for one year only (Juss 1993; Moore and Wallace 1975).

Patriality became the central articulating principle of the 1983 Nationality Act (passed in 1981, it did not come into force until 1983). By inscribing the notion of patriality into nationality law, the Act abolished the dilemmas that had taxed the governments of the 1950s and 1960s. Henceforward, only patrial passport holders could be British citizens; non-patrial passport holders were permanently denied the rights of citizenship. Governments could now no longer be subject to embarrassing scrutiny from bodies such as the European Court or be accused of discriminating between citizens on the grounds of colour. By comprehensively redefining citizens in terms of patriality, the Conservative government had ensured that future citizens would (mostly) be 'white' (Geddes 1996; Juss 1993; Law 1996; Miles and Phizacklea 1984). The aims of the Cabinets of the 1950s would appear then to have been successfully realized.

However, it has been repeatedly emphasized that a key advantage of the realist approach advocated here is that agency, even when apparently successful, changes the structural and cultural conditions for other actors and agents in unpredictable ways. This is partly because agency always entails unintended consequences: it generates emergent outcomes through its interaction with existing structural and cultural conditions. It remains to conclude our account by identifying these outcomes.

Let me begin once more with those outcomes most remote, as it were, from the agents and actors themselves. Ironically, perhaps, in view of the Cabinet's desire to maintain a European and Irish labour supply in order to meet a labour shortage, one of the immediate effects of the 1962 Commonwealth Immigration Act was to restrict the supply of labour. After the early 1950s, especially with European economic recovery, the supply of labour within Britain remained small, and once Commonwealth immigration was reduced the only other source of labour (apart from Ireland) was industry itself. This could only be realized, as Gamble has pointed out, by 'drastically reducing manning levels and eliminating restrictive practices' (Gamble 1985: 116). Any such programme required the co-operation of the trade unions and organized labour and, for reasons that are beyond the scope of this study to outline, this was not easy to obtain in the 1970s.

A second change brought about by the introduction of immigration controls on UKCs was the emergence of constraints on the further development of an immigration policy more suited to the economic needs of UK capitalism and based on a recognition of migration as a structural phenomenon of the contemporary world. Rather, as we have seen, British postwar immigration policy was discriminatory and rested on ideological justifications that trafficked freely in notions about race, culture and assimilability. In this construction of 'coloured' immigration as a social and cultural problem of assimilation, as a moral dilemma of 'race relations', the Cabinet had revivified and legitimated a corpus of race ideas. At its core were notions of unalterable and fixed difference, of character, culture, phenotype and genotype. At its outer fringes it commingled with other corpora of ideas about identity, Britishness, sexuality, nationhood and so on (see, amongst others, Barrett and Roediger 1997; Bederman 1995; Cohen 1992; Gilroy 1993; Goldberg 1990; Guillaumin 1995; Malik 1996; Maynard 1994; Rattansi 1994; Rose 1989; Ware 1996).

Not only did this have some significant effects on the ideational configuration of immigration politics, but it also modified the ideational environment which agents and actors inhabited. This change in cultural conditions was enabling and constraining in different sorts of ways for different groups of actors. In presenting immigration largely in terms of its putative threat to national identity, politicians can continue to play the 'they don't belong here' card (anxieties about asylum seekers and refugees are a case in point; see, for example Geddes 1996; Joly 1997). By the same token, it becomes correspondingly difficult for others to argue for a policy based on international obligations or human needs.

However, it is in the nature of world three propositions as cultural resources that they are available for mobilization in a wide range of settings and for diverse sorts of purposes. All they require is organized sponsors. In bringing discourses about identity, colour, citizenship and controls into the public arena, politicians ran several risks: of exposing the discursive nature of these ideas as well as offering them for elaboration in unwonted directions. In fact both of these risks were actualized during the 1970s and 1980s. The academic field of 'race relations' found itself increasingly subject to professional critique (Bourne and Sivanandan 1980) and the 'common sense' fixity upon which successive Cabinets had built their case for controls came to be viewed as partial and as itself constructed.

Meanwhile, various far right organizations seized the opportunity presented by government insistence that controls on certain types of citizen were necessary if national identity was to be preserved. Significantly, the National Front was not formed until 1967, when:

> it was able to take advantage of a virtual consensus in British politics . . . on the subjects of race and immigration . . . and many of its successes (electoral and otherwise) coincided with periods when these issues were especially salient on the political agenda.
>
> (Husbands 1983:1)

The neo-Nazi grouplets that had struggled throughout the 1950s in a hostile cultural climate finally found their entrée to respectable parliamentary politics once the Cabinet had caused public opinion to 'mature sufficiently'.

Finally, we have to consider the effects of stage 2 on agency, since in bringing about changes in structural and cultural conditions agents change not only themselves but also the conditions under which other actors and agents operate and pursue their interests. These changes may prompt a shift in ideas and a development of organizational resources. The obvious example here is the changes in migrant organization. The enactment of legislation restricting migrant entry into the UK initiates the shift from primary agency to corporate agency (Archer 1995).

As the disillusioning nature of life in Britain became apparent to increasing numbers of colonial UKCs so they began to organize: the Advisory Committee on the Welfare of West Indians in London was founded in 1956, the British Caribbean Association in 1958. The first issue of the *West Indies Gazette*, under the editorship of Claudia Jones, appeared in March 1958, and by 1960 had a monthly circulation of 15,000 copies (Ramdin 1987: 225). Thus, another emergent outcome of the Cabinet's remodelling of immigration law is the reconstitution of immigrant agency. As immigrants respond to the discriminatory effects of legislation and to the government depiction of them as 'not British' and as culturally unassimilable, they develop shared interests, as 'black', say, and begin to organize for the pursuit of these interests. This, in turn, changes the environment in which other agents seek to pursue their interests.

For example, organizations such as CCARD (the Co-ordinating Campaign Against Racial Discrimination), formed in 1963, the Standing Conference of West Indian Organizations, formed shortly after the riots in 1958, and the Indian Workers' Association, campaigned vigorously against the introduction of controls. Governments found themselves having to pursue their restrictionist goals in an environment modified by the responses of primary agents to the context which *they* confronted.

That this is the case is shown particularly starkly in the present example. The Cabinet policy of covert controls accompanied by private manoeuvrings meant that they were diffident about the issue of discrimination, especially in the politically sensitive areas of housing and employment. Consequently, this worsened the situation for migrants themselves, leaving them to face the hostility of prejudiced property owners and employers. This, in turn, prompted a sharper recognition of the problems facing them as 'coloured' and as migrants and of the pressing need to confront these collectively through organizations like the Metropolitan Coloured Peoples Housing Association, founded in 1957. It is also possible to detect the beginnings of a counter ideology to the Cabinet's theme that 'coloured immigration' was a problem. This counter ideology, expressed in the constitutions and programmes of countless social and cultural associations (see Ramdin 1987: 219–6), drew on a variety of discourses and ideas to do with 'inter-racial harmony', with race and colour, and antiracism and anticolonialism.

The move from primary to corporate agency did not only make use of these structural and cultural resources, but also of those of the labour movement and particularly the trade unions. Here the Cabinet's silence on the issue of colonial immigration had other consequences, with 'white' workers sometimes opposing the introduction of 'black' workers, as in the colour bar dispute on the Bristol buses in 1963 (Dresser 1986).

More generally, there was a growth in racist violence and anti-colour sentiments amongst the public during the 1950s. The mutually conditioning effects of agency are especially clear here. As groups such as Oswald Mosley's Union Movement or Colin Jordan's White Defence League argued for 'keeping Britain white', so migrant organizations began to mobilize ideas about race, colour and blackness. This development (certainly not one intended by the Cabinet's decision to pursue a covert policy of restriction) modified the Cabinet's operational context and so further reduced its options.

There are, of course, other social, cultural and agential outcomes of stage 2, although an assessment of their relevance will depend on which aspect of social and cultural elaboration one is interested in and which particular starting point is chosen for the next morphogenetic cycle.

SUMMARY AND CONCLUSION

These two chapters have attempted to demonstrate the explanatory advantages of a sociological realism grounded in an analytical dualism of structure/culture and agency advocated by both Archer and Layder. Using Archer's morphogenetic model they have generated a narrative account of the efforts of postwar British Cabinets to introduce immigration controls on particular categories of British citizens.

Despite changes of government, the Cabinet's attitude towards immigration control of colonial UKCs remained consistent throughout the 1950s and the 1960s. This attitude rested on claims about the alleged unassimilability of people of colour to a British 'way of life' and compelled senior ministers to pursue a revision of the long standing constitutional right of British subjects to freely enter and reside in Britain.

The realist approach adopted here required us to consider the antecedent structural and cultural conditions – stage 1 of the morphogenetic cycle – within which the Cabinet, in 1948, began its project. Attention was drawn to a number of features: the desire of the postwar Labour government for the retention of a world role and the significance of the Empire/Commonwealth to this; the commitment to limited welfare reforms and the demands this placed on the economy; the need for full employment within the framework of a capitalist economy. Alongside this anterior distribution of structural resources was a distribution of cultural resources and values to do with notions of race, with colour and colonial status, democracy, the Empire/Commonwealth and subject status, freedom and the cold war, sexuality. There were, of course, many others (see, for example, Sinfield 1989).

The structural and cultural conditions identified at stage 1 are themselves the emergent products of earlier cycles of interactions and provide the conditioning medium for the interaction considered in our stage 2. That is, this anterior distribution of structural and cultural resources gives us, at the start of stage 2 in 1948, actors and agents differentially placed to pursue projects and realize interests. Different actors and agents are variously constrained and enabled by this distribution and in attempting to change it, or in endeavouring to keep it as it is, they interact with it as well as with each other. In attempting to modify and reshape structure, actors and agents modify and reshape themselves, generating a profoundly relational model of social change. This eschewal of 'single cause' accounts (such as those based, for example, on 'race') is accurately termed by Pretorius as 'methodological relationalism' (Pretorius 1993) and is a direct pay off from a realist perspective with its stress on the emergent properties of structure, culture and agency.

In the example of postwar British immigration policy the Cabinet's project of control and restriction on UKCs suffered various setbacks and reverses. It was the product of a range of factors, some of which not only lay well beyond the influence of the Cabinet but also were not comprehended by its members. Finally, in stage 3 we have seen that even where there is a successful outcome to agency, it is rarely unqualifiedly what actors and agents want. The Cabinet did not secure an end to anxieties about national identity and failed to prevent its corrective work to align colour discrimination with democracy from being scrutinized and condemned.

8 Doing without race: racism, discrimination and realistic measurement

INTRODUCTION

The account of Cabinet responses to postwar Commonwealth and colonial migration to Britain explored in the previous two chapters has pointed to the potential of a realist approach. Such an approach, it was argued, insisted on the inappropriateness of a notion of race *as an explanatory concept* in social science, whilst the example itself showed that such a notion was unnecessary to a *sociological* account of immigration and nationality policies. However, this account has drawn a good deal of attention to the role played by race ideas as a feature of political identities, as a basis for political mobilization and as a resource for the projects of actors and agents. This raises some important questions.

Perhaps the most obvious of these, and one which writers influenced by interpretivist and hermeneutic traditions have persistently brought up, is the relationship between the inconsistencies and inadequacies of race as an explanatory concept within social science and its continued use by racists and non-racists alike. In other words, if, as I have claimed, race is a worthless theoretical concept for sociologists, what are we to make of its continued employment not only by large numbers of lay actors but also by sociologists? This is one question addressed by the present chapter.

A second question has to do with the role played by race ideas in social interaction and in the constitution of subjectivities. Up till now, I have stressed the importance of race ideas as propositional forms, that is their status as claims about the nature of the world (for example, that there are races, that they share identifiable characteristics, that they do not mix, are hierarchically ordered and so forth). As we have seen the propositional forms of ideas are important elements of what Popper terms World Three (Popper 1972), or what Archer refers to as society's 'propositional register' (Archer 1989), and are thus available to actors and agents. Less significance has been attached, though, to race ideas as intersubjective meanings, as sources of psychological sustenance and personal expression of identity, and as interactional resources employed by social actors in accomplishing the routines of everyday life. These are areas left largely untouched by a challenge to the explanatory capacities of race as a sociological concept, that is, as a proposition about the nature of the social world.

The final issue raised by the critique of race developed in earlier chapters, and to some extent implied by these questions about race ideas and race as a sociological concept, is that of policy. There are at least two implications that follow from the above considerations. First, how are we to assess policies based on a notion of race and how might the realist respond to these? Second, what exactly is being measured by empirical and policy studies using a notion of race and how might the realist offer an alternative?

This chapter is structured by these concerns. It begins by developing a stratified approach to race ideas, using Layder's domain theory (Layder 1997). A major claim here will be that the role and relevance of race ideas will vary across different domains and that this requires a sociological approach sensitive to these variations. An examination of social policy research in the area of adoption is then used to identify some of the pitfalls associated with the use of an under-theorised notion of race.

Finally, the chapter returns to the work of Pawson and his insistence that all measurement is theory-driven in order to sketch out a realist approach to measuring discrimination and exclusion.

A 'DOMAIN' APPROACH TO RACE IDEAS

It has been a consistent theme of my argument that human activity is the outcome of the dual influence of structure and agency. This has entailed the rejection of theories that have either reduced one to the other or sought to make them mutually constitutive, on the grounds that such theories, amongst other things, stifle the possibility of a stratified social ontology. What does such an ontology offer in understanding race ideas?

The recent work of Layder (Layder 1997) points to some fruitful applications. He refines the structure-agency dualism by distinguishing four analytically separable 'social domains': psychobiography and situated activity (which, broadly speaking, refer to different aspects of agency), and social settings and contextual resources (which refer to structures).

'The notion of "psychobiography" points to the development of the self as a linked series of evolutionary transitions, or transformations in identity and personality at various significant junctures in the lives of individuals' (Layder 1997: 47). 'Situated activity' involves 'face to face conduct between two or more people who are in each other's "response presence"' (Layder 1997: 85). 'Social settings' are 'the proximate locations of social activities and specific social practices' (Layder 1997: 87). 'Contextual resources' refers to the anterior distributions of material and cultural capital which social actors inherit as a consequence of being born in a particular place at a particular time.

These domains are not experienced by people in their day-to-day existence in this stratified way, since they are always mutually interfused with each other. From a sociological perspective, however, it is possible to see how the influence, significance and relevance of particular elements of social reality will vary empirically according to their position in relation to the social domains. This is the case with ideas about race, as I shall demonstrate. In the discussion that follows I shall concentrate on Layder's first two 'domains'. This is because the implications for notions of race of the two 'structural' domains – those of social settings and contextual resources – have been dealt with extensively in Chapters 6 and 7. My comments on them here will thus be correspondingly brief.

At the level of psychobiography, race ideas may play a major role in the organization of self-identities. Indeed, there is a substantial body of research which has examined the crucial contribution of such ideas in narratives of self (see, for example, Balibar 1991; Barrett and Roediger 1997; Bederman 1995; Bhabha 1990; Cohen 1992; Conzen *et al.* 1992; Hall 1992; Shotter 1993; Small 1994; Ware 1996; Young 1990). At the psychobiographical level, the explanatory reach of sociology 'shades off', as it were, into psychology, biology and other disciplines. These disciplines may point to factors to do with the individual psyche or biology that predispose individuals towards particular sorts of identification; as suggested, for example, by the studies into the 'authoritarian personality'. Yet there is an important role for sociological analyses at the psychobiographical level.

In Chapter 2 it was argued that sociological investigations of identity which were premised on a weak notion of agency struggled to provide plausible accounts of identity. Instead, subjectivities were discursively produced and dealt out: the structuralist fist was frequently hidden within the velvet glove of diversity and difference. I am not denying the importance of discourses of identity. Rather I want to insist that our identity is defined by certain evaluations which are inseparable from ourselves as agents (Taylor 1985a). This, in turn, requires a stronger recognition of self or personhood than is ordinarily found in poststructuralist and postmodernist writing, whereas it presents less of a difficulty for a stratified ontology in which actors are also persons.

The psychobiographical domain is precisely that domain where the uniqueness of persons can be acknowledged – their emotions, anxieties, neuroses and attachments to others. In other words, in realist terms persons have capacities *as persons*, but the concrete realization or expression of these capacities will vary according to the outcome of the interaction between them and the other domains. Self or personhood is understood here to exceed its sociological determinations; in order to interact with the social the self must have some degree of autonomy or independence from it. Discourse does not go 'all the way down', nor does social science account for everything human (see Craib 1997 for a similar argument).

Thus whilst there may be unique factors, or at least ones opaque or refractory to a sociological accounting, that draw an individual towards, say, authoritarian politics, or encourage a psychic security through the denigration of what they perceive as 'outsiders', the politics and the definitions of 'outsiders' will not be the creation of the individual themselves. But we might want to incorporate such unique factors into our account. This suggests a more modest role for discourses than is usually allowed in the Foucauldian influenced work of writers such as Brah or Knowles. A realist account, by insisting on a recognition that the individual subject has biological, psychological and other sorts of capacities that are not reducible to the social, points to the definite limits of discourses in constructing identities and subjectivities. The self (and its identities) are a historically emergent (and conditioned) product of the engagement or interplay *between* persons or selves and the other domains or strata of social life; it is a 'positioned praxis', not a voluntaristic interaction.

It is not possible for us plausibly to carry off any identity we like, since there is a constitutive relation between the individual subject, their psychological needs and dispositions, their biological capacities, and their social milieu. Convincing others that you are a well-known athlete when you are obviously overweight, do not appear on television and have no trophies or obvious material rewards to corroborate your claims is likely to prove an uphill task. A rewarding 'subjective career' (Layder 1997: 48), like the more conventional one, requires social support if it is to be convincing.

I suspect this is one reason why psychobiographical identities based upon notions of race or ethnicity appeal to some groups and not others. Although this is clearly a question of the interplay between culture, structure and agency, it is also the case that we tend to work with the grain of our subjective needs (unless we are prevented from doing so, or wish to experience our lives as failures), seeking social fulfilment for them partly by recognizing the match between them and the potential for their realization in social life. Few 'white' people would find a rewarding subjective career as a 'black' nationalist; few people who regard themselves as part of a society's secure, dominant culture would find much appeal in seeing themselves as ethnically distinct.

This is also why, it seems to me, writers such as Hall, who point out that we are all 'ethnically located', rather miss the point. If we all have ethnic identities then the term loses any specificity as a social category. More importantly the notion that we are all 'ethnically located' does not address the rootedness of a concept of ethnicity in certain ways of life, in which people's subjective careers share some common elements, and the corresponding absence of it in others. Rather than 'uncovering' hidden ethnicities, sociologists should be asking why notions of ethnicity figure prominently in the subjective careers of some but not others. This implies strongly that notions of ethnicity, like notions of race, do not refer to objective features of persons but are discursive products, denizens of World Three. However, my point here is to argue that these discourses do not 'produce' subjectivities; rather it is in the interplay between subjects and those discourses that ethnic and race identities emerge. To explore this more adequately we need to examine Layder's other three domains.

The preceding discussion of the domain of psychobiography may have given an impression that individual subjects assemble identities and pursue their 'subjective careers' in a relatively voluntaristic manner, despite my repeated emphasis on such phenomena as historically emergent products of the interplay between subjects and the social world. As we move away, however, from those domains in which individuals' knowledge and their ability to 'make a difference' in the world encounter the limits imposed by other subjects and social relations stretching away in time and space, this voluntaristic view will be further modified.

Thus, the domain of situated activity 'exists only by virtue of the presence of particular people at specific times and places' (Layder 1997: 85), people whose needs and projects, status and authority have to be negotiated. This domain is irreducible to, and therefore distinct from, the domain of psychobiography. Its irreducibility derives from the fact that the interaction between specific individuals produces emergent features. Situated activity therefore amounts to more than the sum of its constituent parts. Shared agreements and collective understandings are forged in the course of social interaction and can influence subsequent interactions and shape it in particular ways. Significantly, interactants who are unable to 'read' these agreements and understandings – because they missed earlier meetings, say, or because they are unaware of the status and authority relations of others involved or because they do not have access to the cultural codes being drawn upon by the other interactants – may find themselves at a disadvantage.

Here, actors' use of race ideas can be crucial. They can be used to decide who is to be included in the interaction, the terms of their participation and the ways in which that participation is monitored and assessed. Gestures and other body language may be interpreted in terms of race notions. A person's 'race' may thus present serious difficulties for the presentation of self (Goffman 1970, 1971), since 'when an individual appears before others, he knowingly and unwittingly projects a definition of the situation, of which a conception of himself is an important part' (Goffman 1971: 213). In these ways culturalist and race assumptions, racist ideologies and exclusion can all operate at the level of situated activity as integral parts of the dynamic of everyday life and of what Goffman terms the 'basic dialectic of social interaction' (Goffman 1971: 222).

In terms of our earlier discussion in Chapter 3, what the distinction between the psychobiographical and situated activity domains entails is a stratified view of 'the people' (as opposed to 'the parts' of the social system). People are simultaneously persons (individual subjects with various capacities); social actors (engaged in the stream of daily life and negotiating various situated activities and social settings in doing so); and social agents (the constituents of collectivities sharing the same life chances). In the present chapter, though, our concern is more with the methodological implications of these distinctions. The identification of the domains of psychobiography and situated activity allows researchers to discriminate between the personal, psychic commitment to various ways of finding our feet in the world and the use of race ideas as interactional resources and as sources of personal evaluation, where other interactants may challenge or endorse the view of oneself as white, black, Jewish, middle aged, unattractive and so on.

Since talk of personhood and human nature can produce a shuffling embarrassment in the mixed company of some sociologists, let me repeat as plainly as I can what is being argued here. First, human beings, as organic, animate beings, possess certain biological and psychological capacities. Our scientific knowledge of these is, of course, fallible and revisable. Nevertheless, the capacity to walk upright, to communicate through language, to engage in conscious reflection, to labour and so on are all human capacities. Second, such capacities are both enabling (language enables literacy and the development of a 'World Three' of ideas) and constraining (our dependence on oxygenated air rules out an amphibious life). Third, and most importantly, which of these possibilities of constraint or enablement are realized, and the specific manner in which they are realized, will depend on the social context in which they are historically emergent. No human capacities are realized in the abstract; they can only be realized historically and socially, that is within determinate historical conditions. This is the sense in which psychobiography is an emergent outcome of the interplay between human capacities and social structure. This interplay also implies the irreducibility of the interacting elements, hence the insistence on a human nature which provides a resistance to the social, and places limits upon the extent of social scientific explanation.

Now it seems to me that to use a notion of race without recognizing these distinctions leads to some serious errors. The scientific critique of biological and genetic notions of race, alluded to earlier, has ruled out race as a meaningful determinant of human capacities: there are no significant differences between human beings that can be adequately described as 'race-ial', or as deriving from genetic 'race' features (Jones 1997). However, human capacities are always socially mediated; their concrete expression is always an emergent outcome of the engagement between persons and the social world. In a social world in which race ideas are the common currency of interactional exchange and are powerful discursive features of the cultural field, then human capacities may be expressed or grasped by actors and agents in race terms.

The use of a concept of race makes it difficult to discriminate between these ontological levels methodologically, whereas an implication of the approach urged here is that, from a social scientific point of view, it is essential to do so. Once more, race obfuscates social analysis. It has no relevance to an account of human capacities and it is more exact to refer to race ideas (used in the loose sense outlined above, referring not only to racism and other propositional forms of race ideas but also to their quotidian, taken for granted expressions) precisely in order to examine the interplay between these and the psychobiographical domain. This is particularly important when it comes to empirical research, as we shall see presently.

As I noted in the introduction to this chapter, I shall deal only cursorily with Layder's remaining domains of 'social settings' and 'contextual resources'. These were dealt with fully in Chapters 4, 5 and 6, where the following propositions were advanced:

1 race ideas, as cultural capital, are a discursive resource available to actors and agents;
2 race ideas, as ideas, cannot distribute material or cultural resources. Such distributions are always the historically emergent outcome of the interplay between structure and agency and the partly autonomous structural and cultural emergent properties that result from this.
3 partly as a direct consequence of 2, discriminatory and exclusionary practices often have a complexly mediated relation to race ideas.
4 the use by social scientists of a notion of race collapses these distinctions.

I now want to examine some examples of empirical research in which these propositions are neglected, largely through the employment of an under-theorized notion of race. This will serve both as a means of highlighting the problems raised by such research (What are social scientists measuring when they measure race?) and of preparing the way for the discussion of an alternative realist approach to empirical measurement based on the work of Pawson.

For some commentators, research into race is the paradigm example of modernist, Enlightenment reason run amok. Bauman, for instance, has argued that the Holocaust was the outcome of a bureaucratic rational culture and the ideas about race that it engendered and to some extent based itself upon. Bureaucratic rational culture is characterized by two key processes, a material and functional division of labour and the substitution of technical for moral responsibility, which together reduce the ambit of our moral responsibilities and produce indifference towards others (Bauman 1989: 98). This makes available the possibility of large scale social engineering – through death camps, genocide, ethnic cleansing, enforced migration and the like – a possibility realized through organization, management and experts and rationalized by racism: 'Racism is a policy first, ideology second' (Bauman 1989: 74).

At first take, Bauman seems to have a strong case. A full account of race research is beyond the scope of the present thesis, and reference has been made in Chapter 4 to some of the political consequences of such research. Nevertheless it might be helpful to dwell for a moment on the connections between reason, scientific rationality and empirical research into race. In his study of the politics of race research, Tucker reaffirms Bauman's claim about racism as policy first, ideology second.

> The question of genetic differences between races has arisen not out of purely scientific curiosity or the desire to find some important scientific truth or to solve some significant scientific problems but only because of the belief, explicit or unstated, that the answer has political consequences.
>
> (Tucker 1994: 5)

There may be any number of contingent political reasons for wanting to establish the scientific credibility of race ideas. Malik, for example, suggests *contra* Bauman that race ideas are invoked to justify the contradiction between inequalities associated with capitalism and the claims for equality made by the Enlightenment (Malik 1996: 6). Yet it is hard to disagree with Tucker's conclusion that in many of its forms race thinking represented 'the natural extension of the Enlightenment's faith in the instrumental use of reason, the conviction that rationalism could liberate the human mind from the bonds of myth, superstition, and revealed religion in favor of the truths derived from science' (Tucker 1994: 54). Underlying race research, from Blumenbach's rudimentary efforts at craniology in the eighteenth century, through the eugenics movement to Jensenism and the contemporary Bell Curve debate, has been the positivist presumption that science can provide the basis for the rational conduct of human affairs.

Given the close relationship between positivistic views of science and empiricism (Benton 1977; Bhaskar 1979; Doyal and Harris 1986; Hollis 1994; Hughes and

Sharrock 1997; Outhwaite 1987; Trigg 1985) it is, on the face of it, perhaps surprising that race should figure so prominently in scientific efforts to legislate for social behaviour. After all, as Banton has drily noted, no one has ever seen another person's race – what they see are particular phenotypical characteristics, which are taken as signs of expected behaviour and then used to classify individuals and groups 'race-ially'. Race suffers from a serious handicap as an empirical concept, namely that it is not directly observable.

This has not discouraged researchers from treating race as though it was an independent, empirically verifiable variable. I have discussed some examples of this in earlier chapters, but in the present chapter I want to look more specifically at social research directed at policy reform. In particular, I want to explore the continued vitality of race as a variable within empirical research, and to indicate some of the problems that flow from its use as a research concept, not the least of which are the effects that race classifications can have on actors and agents. More positively, it allows the stage to be set for the outline of an alternative realist approach to empirical research into racism, discrimination and social policy.

RACE CONCEPTS AND SOCIAL POLICY: THE CASE OF TRANSRACIAL ADOPTION

As we have seen from the previous section, concepts of race have played a notorious role in the advocacy of social reform in the past century and a half. The arguments of the eugenics movement, as Tucker and others have shown, were influential in political projects and campaigns that issued in a terrifying range of social policies, from death camps in Nazi Germany to enforced sterilization and discriminatory immigration controls in the USA (Barkan 1991; Higham 1994; Malik 1996; Stepan 1982; Tucker 1994). More recently, the work of Jensen and the 'Bell Curve' authors, Herrnstein and Murray, have demonstrated the continuing relevance of race concepts to contemporary efforts to influence public policy in an inegalitarian direction (Herrnstein and Murray 1994).

In considering social policy, we are examining the effects that the employment of race categories in political projects may have on people's lives. To some extent the examination of immigration and nationality legislation in postwar Britain did this, although it is not the concern of the present book to explore the damaging effects of such legislation on the lives of migrants and their families (but see, for example, (Dummett and Nicol 1990; Humphry and Ward 1974 ; Joly 1997; Miles and Phizacklea 1984; Moore and Wallace 1975; WING 1985). I wish to explore the more mundane use of race categories, what we might describe in Foucauldian terms as an aspect of 'governance', their use as a means of regulating and surveying populations. To this end, I have selected an area of social policy – so called transracial adoption – with the objective of (a) examining the role and use of race concepts; (b) seeing how such concepts are mobilized in the context of empirical research; and (c) drawing out and assessing the policy implications. I could, of course, have used other areas of social policy, such as housing or poverty: the example I have chosen is illustrative. The point is twofold: to emphasize the consequences for empirical research and social policy of employing an under-theorized concept of race; and to reinforce the central argument that a concept of race does not belong in social scientific research.

An important area of social policy in which race concepts have figured prominently has been adoption. Here the empirical verifiability of race has been a tacit assumption of debates about who should adopt whom and how this may best be regulated. Indeed, in the discussion both in the UK and the USA about what has come to be called 'trans-racial adoption' (hereafter TRA), the identification of race is frequently regarded as unproblematic (although there are distinctions to be made between the USA, where race is usually signified by skin colour, and the UK, where practitioners and academics are more cautious about what is meant by race).

TRA – adoption policy that tended to disregard race as a criterion for allocating children to adoptive parents – was first mooted as a policy strategy in the 1960s in the USA and Canada. Between 1958 and 1968, approximately four hundred children of Native American parents were placed with 'white' families in a joint venture between the Bureau of Indian Affairs and the Child Welfare League of America (CWLA) (McRoy 1989). As TRA gained acceptance, the practice became more widespread and was extended to 'children of colour'. In 1968, McRoy notes, '23% of the black children adopted were placed in white homes, and by 1971 this figure had increased to 35%' (McRoy 1989: 150). Given the salience of colour in US political culture it was only a matter of time before adoption policy came to be viewed critically in terms of race ideas.

The first public hostility to TRA was expressed at the National Association of Black Social Workers conference in Atlanta, USA in 1972. Following intense lobbying, the major professional child care organization in the USA, the Child Welfare League of America, also began to advocate 'in-race' adoption (this was actually a reversion to the position it had held during the Jim Crow years of segregation). In the 1980s several US states passed legislation that prohibited or regulated TRA; by the 1990s opposition to TRA had become 'a virtually unchallenged orthodoxy amongst child care professionals' and one that was 'constantly reflected in adoption practice' (Hayes 1995: 3–4). Instead policy emphasis was placed on SRA (same race adoption).

In Britain in 1983, and taking its lead from the US, the Association of Black Social Workers and Allied Professions reported to the House of Commons Social Services committee that:

> Transracial placement as an aspect of current child care policy is in essence a microcosm of the oppression of black people in society; the most valuable resources of any ethnic groups are its children . . . Transracial placement poses the most dangerous threat to the harmonious society to which we aspire. It is in essence 'internal colonization'.

> (Small 1991: 66)

By the time the 1993 white paper on adoption was published 'the placement of black children for adoption [had] become a battleground between those who believe that skin colour should not be a major consideration in such decisions and those for whom it is the single most important factor' (Macey 1995: 475).

Hayes has usefully summarized the key propositions of the argument against TRA. They are

> that minority children have a *right and need* to develop a *positive ethnic identity* and awareness of their *cultural heritage* within their own *community*. Without this identity they will face *inevitable problems* as they get older and will be unable to develop *survival skills or coping mechanisms* to deal with *the reality of racism*.
>
> (Hayes 1995: 4, original emphasis)

These propositions reflect many of the weaknesses associated with lay discourses of race, particularly the imprecision that accompanies the use of race notions. The adoption by parents of one race of children belonging to another is to be deprecated on the basis of a universal psychological need for a strong ethnic identity which can only be met by those who have an 'awareness of their cultural heritage within their own community.' Ethnicity, culture and community, themselves the impermeable offspring of the 'myth of cultural integration' adopted by public policy discourses, become entangled with notions of colour, race and racism. A few examples will serve to emphasize the point.

In 1989, the British Association for Adoption and Fostering (BAAF) summarized the professional position on TRA. Reviewing recent research and debate 'on the placement needs of black children', they noted that 'it seems to have produced a broad consensus: that a child's needs are best met in a family of the same race' (BAAF 1989: 1). The basis for this claim was again the insistence that one of the needs of the adopted child 'is unquestionably to develop a positive sense of racial identity'. Its chief policy conclusion was a call for more black social workers, especially ones 'with a respect and understanding for black communities and the particular problems they face, including the threat that policies of trans-racial placement pose to the survival of their communities' (BAAF 1989: 1–2).

Other practitioners have repeated these arguments. Waltham Forest Council made 'same race adoption' official policy in 1986. Its statement in justification of the policy mentioned two key principles: that the council should provide a service to meet the needs of children and families which will 'maintain and support the cultural and racial identity of the child and family'; and that children in care should be 'placed with families of the same ethnic background unless this is not in the best interests of the child' (Heywood 1990: 9).

One of its senior adoption workers made the implications of these principles and the policy derived from them quite explicit. 'It is self-evident to us,' she insisted, 'that the race and culture of substitute carers should be as close as possible to that of the child needing a new permanent family' (Heywood 1990: 9). SRA helps children cope with 'being black and brought up in a white environment' and it does so partly by helping children recognize their 'blackness'. Its essential, biological character is caught nicely in the anecdote Heywood employs as an illustration of the benign effects of SRA:

> I remember some children who had lived with their white mother and had been in and out of care repeatedly. When they came into care permanently they *had no sense of being black* (their father is Afro-Caribbean). They were placed with a black family and have blossomed in confidence . . . They now *know they are black* and feel good about it.
>
> (Heywood 1990: 10, my emphasis)

Occasionally, these arguments for SRA are buttressed by stressing the uniqueness of the 'black experience'. According to Small for example,

> white norms are used to measure the black person . . . There is a duality, the 'private' and the 'public self', a survival skill which is transmitted by black families . . . Duality is . . . a technique which has consequences for the child's ego and these adaptive techniques are not within the construction of reality by white families.
>
> (Small 1991: 65)

Now, it is not my present purpose to assess the effectiveness of TRA or SRA as social policies, although it should perhaps be noted that there has been a recent reversal of SRA policy both in Britain and in the USA, where the 1994 Multiethnic Placement Act forbids discrimination in foster care and placement (Alexander and Curtis 1996; Hugill and Mills 1998). (A range of opinions can be found in Hayes 1993, 1995; Kirton 1996; Macey 1995; Richards 1987.) Rather, I want to note some features of the race concepts employed by social practitioners and relate these to the realist arguments outlined at the beginning of the chapter.

The notions of race employed in the debates about TRA provide an example of the meaning in use of race. What does this example tell us? First, the debate about TRA sees race as something people have, an essential feature of which they may even be unaware but may later come to see. It does not regard race as a relational concept, a notion that emerges from social interaction and which actors and agents can deploy in various social settings and situated social activities.

Second, the meaning of race in these social policy contexts is only ever indexical or given in use: it is 'experience'; it is something derived from 'the community'; it is about skin colour; it is about culture or ethnicity; it is about all or some of these things. This lack of precision about what a concept of race refers to licences, as we have seen, some very bold claims as well as giving rise to definite social policies. It also encourages a disregard for social research findings and their possible relevance to policy issues. As Rowe has pointed out:

> We do not yet know from research how many black children are being placed transracially; exactly how black children develop a positive sense of black identity or what effect family and environmental circumstances may have; how

a representative group of transracially adopted adults would describe their experiences and feelings or how they have dealt with ethnic issues, or what is their current state of well-being and mental health.

(Rowe 1990: 8)

Similarly, Alexander and Curtis, noting the role played by research evidence in the move away from SRA in the United States, suggest that the weight of such evidence 'favors proponents of transracial adoption', whilst 'opponents of transracial adoption . . . had no empirical support for their position' (Alexander and Curtis 1996: 231–2). As we have seen, this has not inhibited the claims of policy practitioners, nor encouraged a more cautious approach to policy. On the contrary, since race takes its meaning here from lay discourses about colour, cultures, language, dress, habits and so forth, its place as a theoretical concept, and its connections with other theoretical concepts to do, for example, with identity or social relations, are left unexamined. The protean character of the concept, of course, derives from this dense accretion of lay meanings; these in turn are what contribute to its richness as a discursive resource for actors and agents in their pursuit of political interests and agendas.

This will not do for social science, as I argued in Chapter 3. Social scientific terms, locked into formal networks, have to be justified and proved *conceptually*. They have to be defended logically and be made to point to the means of measuring what would count as adjudicatory evidence. One of the reasons why the discussion of TRA and SRA appears impossible to adjudicate is because the key concept in that debate – race – does not have to be defended conceptually; it is simply taken for granted. Whilst supporters and critics of TRA cast their arguments in terms of a pre-theoretical concept, the possibility of an adjudication between them remains chimerical. In other words, if, as was argued in Chapter 3, the construction of evidence consists in the search for intersection between rival theories (Pawson 1989a: 257), concepts whose place within a theoretical scheme is obscured or impossible to identify are worthless. Race is such a concept.

Lest this be seen as a case of the ivory tower theorist scornfully dismissing the uninformed antics of those living in the real world, let me add that I am not claiming that if only social actors could get their concepts adequately theorized they would see the error of their ways. Clearly the interests of those involved in pursuing policies of TRA or SRA have to do, amongst other things, with personal careers, political status, authority, power and so on. None of these, of course, rule out an interest in arriving at an adequate sociological account of adoption of children by parents of a different colour, but this is unlikely to be a priority. However, although TRA may be an issue of public political debate my point is that it is an issue to which sociologists can make a contribution. The question, then, is what is the nature of this contribution? If a realist social science rejects the notion of race, how might it address policy issues such as discrimination and exclusion, racist violence or indeed TRA?

RACISM, DISCRIMINATION AND SOCIAL POLICY: REALISTIC MEASURES

This concluding section of the chapter is divided into two parts. In the first I will draw out some of the implications for policy of the realist position. These will focus on the issues raised for policy interventions and programmes of the revision of race concepts proposed earlier in this chapter. The second, longer section will indicate the possibilities for empirical research into discrimination and exclusion offered by a realist approach by drawing on the work of Pawson, and Pawson and Tilley (Pawson 1989a, 1989b; Pawson and Tilley 1997).

In the hope that it does not sound too manifesto-like, let me reiterate the conclusions about race that I have insisted follow from its inutility as a sociological concept. First of all, and contrary to much received wisdom on the topic, I have defined racism as a view of the world – ranging from the explicit and fully formed such as Nazism to the inexplicit and half-baked such as the belief that 'Asians can't play football' – which posits the existence of races. Two objections may be raised to this first conclusion.

One is that it fails to distinguish between what we might term 'reactionary' forms of racism, for example Nazism, apartheid or anti-Semitism, and 'progressive' forms of racism such as that expressed in various currents of black nationalism or by the rhetoric of 'race relations' agencies. This objection takes some of its force from the pejorative connotations that have become attached to the concept of racism. However, as sociologists we need to be consistent in our use of terms. At the risk of introducing more fancy terminology into an area of research that has already been overburdened in this respect, I propose that the term 'race-ism' would more accurately capture the idea, namely that it is a belief in 'races' as discrete human groupings. Like all propositional forms, they are *as ideas* neither 'reactionary', nor 'progressive'. Rather it is the purposes for which actors and agents employ them that may be evaluated in these terms.

A second objection is that defining race-ism as the belief in races is too narrow a view, and one that excludes important contemporary forms of race-ism in which notions of culture perform a similar function to notions of race in ascribing unalterable characteristics to human groups. This 'new racism' has been a central theme of Barker's work (Barker 1981). He argues that at the core of the 'new racism' is a theory of human nature which asserts the 'naturalness' of group exclusiveness and xenophobia; it is 'merely common sense' to reject outsiders. Barker's claim for the distinctiveness of the 'new racism' has been challenged (see, for example, Miles 1993), but the point I wish to establish is that Barker's efforts to describe as racism ideas that do not make explicit reference to race is needlessly confusing.

We have already seen in Chapter 4 that analytical dualism allows a view of race ideas as cultural system elements encountered by actors and agents who modify and customize these elements for their own purposes. It is unremarkable that in this process of culture-agency engagement race ideas are often displaced by other sorts of ideas – to do with human nature, say – as a basis for dividing human populations. It is, though, always human beings who do this dividing – not the ideas. The difficulty with notions of a 'new racism' is that they seem to rest upon an ideational essentialism; no matter what terms actors actually employ, really, 'underneath it all', these are expressions of racism, or, as one writer has it, 'race' gets coded as culture (Witte 1996: 195). This can only make sense if race ideas have (unique) properties which somehow survive their expression as something else (the debates about whether or not Enoch Powell was a racist, or a nationalist, illustrate many of these themes (Nairn 1981)).

If we abandon this specious notion of race as some sort of transhistorical essence, then we can develop an alternative account in which actors and agents seek to exclude, or discriminate against, certain groups and deploy various cultural resources as part of their efforts to do this. However, it is not the case that any old ideas will do: certain ideas will be politically unacceptable, others will carry the wrong sorts of connotations or will be monopolized by other groups or will entail certain sorts of relations with other ideas and so on. Thus the content of exclusionary ideas will be historically contingent – actors and agents are innovative and, depending on their level of political competence and capacities for mobilization, astute enough to go with what works. Sometimes this will be racism, at others it will be xenophobia or nativism (Higham 1994). It is hard to see what is gained by reducing these different ideational resources to expressions of an essential racism, new or otherwise, especially as this also obscures the ways in which the specific features of these ideas vary with the changing strategic collective interests of different groups of agents and actors.

Confining racism to the use of race ideas in this way has some further implications. Clearly, for instance, one cannot in this sense be an unconscious racist, any more than one can be an unconscious Marxist or an unconscious Muslim. More significantly, if we add the realist's stratified social ontology to the claim that race ideas are part of society's cultural register we obtain a more complex and subtle view of the role of such ideas. We can regard race ideas as a psycho-biographical resource, a means of expressing one's (frequently ill understood) psychic needs for identification, for example, as a 'white' person. We can also view them as a situational resource, expressed in prejudice, harassment and abuse and discrimination, or in group enterprises concerned with cultural solidarity. They can be an element of social settings, in the form of systematically reproduced discrimination and political definitions of citizenship and entitlement through immigration controls and nationality laws. Finally, race ideas may be seen as a contextual resource, that is, as a part of society's 'cultural capital'.

We are now in a position to move on to the second part of this section. It is a core element of morphogenetic theory that actors' readiness and capacity to employ cultural resources, as well as the adequacy of those resources to making sense of their lived experience, are themselves the outcome of the interplay of structure and agency. In other words, actors' take-up of race ideas is, to use Pawson's phrase, a matter of 'differently resourced subjects making constrained choices amongst the range of opportunities provided' (Pawson and Tilley 1997: 46). Policy designed to influence these choices, or research designed to understand them, will be less effective and less perspicuous to the extent that it neglects this insight. In order to examine how research (and by extension, policy) might avoid doing this, we need to return briefly to the realist principles outlined in Chapter 3 and develop their methodological implications.

Starting from the claim that 'society as an object of enquiry is necessarily theoretical' (Bhaskar 1979: 57), realism offers a radical revision of conventional models of empirical research. This derives from its notion of generative causality (Harré 1972, 1986) and its associated core principle that 'science is the business of understanding the unobservable structures and mechanisms that stand behind and produce concrete features of social reality' (Pawson 1989a: 168). An important methodological corollary of this ontological claim is that 'measurement in social research will always be an act of translation' (Pawson 1989a: 287). This is to say that empirical data should be constructed from a grounding within the conceptual networks of sociological theory, since the social regularities described by such data are themselves the product of scores of distant social processes and mechanisms. In short, measurement in social science is theory-driven.

Now we have already seen that this view of empirical regularities and the role of theory in social science entail serious reservations about sociological concepts of race. Without labouring the point made earlier, if empirical research and measurement is theory-driven then social scientists (like their natural science counterparts) require a logically consistent network of concepts capable of formulating and describing the real connections between social phenomena which we regard as causally connected. This then permits the construction of evidence that enables adjudication between rival theories. Race is not such a concept, as has been amply demonstrated; it neither refers to biological or genetic groupings of any social significance nor does it capture with coherence the 'forms of life' in which everyday uses of race ideas are embedded.

Race is thus a prescientific, routine description employed by lay actors. More significantly, it carries its theoretical assumptions directly into what is to be measured; its residual essentialism simply cannot be extirpated. This is the source of its incoherence once it is put to work as an instrument of social research, where it unavoidably appears as an empirical variable. This leads to a second methodological observation about realist social research. It requires us to specify accurately what it is we wish to measure or evaluate (not race, for this cannot be measured, but colour discrimination in the housing market, say), whilst recognizing that this will itself be the outcome of a series of generative processes. Grasping these processes requires the sort of conceptual framework alluded to above. Pawson has described this form of realist measurement as transduction (Pawson 1989a).

At the heart of the transduction principle is the notion of generative causality and the claim, discussed above, that it is therefore the 'theoretical precision with which models of generative mechanisms are constructed in natural science which lends exactitude to the measurement process itself' (Pawson 1989a: 159). Since generative properties do not reveal themselves, the natural scientist sets up experiments as situations in which properties can be 'triggered' to perform. Thus measurement is never direct, since a range of theories is needed to transform what is measured into knowledge about causal capacities and relations. Thus the properties of heat are not measured directly but indirectly by a thermometer, itself the product of a host of theories about kinetic energy and so on (Pawson 1989a).

The need to transduce requires the use of theories to make the connections between data and properties. This makes it common in natural science for competing theories to employ shared procedures and assumptions in their attempts to verify their own position. It is these points of theory intersection, rather than the supposedly neutral language of direct observation, that become vital in theory choice and prevent the lapse into complete relativism (Pawson 1989a). Pawson suggests that this is also the model that realist social research should emulate.

The first step in applying the transduction approach to the issues of racism and discrimination is the critique of race as a sociological concept. For reasons that have been argued at length in earlier chapters, the lay category of race has no place in sociological research. Instead the phenomena that it inconsistently delineates at the level of lay discourse have to be dis-aggregated and broken down. Race in sociological and lay discourses can variously be taken to refer to: perceived differences in skin colour, 'culture', religion and so on; forms of mutual knowledge and theoretical ideologies; processes of exclusion and discrimination, in the domains of situated activity and social settings; and systematically reproduced inequalities, such as distributions of material and cultural capital, in the domain of contextual resources.

As a second step, the measurement of these distinct types of phenomena requires a theory that recognizes their distinctiveness as well as their connections and their embeddedness within a stratified social reality. In short, this cannot be the measurement of race, but the use of empirical research as a means of testing theoretical knowledge of the causal processes generating domain-specific events, properties and regularities. 'The general thesis here is that sociological theory determines the conceptual structures of explanation, which in turn determine the measurement parameters into which we should encode empirical evidence' (Pawson 1989a: 192).

This view of the relationship between social theory and social research enables the third step linking realist ontology, epistemology and methodology, namely the elaboration of a realist research programme. Here we need to remind ourselves of the core components of the realist ontology. Briefly, it was argued in Chapter 3 that the realist notion of causative generality rests on the recognition of the powers, capacities and liabilities of agents and actors, structure and culture. Through the interplay between these elements such powers, capacities and liabilities are realized (or not) and are modified (or not). Realism thus stresses change as an internal potential of a structure or system that may be activated by the right sorts of conditions. This provides us with a model for realist measurement and evaluation within social science, a model that Pawson and Tilley have explored (Pawson and Tilley 1997).

Realist measurement, argue Pawson and Tilley, rests on the axiom 'regularity = mechanism + context'. Empirical regularities are the product of particular causal relations operating in particular contexts, that is the contexts in which their causal powers and capacities are triggered. Sociological explanation, then, consists of the identification of empirical regularities (ethnographically, ethnomethodologically, statistically or whatever, depending on which domain of social life is being examined), the identification of the causal mechanisms and processes that generate these and the context within which these processes become operative. The whole operation, as we have seen, is theory-driven, since

> 'A mechanism is . . . not a variable but an account of the make-up, behaviour and interrelationships of those processes which are responsible for the regularity. A mechanism is thus a theory – a theory which spells out the potential of human resources and reasoning'
>
> (Pawson and Tilley 1997: 68)

Further, this form of measurement has to be firmly anchored in analytical dualism, because 'Social mechanisms are . . . about people's *choices* and the *capacities* they derive from group membership' (Pawson and Tilley 1997: 66), and in a stratified social ontology, because the realization (or not) of people's choices and capacities is socially enacted.

The account of immigration legislation and definitions of citizenship in Chapters 6 and 7 has been based on this model. However, whilst it is beyond the scope of the present book to explore in detail the implications of the Pawson and Tilley approach for policy, it might be helpful to suggest some lines of further enquiry for realist social research. Take, for example, patterns of colour discrimination. Let us leave aside for the moment the issue of how technically such discrimination might be measured, since, as we shall see, our encoding of empirical variables (what it is we want to measure) is itself determined by the conceptual structures of explanation. Patterns of colour discrimination represent systematically reproduced phenomenal forms of inequality, irreducible to personal prejudice and individual acts of discrimination on the basis of race ideas.

Our next task, having identified this particular empirical regularity, is to seek for the mechanism(s) responsible for generating these and to specify the contexts within which they are triggered into producing the particular outcome of systematic inequality. How might we account for systematic colour discrimination? Again, the different social domains will have relevant mechanisms. An obvious starting point, for instance, is the level of situated activity, where the prevalence of race ideas as common sense may encourage colour discrimination (see, for example, Willis 1977).

Our insistence on a proper realist regard for the interplay between structure, culture and agency, however, suggests that the readiness to draw on race ideas in order to discriminate will depend on people's choices and capacities. For instance, people may choose not to discriminate because they believe it to be wrong for moral reasons. They may discriminate simply because it is easier to go along with the workplace mores of the discriminating group. Alternatively, people may display prejudice and discriminate in order to further their careers; they may do the opposite to further their careers, and some people will not be in a position to discriminate. There are plenty of other contextual conditions that will inhibit or encourage the expression of prejudiced and racist sentiments and discriminatory behaviour. The point is that the research methods we employ to examine these processes is a matter of appropriateness – which works best to get at what we want – and that a notion of race is irrelevant to explaining them.

Mechanisms operating predominantly in one domain may influence the operation of mechanisms and relations dominant in other domains, inhibiting them, suppressing them, facilitating them. Continuing with the discrimination example, the existence of a company or institution policy on discrimination may discourage public discrimination, whilst encouraging informal means of arriving at the same end. It may become a resource in the struggles between groups with conflicting or divergent interests. The use by Willis's 'lads' of their secondary school's taboo about references to colour and the overt expression of racist language is a case in point. The casual use of racist terms was partly a resource for embarrassing teachers and for furthering one's peer group career (Willis 1977). The policy point of this is not that anti-discrimination policies should be abandoned, but that their effectiveness is always socially mediated so that whilst addressing the contexts in which some mechanisms operate, such policies frequently fail to address the contexts in which others operate. A stratified social reality means refining policy to ask for whom it might be effective and under what conditions.

This is especially the case when we incorporate other domain levels into the analysis. Whilst, as we have seen, discrimination is possible and advantageous in some settings and not possible and disadvantageous in others, the capacity to discriminate is a group and social capacity which is itself the consequence of a particular agential location (owning property, being an employer, operating an admissions policy). Further, these locations are themselves the outcome of particular distributions of material and cultural capital and of antecedent interaction between structure and agency.

We might take a similar line with TRA. This debate starts from an assumed empirical variable derived from lay discourses – race. It then measures the distribution of this variable in different settings, and finds a putative mismatch between the needs of children of one race with the parenting skills of adults belonging to another race. The policy solution then is to match children with carers on the basis of 'race'.

Against this the realist would favour placing empirical strategy firmly within a theoretical discourse, rejecting race as an inadequately defined theoretical object and identifying more appropriate regularities – inequalities associated with colour, for example, or class distributions of adoptive strategies, or the numbers of black children in institutional care – to measure transductively the causal relations that may be operating (such as economic and other pressures on black families creating a disproportionate number of children in care) and the contexts in which they may be activated.

SUMMARY AND CONCLUSION

This chapter has explored the methodological and policy consequences of abandoning a sociological notion of race. The general theoretical argument for this was that race is not an adequately defined theoretical object within social science. That it should be so defined follows from the position outlined elsewhere in this study, namely that a realist theory of knowledge must recognize the reality of the object of knowledge and its relative independence from the 'knowing subject'. It follows from this that the source of objectivity of scientific knowledge lies in the referential character of its theoretical concepts and that therefore empirical evidence should be constructed from a grounding within the language of sociological theory. Yet sociologists find themselves unable to agree on the object of race. More often than not they ontologize it, making race capable of autonomous interaction and so dragging empiricist conceptions of knowledge into social scientific discourse.

After noting some of the effects of race research, the chapter has argued that not only is the abandonment of a sociological concept of race necessary for social science but that doing so opens the way for a properly realist social research. Layder's domain perspective was seen as offering a practical means of grasping the embeddedness of social life in a manner that recognized a stratified social reality. The possibilities of such an approach were developed by contrasting it with an account of TRA, a policy debate conducted almost entirely in race terms. Finally, a realist model of measurement and evaluation was outlined, based on the work of Pawson and Tilley. This suggested avenues for social research into discrimination, inequality and racism that required no concept of race.

In an important sense this has brought us full circle, since this book began with the question of what was wrong with the concept of race. The arguments for abandoning the concept have always been shadowed by larger debates about the future of social science and particularly its claim to privileged knowledge; indeed some would question strongly the very notion of a science of the social. It is to these doubts and debates that I turn in the final chapter.

9 Defending a science of the social

It is a testament, perhaps, to the force of postmodern ideas in the West that the very idea of a science of society should require defending. In fact, it is hard not to agree with two recent commentators that postmodernism's critique of science as a 'grand narrative', as a particularly overweaning instance of the ambitions of reason, has led to a 'loss of faith in the capacity of our schemes of thought, especially science, to represent the truth about reality' (Hughes and Sharrock 1997: 184–5).

Rather than square up directly to the challenge of postmodernism, I have adopted an approach by stealth. This strategy has been chosen not in order to minimize the risk of injury, but because the protagonists in the debates about a social science do not come solely from the postmodern camp (see, for example, Benton 1977; Cottingham 1984; Doyal and Harris 1986; Gellner 1985; Giddens 1984; Harré 1972; Hughes and Sharrock 1997; Kirk 1999; Manicas 1987; Phillips 1996; Williams 2000). Thus I have preferred not to pick a straightforward fight. Instead I have selected a topic about which sociologists of all stripes have had something to say (even if they did not intend to say it), namely race, and pointed out some of the difficulties entailed in providing an adequate sociological account of the phenomena to which this term is taken to apply. I have then suggested that these difficulties stem from an unwillingness, or a plain desire to avoid, the theoretical issues associated with the notion of a social science, particularly the issue of structure and agency.

This concluding chapter falls into two parts. In the first, I shall provide a detailed recapitulation of the argument, taking the opportunity to highlight and reinforce some of its central points, whilst also indicating some of its limitations. The second part will claim author's privilege in suggesting to those who are persuaded by the argument some possible directions for social science and research.

WHAT'S IN A WORD? RACE, RACISM AND RACIALIZATION

I began by querying the privileged status of the concept of race. Almost alone in the densely populated nation of sociological terms, this concept invariably appears with a trim of scare quotes ('race'), a decoration rarely awarded to other denizens and one oddly out of place in such a staunchly republican realm. Old-timers such as class, bureaucracy or rationalization do not get this privilege; new hands such as gender or discourse are overlooked. In fact, race receives this embellishment not because it is an especially powerful, relevant or perspicuous concept, but rather because its status as a *sociological* concept is obscure.

Many, perhaps most, sociological terms possess dual citizenship of the realms of lay and social scientific discourses and sociologists seem to have little difficulty in getting them to acknowledge their different responsibilities in each. Social researchers, for example, generally regard common sense notions of class as providing partial, limited and occasionally misleading accounts of the social world. Accordingly, whilst not dismissing the authenticity of these accounts (after all, if we are interested in how actors experience or live class relations, this is the best place to start), sociologists nevertheless realize that the job they want to undertake requires a more rigorously defined category of class. This will be defined by sociologists for sociological purposes.

Why can we not perform a similar operation on the concept of race? I have suggested a number of reasons for this, some of which I will return to presently. The central reason, though, is that the notion of race cannot generate an adequate theoretical description of social reality. Few would now posit races as distinct and discrete biological categories transmitting genetically sociologically relevant characteristics. The status of race as a theoretical concept therefore remains dubious.

The perdurable place of race in lay discourses means that we should question its admission to social science discourses; sociologists should not extend dual citizenship to race and its passport should be revoked. However, sociologists have in the main been reluctant to take such measures and in Chapters 1 and 2 I have explored some of the reasons for this. In order to make the case more sharply for a realist alternative, let me return to these once more.

One important objection to my claim for more active border patrols between social scientific and lay discourses with regard to race is that such measures render it difficult to acknowledge the force, or explore the extent, of race ideas within lay discourses. There are several aspects to this argument. First, there is the point that the distinction between lay and social science discourses does not matter greatly, partly because there are many sociological terms whose meaning is imprecise and unstable; partly because we should recognize the organic connections between social science language and lay languages; partly because race concepts are simply elements of society's symbolic order and to insist that they refer to something beyond this is unrealistic and unnecessary. Second, writers influenced by interactionist traditions of sociology have insisted that notions of race have a common sense validity and, to this extent, they influence the behaviour of social actors. In so far as the belief in races is real, then such belief has real consequences.

Chapter 1 dealt in some detail with the second of these objections. Leaving aside the more general reservations about interactionist approaches (Anderson, Hughes and Sharrock 1987; Benton 1977; Foucault 1977; Giddens 1979; Hughes and Sharrock 1997; Layder 1990; Mouzelis 1997; Sharrock 1987), the chief problem with the 'race is real because actors believe it to be so' line was that, paradoxically, it found it difficult to avoid reifying race ideas. There are several reasons for this, some empirical, some theoretical.

In so far as the social world is constituted in part by what actors and agents do and has meaning by virtue of this, then the cognitive resources of actors and agents must be a crucial element of any adequate description of that world. Actors and agents act on the basis of reasons and motives which are presumably existentially real for them but which, as Taylor has argued, are rooted in social practices and thus not reducible to individuals (Taylor 1985b). They are inter-subjective and, in terms of our realist perspective, part of culture and the cultural system (society's 'propositional register'). Actors and agents encounter these meanings as resources, and in the course of deploying them, modify them or leave them unaltered. The irreducibility of inter-subjectivity recognizes both unacknowledged conditions of action – we do not always know why we do what we do or understand our own motives – and the unintended consequences of action.

All of these distinctions are simply erased in the 'race is real because actors believe it to be so' approach. Without repeating the arguments advanced in Chapter 1, the chief weakness of this approach is its ontological reduction of social reality to actors' beliefs about it. Not only is the claim empirically difficult to verify but it also makes analysis and explanation of the structuring of beliefs formidable. In short, it makes a critical account of racism and race ideas well nigh impossible precisely because it conflates culture, structure and agency. This restricts social science to providing a (circular and largely otiose) description of the social world as seen by its members: race is a part of the social world because people believe in race. Questions about the adequacy of actors' descriptions of their social world tend to be squeezed out by this sort of conflationary thinking.

Miles' notion of *racialization* represents an important advance in formulating the connections between actors' beliefs and structure. As we saw in Chapter 4, Miles uses the term to address the shifts in systems of signification whereby aspects of the social world come to be understood in terms of ideas about race. The reintroduction of structures both allows for a critical view of the concept of race and raises the (realist) possibility of explaining the prevalence or otherwise of race ideas in terms of irreducible causal social relations and processes. However, the concept of racialization, I suggested, is itself conflationary, referring as it does to both the structuring *of* social relations and to the structuring of ideas *about* social relations. This imparts to the term a hamstringing ambiguity, reflected in the way it hobbles onto the playing fields of theorists less rigorous than Miles and performs a few perfunctory runs as a substitute for notions such as ideology or discourse.

It will be recalled that we identified two objections to the expulsion of the notion of race from the sociological lexicon. The second of these we have just considered, so let us now turn to the first. This has two components, both associated with postmodernism. There is the claim that since all theoretical terms are social constructs, insisting on a spurious scientific exactitude is futile, delusional and irrelevant. All meanings are endlessly deferred, and the rough democracy of language ensures that this will be just as true for the social science aristocrats as it is for the lay discourse plebeians. Second, there are those writers who regard race concepts simply as elements of society's symbolic order; to insist that they refer *to* something is unrealistic and unnecessary.

Chapter 2 set these arguments in the broader context of the rise of post-structuralist and postmodernist ideas. There, following Rosenau, I distinguished between sceptical and affirmative postmodernism (Rosenau 1992) and added a further distinction of my own between 'weak' and 'strong' interpretations of Foucault's notion of discourse. Theorists working in the sceptical and 'weak' camps have made some important contributions to the analysis of racism and race ideas, highlighting the role played by discourses of race as 'regimes of truth' and pointing to the significance of race ideas as interactional and affective resources for actors and agents. The contribution of the 'strong' affirmatives was seen to be less helpful and far less accommodating to the realist perspective.

In the hands of the 'strong' affirmatives, notions of endlessly deferred meanings effectively become a means of avoiding, in Manicas's words 'the most pressing problem for a viable philosophy of social science, that of formulating in a clear and adequate way the 'object' of theory in social science' (Manicas 1987: 270). 'Endlessly deferred' frequently comes to mean 'rarely theorized', with its inescapable proliferation of common sense notions of race. This is why, as Chapter 2 demonstrated, 'strong' affirmatives found it difficult to develop a convincing sociological critique of race ideas: the withdrawal from the social practices of critique and objectivity entailed by a notion of social science brings them precipitously close to irrationalism. These tendencies are most marked in the discussion of identity. Here postmodern epistemologies often rely on a mixture of experiential empiricism (some people have 'common' experiences and therefore come to 'share' an identity based on certain common perceptions of these experiences) with reductionist romanticism (and therefore they have privileged access to knowledge of these experiences).

In various ways, and under various guises, then, race survives as a sociological category: as something people believe in and therefore make real: as a discourse; as a symbolic form; as a source of privileged knowledge. Theorists cannot agree on what it refers to, and yet it interacts with, amongst other things, class, gender and politics. It forms the basis of adoption policy in the USA and Britain; nobody has seen it and yet it is 'One of the first things we notice about people when we meet ... them' (Omi and Winant 1994). As Chapters 1 and 2 have shown, this absence of an object is a recipe for incoherence and as is commonly the case with such recipes the end product is often half-baked.

BEING REALISTIC ABOUT RACE

These difficulties with the race concept are not merely local disciplinary scuffles, of little interest to those choosing to avert their gaze whilst continuing to plough their own academic furrows. The equivocation about race concepts is connected to the wider uncertainty amongst sociologists about the status, meaning and viability of a notion of social science. There are, of course, traditions within the human sciences that may be seen as challenging the very notion of a social science at the outset, especially those associated with the various schools of interpretivism and hermeneutics.

An assessment of this debate is clearly beyond the scope of the present work, but I would suggest that it reflects a concern with *scientism* rather than science. Scientism refers to the (positivistic) view that science produces objective knowledge through the consistent application of the hypothetico-deductive method, that is through neutral observation of reality and the accumulation of the data arrived at to the point at which some general law or pattern can be discerned (Hughes and Sharrock 1997: 208).

The blurring of science with scientism has had some crippling effects within social science. These have been aggravated by poststructuralist and postmodern emphases on reflexivity, representation and discourse, which have tended to collapse the distinction between science and ideology by developing a critique of science as 'an instance of the ambitions of reason' (Hughes and Sharrock 1997: 184). Disentangling scientism from science is the first step in the recuperation of science.

Some of the objections to scientism have been aired in earlier chapters, sufficient to make it clear that the realism advocated here is radically antithetical to the empiricism on which scientism rests. This is especially clear in realism's commitment to 'ontological depth', to the empirically unobservable nature of social relations and processes and to the role of retroduction as an analytical strategy. However, as Chapter 3 noted, these rather general philosophical claims do not provide much in the way of concrete help for the jobbing sociologist; frequently, they simply get in the way. Nevertheless, a version of realism, I have argued, is indispensable for social science.

The elements of a distinctively *sociological* realism are to be found in the work of Archer, Layder, Pawson and Sayer. Collectively their work offers a cogent and powerful defence of a social science and provides the basic components of a realist programme for social research. Five themes were identified as central to sociological realism: analytical dualism; a stratified social ontology; the distinction between scientific and lay discourse; mechanism, processes and empirical research; and morphogenesis and history.

Analytical dualism is the core principle of sociological realism. In recognizing an analytic distinction between structure and agency (and simultaneously resisting efforts to reduce either one to the other or to see them as mutually constitutive), realism also recognizes their distinctive emergent properties and powers and their irreducibility. This basic ontological division licenses two important refinements to the agency-structure dualism. First, we can appropriate to our sociological armoury the distinction between social integration and system integration.

Second, analytical dualism not only allows a view of 'people' and 'parts' as having irreducible properties and powers and as operating within different temporalities. It also facilitates a notion of them as internally differentiated, as comprising a series of 'domains' extending from the psycho-biographical through the domains of situated activity and social settings to that of contextual resources. Each of these domains has its own temporal rhythms and its own properties and powers and is not reducible to the other domains (although, of course, they are connected to each other in all sorts of ways).

Analytical dualism entails a stratified social ontology, our second key theme. The term *entails* is deliberate, because the notion of emergence as the engine of realist epistemology methodologically compels the recognition of the irreducibility of the different levels of the social world. We can map onto the four 'domains' of the social world a stratified view of agency. Thus our second theme – that social reality is stratified – is seen to entail a more complex view of the proposition that agency and structure, 'parts' and 'people', have ontologically distinct properties and powers. Whatever loss of popular support may be prompted by this complexity, it does allow a fundamental sociological question to emerge with precision and force, namely 'whose activities are responsible for what and when?' (Archer 1995: 141). This is the question social science should be attempting to answer and a realist view of structure and agency, on the present view, makes this possible.

In order to realize this possibility, however, social science must develop a conceptual vocabulary adequate to an account of a stratified social reality. This is our third theme. We have already seen that agency is in a sense 'blind', or at least dumb, when it comes to cognizing the distribution of material and cultural capital and its consequences. Further, this is not merely a matter of spatial and temporal limits, of not seeing far enough for long enough to cover all the angles of social life. It is implicit in the realist ontology of emergent properties and powers and their contingent realization in various causal relations that our grasp of the world must be theory driven, since empirical observation alone cannot yield an understanding of these relations. Unsurprisingly, then, lay discourses are the product of actors' and agents' necessarily limited experience and partial knowledge. They are practically adequate. They are not necessarily adequate at the level of theory, and this is perhaps nowhere more obvious than with the lay concept of race.

As a lay concept race is polysemic and all purpose, as a number of writers have pointed out (Cohen 1992; Gilroy 1987; Goldberg 1990). That is to say, its 'meaning in use' encompasses a broad variety of propositional and symbolic forms. Like the company car, which can simultaneously be a means of doing a job, demonstrating status, avoiding tax restrictions or conducting an affair, race concepts in lay discourse can be, amongst other things, a means of self definition and identification, an objectification of affective commitment, a rationalization of inequality, a justification for violence and discrimination and a means of getting elected. And also like the company car, lay race concepts are widely available and come with all sorts of discounts and free gifts: flags, symbols, communities, the whole paraphernalia of 'banal nationalism' (Billig 1995). Note that this is not to suggest that race concepts in lay discourse are 'merely' symbols, or even 'only' symbols. As we have seen in Chapter 5, race concepts, as cultural items, have emergent properties and these too must be incorporated into a sociological explanation and, as Smaje has recently and rightly argued, not dismissed as simply a social construct (Smaje 1997).

Another way of putting this is to say that lay race concepts are conflationary; they run together, often in a deceptively seamless way, propositions, meanings and symbols. Of course, actors and agents frequently only buy parts of the package –

standing for the playing of a national anthem does not make you a neo-Nazi – but the proto-theoretical status of lay concepts (not only race concepts) means that their 'meaning in use' is de facto. In this sense, part of the utility of lay concepts is the flexibility of their meaning in use, their lack of constraint by theoretical discipline. This is a feature of 'practical consciousness' and it is exactly why lay concepts will not do for social science.

Such a claim follows directly from a stratified social ontology and the realist insistence that 'science is the business of understanding the unobservable structures and mechanisms that stand behind and produce concrete features of social reality' (Pawson 1989a: 168). However, this is not a matter of getting down to the 'real' structures that underlie appearances; rather it is a question of developing generative models, through retroduction, capable of constituting research hypotheses and providing appropriate strategies for empirical research. The generation of models is a *theoretical* enterprise and this requires a social scientific language of social analysis.

Chapter 3 used the work of Layder as the basis for exploring such a language (Layder 1990). Here it was argued that the depiction and description of actors' and agents' lay accounts, or of their knowledge of 'how to go on' in situated social activities, will require reference to the terms in which those accounts are experientially grasped and shaped. This, it seems to me, is the nub of the 1980s debate about the irreducibility of race and the relationship of race to class (Gabriel and Ben-Tovim 1979; Gilroy 1987; Hall *et al.* 1978; Miles 1982; Miles and Phizacklea 1984). Briefly, the argument went that if race was a social construction then it was epiphenomenal and could be 'reduced without remainder' to an expression of more fundamental, material interests, usually those of class. Against this it was charged that race had an autonomy from class relations, reflected in the vigour of popular political and cultural movements built around it.

From the realist point of view, this is something of a phoney debate. Race ideas and symbols, as cultural system items, do have some autonomy from structural relations since they have emergent properties and features. As we saw in Chapter 5, race ideas have a specificity of meaning that partly derives from the logical relations they have with other ideas and propositions. These relations are contingently realized through actors and agents. This means that the meaning and content of race ideas is important and is not reducible to material interests or agential location.

On the other hand, the deployment of cultural items such as propositions and ideas about race in lay discourse, and their symbolic representations in flags and so forth, does not constitute race as a social scientific category. The intersubjective reality of race symbols and ideas, the fact that at the psycho-biographical level they can provide powerful sources of affective identification and emotional security, cannot be *explained* in terms of race. Explanation requires theory; theory requires self-conscious conceptual formation grounded in the language of social science.

This returns us to the phoney debate. The concept of race *only* has meaning in lay discourse. The point is worth emphasizing. There are no reputable theoretical frameworks in social science that establish or develop a *sociological* concept of race.

There are theories a-plenty about the role and relevance of race ideas, propositions and symbols in the psychobiographies of individuals, in the rules and normative frames of situated activities and social settings, theories in which these different domains with their distinctive properties and features are conflated under the term race. But there is no theoretical definition of race, for the simple reason that whatever meanings the term race has are those given it in use by lay actors.

Attempting to assess the relative weighting one has to give to race or to class in sociological explanations is thus rather like trying to measure a pound of potatoes using a ruler; the two categories are incommensurable. Class, like other theoretical terms within social science is, of course, a social construction, if by that we mean that it is not a category naturally given in experience, but is a product of human cognition and rationality. Class as a social science concept is a human invention. But it is a concept drawing explicitly on consciously formulated ontological and epistemological claims about the nature of social reality. In using it sociologists attempt to capture analytically the structural features of social life. This is why they do not place it in scare quotes.

Race, however, is an altogether different matter. Not only does it not get the technical backup from other conceptual frameworks – there is no functionalist concept of race, for example, to contrast with a Marxist or interpretivist one – but its embeddedness in the experiential world of everyday activity renders it unsuitable for analysing social scientifically the contextual conditions of action because this again requires that our concepts are coherent and consistent attempts to describe social reality.

Why can we not make a sociological concept of race? After all, the fact that terms have lay meanings does not disqualify them from also acquiring social science meanings. Examples such as social class, bureaucracy, fascism, interaction abound; indeed the traffic is far from one way, as writers such as Giddens have pointed out (Giddens 1979, 1984), with plenty of terms doing the round trip and becoming exemplars of reflexivity. However, a consistent realism will help us to see that some terms and vocabularies are better travellers than others. This is because inter-subjective meanings are irreducible and have emergent features and properties of their own.

Several insights follow from this. First the meanings of terms and concepts cannot simply be amended or altered at will by individuals, partly because of this irreducibility – you might use these words and terms but their meaning is not given by you or exhausted by your use of them – and partly because terms and concepts have all sorts of symbolic and logical connections with other terms and concepts. To use Taylor's analogy, language is like a web which we can never fully dominate and oversee; it can never be just *my* language, it is always largely *our* language (Taylor 1985a: 234). 'To speak', says Taylor, 'is to touch a bit of the web, and this is to make the whole resonate' (Taylor 1985a: 231). This is a compelling argument for theoretical language. It is because language enables us to place matters in public space that, in the case of the small part of World Three occupied by the ideas and propositions of social science, we need to be careful about the parts of the language web we employ when doing so.

Second, the irreducibility and the emergent features of intersubjectivity, means that words, concepts, ideas have histories. Whilst we might not wish to go as far as Taylor in claiming that 'the idea of a science which could ignore culture and history, which could simply by-pass the historically developed languages of political and social self-understanding, has been one of the great recurring illusions of modern Western civilization', it is obvious that there are limits to the extent to which language can be re-fashioned for any sort of purpose (Taylor 1985b: 131). Words, concepts and ideas often have their CVs assessed to see whether they are sufficiently versatile to fill a suitable vacancy (rather than the job being given to some bright young neologism). The employment history of race ideas is a serious handicap: a failed career as a scientific concept in the nineteenth century and various spells fronting right wing, genocidal politics in the twentieth should make future employers extremely wary.

The argument for a more circumspect employment policy towards the language that we employ as social scientists is reinforced by the contemporary emphasis on the constitutive aspects of language. Language, as postmodernists and social constructionists frequently point out, does not only represent, but enters also some of the realities it is about. It is through language that we formulate things, come to have an articulated and explicit awareness of things.

This is a key insight of the interactionist and postmodernist accounts that were considered in Chapters 1 and 2. If people believe race to be real, that is, if race ideas are a means of understanding, and 'getting on', in the phenomenal world, then in this sense race ideas and terms have an intersubjective reality. But this, it seems to me, is an argument for recognizing the reality of race ideas as an object of social scientific inquiry, not for employing race ideas or a notion of race as conceptual tools in such an inquiry. People's belief in witches does not make magic real; people's belief in their horoscopes does not substantiate astrology; people's belief in race does not validate it as an analytical category. This does not prevent any of these beliefs from being the object of social research but we are unlikely to arrive at any explanation of why some people hold certain beliefs if we cannot constitute their beliefs as an object of inquiry to begin with. It is a truism that whilst the partisan produce their own truths, they are ones that can seldom be shared with the rest of us. In theory, as in many other things, a little disengagement goes a long way.

Thus our third theme, the development of a vocabulary adequate to an account of a stratified social reality, sheds some realist light on discussion of the meanings of race. This raises the issue of methodological implications. If race is a lay category that does not belong in the sociological lexicon, how are we to develop research strategies to investigate the use of race ideas and symbols, or discrimination and inequality? This is my fourth theme.

Pawson (1989a and b) and Pawson and Tilley (Pawson and Tilley 1997) have developed a model for realist empirical research, neatly summarized in the formulation, outcome or regularity = mechanism + context. This is what they call a CMO (context, mechanism, outcome) configuration (Pawson and Tilley 1997: 56). This follows the pattern of realist explanation I have outlined and the generative logic associated with it. Briefly, it sees observable outcomes or regularities – certain groups, for instance, perhaps identified by their colour, are seen to earn less than other groups, to live in certain deprived areas of the city, to be less prominent in public office, or to suffer from violence and harassment – as the product of mechanisms acting in particular contexts. Mechanisms have a specific realist meaning, as Pawson and Tilley explain:

> A mechanism is . . . not a variable but an account of the make-up, behaviour and interrelationships of those processes which are responsible for the regularity. A mechanism is thus a theory – a theory which spells out the potential of human resources and reasoning.

> (Pawson and Tilley 1997: 68)

Furthermore, the analytical dualism of structure and agency that is at the core of sociological realism ensures that these mechanisms in the social world are 'about people's *choices* and the *capacities* they derive from group membership' (Pawson and Tilley 1997: 66). Realist information gathering is, then, radically innovative. By contrast orthodox, positivist forms of empirical research usually start by isolating a discrete variable and randomly selecting populations on the basis of it. An experimental and a control group are then identified within this population and certain dependent variables introduced to the experimental group. Various counting operations are then performed on the outcomes to see whether the introduction of the dependent variables has resulted in any differences between the experimental group and the control group.

The earlier discussion of the debates about TRA provides a good example of the standard experimental approach to empirical research. Almost all the empirical studies of TRA start from the assumption that race (invariably identified by skin colour, since most of the studies are US based) is the key defining variable of the study population (see, for example, the 'meta-analytic review' of such studies in Hollingsworth 1997). The empirical proposition is then advanced that the 'racial identity' and self-esteem of children of one race (black, but sometimes Korean, 'Asian' or even 'Oriental') are in some manner impaired or damaged if they are fostered to carers of another race (white). Research design then follows a basic pattern. Identify two groups of same race children, one of whom has been fostered to white carers (the experimental group), the other of which has been fostered to black (or Korean, etc.) carers (the control group), whose 'racial identity' and self-esteem are taken as the norm. The dependent variable is the effect of transracial adoption on racial identity and self-esteem. Usually this is measured by getting the children to choose different coloured dolls (if 'black' children choose 'white' dolls this is evidence of negative 'racial identity') or to express attitudes towards their own colour or race (if 'black' children do not explicitly identify themselves as 'black' this is evidence of negative self-esteem).

One effect of having to convert race into an empirical variable in this way is the unsubtle shepherding of complex social relations into the narrow pens of empiricist categories. Experimental research of this sort must be able to rely on an unambiguous definition of a child's race, but as we have seen, such a definition is not possible.

Children of 'mixed parentage' present an acute problem for this type of research, one that is overcome by setting aside biological determinism in the case of the 'mixed' category in order to reinstall it in the case of the 'racially pure' categories. Thus in the studies reviewed by Hollingsworth 'Bi-racial children were categorized according to the biological parent whose race or ethnic group was considered an ethnic minority in this society' (Hollingsworth 1997:109), that is children of 'mixed parentage' were considered 'black'. They are not allowed to *be* in any existentially valid sense; instead they must *belong* to one race or another.

It is perhaps not surprising that a recent summary of studies of this sort (and they are frequently regarded as the only valid sort of relevant data by academics and policy practitioners) concluded that opponents of TRA had been unable to produce any empirical studies supporting their position or demonstrating any of their central claims about the signficant mental health problems faced by children of colour placed with 'white' families (Alexander and Curtis 1996: 232). To a significant extent this failure has to do with the operationalization of some very dubious concepts: race, racial identity, self-esteem and so on. Equally, though, the (empiricist) research strategy is profoundly flawed.

This sort of research, much of which was considered in Chapter 8, in setting out to measure some aspect of race, finds itself quite unable to come up with measurement parameters capable of forming the basis for empirical evidence. In fact much of the debate between proponents and antagonists of TRA was about contextual resources (who gets what in contemporary USA and what part does a person's colour play in this); about social settings (distribution of carers, the role of institutional care and the reasons for the disproportionately high number of children of colour in such care); about situated activity (self-esteem and racial identity as interactional resources); and psycho-biography (who is damaged and in what ways by adoption by carers of a different colour). The concept of race conflates all of these domains.

The realist CMO approach of Pawson and Tilley offers an alternative research strategy. Since all measurement is an 'act of translation', data collection priorities are established within theory. So rather than set off with 'let's measure the effects of race on adoption', our model realist would want to scrutinize the theoretical assumptions underlying both the terms employed and the theoretical networks from which they are derived. As we have seen there are grave difficulties facing the socio-logical user of race concepts. Such a scrutiny might suggest not only more adequate sociological questions (e.g. 'In a colour-conscious and unequal society what are the effects at the various domain levels of placing children with parents of a different colour to themselves?') but also enable us to identify more precisely what particular outcome or regularity it is that we are trying to explain: the existence of racism and discrimination in US society; the reasons why some parents make successful carers and other do not; how to develop colour consciousness amongst children placed with other colour carers.

Without such a specification, empirical research is largely bound to be inconclusive and poorly generalizable (the example of empirical research into TRA, as Chapter 8 showed, is a case in point; see also Triseliotis 1991). The realist, on the other hand, sees knowledge acquisition as organized around realist propositions connecting agency and structure via mechanisms, contexts and outcomes. What it is we want to measure is derived from a theoretical discourse as is our overall empirical strategy. Thus hypothesizing CMO configurations is a theoretical exercise. Let us pursue the example of TRA further in this context.

What we take to be the outcome that needs explaining will depend on theoretical assumptions. For instance, we might as policy makers want to explain why some adoptions are successful and others not. The empiricist would at this point compile data on all successful adoptions and then set about identifying the characteristics they shared in common, such as social class, neighbourhood placement, colour and so forth. These characteristics would then be compared and contrasted with the characteristics of the population of unsuccessful adoptees. The point is that no matter how sophisticated the statistical techniques employed, such an approach can only identify variables; it cannot tell us about the processes or mechanisms that are responsible for the particular distributions. Nor as a consequence can it tell us about the contexts in which some mechanisms will operate, or the contexts in which either they do not, or their effects are muted or suppressed by the operation of other processes and mechanisms.

Suppose that we hypothesize that the central causal relation governing successful adoption is parental love and commitment to adoption. As a social process this will involve people's choices and the powers and liabilities they possess as agents and actors and so will not operate mechanically. The purpose of an empirical research strategy would be to identify those contexts in which the relation operates and those where it does not and, from the policy point of view, to maximize the former whilst minimizing the latter. Thus it may well be the case that the love and commitment of some parents is less than wholehearted towards children whom they perceive as black or as poor or as difficult; their ability to foster may be influenced by their reasons for adoption, by their age or by their neighbourhood or by some combination of any or all of these.

The purpose of our empirical work should be to devise and implement research strategies that will yield the expected outcome. In other words if we maintain that the crucial mechanism determining the success of an adoption is carer response, then unsuccessful adoptions provide instances where the contextual conditions are such that the mechanism is suppressed; people have made different sorts of choices and decisions. Empirical research can then be directed towards discovering in greater and greater detail what Pawson and Tilley summarize as the three Ws – *what* works for *whom* in *what* circumstances (Pawson and Tilley 1997: 210). Discovering which carers are successful adopters in which circumstances is a task beyond empiricist research.

Ironically, the opponents of TRA might have presented a better case if they had pursued such an approach. After all, the hypothesized outcome – that children of colour would get a worse deal from white carers than from carers of a similar colour – is not unreasonable in the context of the contemporary USA. However, rather than specify the processes which would link TRA with outcomes in other domains (high levels of long term unemployment, concentration in particular urban areas, disruption of family life and so on) and identifying the contexts in which these might become operative, those objecting to TRA have done so on the grounds of a-priori assumptions about race and identity. This has been a major factor in their failure to provide empirical evidence in support of their case.

Finally, it is worth noting that realist research strategies are not methodologically prescriptive (Layder 1993). Indeed it could be said to encourage sophistication in such matters, since knowing what you want to find out before determining how to go about finding it is surely an improvement on the 'if it moves, measure it' school of thinking which, oddly enough, always seems to require further research in order to arrive at a conclusion.

The emphasis on processes, on agency and structure and on the contexts in which these combine in specific ways brings us to the fifth and final theme in the development of a sociological realism, namely that of morphogenesis and history.

Reference has already been made to the dynamic, generative view of causality at the heart of realist explanation. In contrast to the static, successionist view embodied in much sociological research, the generative view of causality, by according time a central place in social theory, allows a purchase on the structuring of social systems over time. Chapter 4 elaborated a realist perspective on the dynamics of societal change using the work of Archer and particularly her conception of morphogenesis. Morphogenesis is based squarely on the analytical dualism of structure and agency. It emphasizes the analytical distinctiveness of structure, culture and agency, seeing each as relatively autonomous, relatively enduring and as irreducible to the others. It thus allows the development of a three stage morphogenetic cycle in which structural conditions are encountered by agents and actors, leading to efforts by these actors and agents to either maintain or transform these conditions, which results in structural elaboration or modification of the original structural conditions. These, of course, form the initial structural conditions for subsequent agents and actors.

This basic analytical cycle of conditioning, interaction and elaboration was applied in Chapters 5, 6 and 7 to an account of the development of race ideas and immigration controls in postwar Britain. Combining this with the CMO strategy for empirical research provides a powerful sociological tool for examining the dynamic interplay between 'parts' and 'people' across time and across different domains of social life.

BEING REALISTIC ABOUT REALISM

Making a case in social theory is not unlike standing for election: you tend to make promises that you are not sure how to keep; you play to the audience with rhetorical devices hoping that a vivid image or an authoritative phrase will discourage close questioning; and you point to the crisis or malaise which supporting your policies will swiftly remedy. Unlike most politicians, however, social theorists tend not to have to toe a party line and can take the opportunity to speak frankly to their constituents. This is the intention of this section.

One of the problems facing realist sociology lies in developing a body of methodological work. Whilst realism has established a respectable foothold as a philosophy of science, its impact within the practice of social science has been much less significant. There are a number of reasons for this, and it is clearly not the task of the present book to examine these, but among them we might cite the unfashionable status of notions of science and the advent of various forms of relativism associated with the rise of postmodern and poststructuralist ideas. Amongst other things, this has led to a waning of confidence amongst social scientists in the ability of their discipline to offer anything much beyond 'stories and narratives'. As Pawson and Tilley observe, 'once researchers abdicate the claim for privileged knowledge based upon their methodological strategy, then someone else will claim the warrant for them' (Pawson and Tilley 1997: 14). And there has been no shortage of usurpers.

In my view, realism provides the basis for a claim to privileged knowledge, but with the notable exceptions mentioned here, social scientists have done relatively little in the way of translating the general philosophical claims of realism into practical strategies for social research. The question is, perhaps, how much this has to do with disciplinary division of labour and professional circumscription and how much to do with the shortcomings of a realist approach to sociological knowledge and social research. Some of these shortcomings derive from the naturalist 'pull' in realism and I have identified some of these. In particular, the epistemological difficulties encountered in developing realist accounts of social causation and social relations are sometimes underestimated in realist work (which is why, I suspect, many of the illustrative analogies realists employ are taken from the world of the physical sciences). There can also be a corresponding neglect of the powerful insights of hermeneutics, whilst a realist position on subjectivity – the existential validity of human *being* – remains underdeveloped (although see Craib 1998 and Soper 1995).

So, not only are more examples of realist social research needed, but also such research needs to consider these tensions within realism itself. This is especially urgent when we consider the benefits of a sociological realism. First, as many writers have made plain, realism provides a cogent defence of objectivity and an evolutionary view of the growth of knowledge (see, for example, Layder 1990; Mouzelis 1995; Norris 1996; Norris 1997; Sayer 1994; Trigg 1993; Williams 2000). To insist that social scientific knowledge is knowledge *of* an ontologically stratified social reality is, it seems to me, the most compelling means of disposing of the relativist claim that our theories are entirely self-referential.

However, and second, realism is resolutely post-empiricist in its stress on the theory-driven nature of social scientific knowledge. The prominence of theory leads to both a distinctive view of empirical research as the identification of mechanisms and contexts responsible for regularities, and to a sharp break with those forms of sociological thinking which insist on the commonality of social scientific and lay languages or discourses. Whilst acknowledging their common sources, realism retains the view that theoretical languages serve different purposes to those of the language of everyday life.

Finally, Mouzelis has recently summed up the major task of sociological theory 'as not only providing fully worked-out, conceptual edifices (à la Parsons or Giddens), but also as providing tentative, flexible, open-ended, transitional frameworks useful for the empirical, comparative investigation of specific sociological problems' (Mouzelis 1995: 152). A sociological realism of the kind I have defended and elaborated offers us the resources to meet this task.

Bibliography

Archival collections: Public Records Office (PRO), Kew, London. PRO documents are given by Department (Colonial Office, Dominion Office, Home Office), box and file number (e.g. DO 335/77981).

Afary, J. (1997) 'The war against feminism in the name of the Almighty: making sense of gender and Muslim fundamentalism', *New Left Review* 224: 89–110.

Afshar, H. and Maynard, M. (eds) (1994) *The Dynamics of 'Race' and Gender: Some Feminist Interventions*, London: Taylor & Francis.

Alexander, R.J. and Curtis, C.M. (1996) 'A review of empirical research involving the transracial adoption of African American children', *Journal of Black Psychology* 22(2): 223–35.

Anderson, B. (1983) *Imagined Communities: Reflections on the Origins and Spread of Nationalism*, London: Verso.

Anderson, R.J., Hughes, J.A. and Sharrock, W.W. (eds) (1987) *Classic Disputes in Sociology*, London: Allen & Unwin.

Andreasen, R.O. (1998) 'A new perspective on the race debate', *British Journal for the Philosophy of Science* 49: 199–225.

Anthias, F. and Yuval-Davis, N. (1993) *Racialized Boundaries: Race, Nation, Gender, Colour and the Anti-Racist Struggle*, London: Routledge.

Appiah, K.A. (1986) 'The uncompleted argument: DuBois and the illusion of race' in H. L. Gates (ed.) *'Race', Writing and Difference*, Chicago: University of Chicago Press.

Appiah, K.A. (1992) *In My Father's House: Africa in the Philosophy of Culture*, Oxford: Oxford University Press.

Archer, M.S. (1979) *Social Origins of Educational Systems*, London: Sage.

Archer, M.S. (1989) *Culture and Agency: The Place of Culture in Social Theory*, Cambridge: Cambridge University Press.

Archer, M.S. (1995) *Realist Social Theory: A Morphogenetic Approach*, Cambridge: Cambridge University Press.

Archer, M.S. (1996) 'Social integration and system integration: developing the distinction', *Sociology* 30(4): 679–99.

BAAF (1989) 'Editorial – placement needs of black children', *Adoption and Fostering* 13(4): 1–2.

Back, L. (1996) *New Ethnicities and Urban Culture: Racisms and Multiculture in Young Lives*, London: UCL Press.

Balibar, E. and Wallerstein, I. (1991) *Race, Nation, Class: Ambiguous Identities*, London: Verso.

Banton, M. (1997) *Ethnic and Racial Consciousness*, Harlow: Addison Wesley Longman.

Banton, M. and Harwood, J. (1975) *The Race Concept*, Newton Abbot: David & Charles.

Barkan, E. (1991) *The Retreat of Scientific Racism: Changing Concepts of Race in Britain and the United States Between the World Wars*, Cambridge: Cambridge University Press.

Barker, M. (1981) *The New Racism*, London: Junction Books.

Barratt, M. (1991) *The Politics of Truth: From Marx to Foucault*, Cambridge: Polity Press.

Barrett, J.R. and Roediger, D. (1997) 'Inbetween peoples: race, nationality and the new immigrant working class', in R. Halpern and J. Morris (eds) *American Exceptionalism? US Working Class Formation in an International Context*, London: Macmillan.

Bauman, Z. (1987) *Legislators and Interpreters: On Modernity, Post-Modernity and Intellectuals*, Cambridge: Polity Press.

Bauman, Z. (1989) *Modernity and the Holocaust*, Cambridge: Polity Press.

Bederman, G. (1995) *Manliness and Civilization: A Cultural History of Gender and Race in the United States 1880–1917*, Chicago: Chicago University Press.

Benton, T. (1977) *Philosophical Foundations of the Three Sociologies*, London: Routledge & Kegan Paul.

Bhabha, H.K. (ed.) (1990) *Nations and Narration*, London: Routledge.

Bhaskar, R. (1979) *The Possibility of Naturalism: A Philosophical Critique of the Contemporary Human Sciences*, Brighton: Harvester Press.

Bhaskar, R. (1989) *Reclaiming Reality: A Critical Introduction to Contemporary Philosophy*, London: Verso.

Bhavnani, K-K. (1994) 'Tracing the contours: feminist research and feminist objectivity' in H. Afshar and M. Maynard (eds) *The Dynamics of 'Race' and Gender: Some Feminist Interventions*, London: Taylor & Francis.

Billig, M. (1993) 'Nationalism and Richard Rorty: the text as a flag for Pax Americana', *New Left Review* 202: 69–83.

Billig, M. (1995) *Banal Nationalism*, London: Sage.

Bloor, T. and Bloor, M. (1995) *The Functional Analysis of English: A Hallidayan Approach*, London: Arnold.

Bolt, C. (1971) *Victorian Attitudes to Race*, London: Routledge & Kegan Paul.

Bourne, J. and Sivanandan, A. (1980) 'Cheerleaders and ombudsmen: the sociology of race relations in Britain', *Race and Class* XXI, 4331–52.

Brah, A. (1996) *Cartographies of Diaspora: Contesting Identities*, London: Routledge.

Burke, P. (1992) *History and Social Theory*, Cambridge: Polity.

Butler, J. (1990) *Gender Trouble: Feminism and the Subversion of Identity*, London: Routledge.

Byrne, D. (1998) *Complexity Theory and the Social Sciences*, London: Routledge.

Cain, P.J. and Hopkins, A.G. (1993) *British Imperialism*, vol. 1, London: Longman.

Callinicos, A. (1993) *Race and Class*, London: Bookmarks.

Callinicos, A. (1995) *Theories and Narratives*, Cambridge: Polity.

Carter, B. (1996) 'Rejecting truthful identities: Foucault, "race" and politics', in M. Lloyd and A. Thacker (eds) *The Impact of Michel Foucault on the Social Sciences and the Humanities*, London: Macmillan.

Carter, B. (1998) 'Out of Africa: philosophy, "race" and agency', *Radical Philosophy* 89: 8–15.

Carter, B., Green, M. and Halpern, R. (1996) 'Immigration policy and the racialisation of migrant labour: the construction of national identities in the USA and Britain', *Ethnic and Racial Studies* 19(1): 135–57.

Carter, B., Harris, C. and Joshi, S. (1993) 'The racialisation of black immigration: the Conservative government 1951–1955', in W. James and C. Harris (eds) *Inside Babylon: The Caribbean Diaspora in Britain*, London: Verso.

Carter, B. and Williams, J. (1987) 'Attacking racism in education', in B. Troyna (ed.) *Racial Inequality in Education*, London: Tavistock.

Cashmore, E. and Troyna, B. (1990) *Introduction to Race Relations*, Basingstoke: Falmer Press.

Childs, D. (1992) *Britain Since 1945: A Political History*, London: Routledge.

Cohen, P. (1992) 'It's racism what dunnit: hidden narratives in theories of racism', in J. Donald and A. Rattansi (eds) *'Race', Culture and Difference*, London: Sage/Open University Press.

Cohen, S. (1984) *That's Funny, You Don't Look Anti-Semitic*, Leeds: Beyond the Pale Collective.

Collier, A. (1994) *Critical Realism: An Introduction to Roy Bhaskar's Philosophy*, London: Verso.

Conzen, K.N., Gerber, D.A., Morawska, E., Pozzetta, G.E. and Vecoli, R.J. (1992) 'The invention of ethnicity: a perspective from the USA', *Journal of American Ethnic History* 12(1): 3–41.

Cooley, C.H. (1964) *Human Nature and the Social Order*, New York: Schocken Books.

Cottingham, J. (1984) *Rationalism*, London: Paladin.

Craib, I. (1997) 'Social constructionism as a social psychosis', *Sociology* 31(1): 1–15.

Craib, I. (1998) *Experiencing Identity*, London: Sage.

Darwin, J. (1988) *Britain and Decolonisation: The Retreat From Empire in the Post War World*, London: Macmillan.

Davis J.F. (1991) *Who Is Black? One Nation's Definition*, Pennsylvania USA: Pennsylvania State University Press.

Dean, D. (1993) 'The Conservative government and the 1961 Commonwealth Immigration Act: the inside story', *Race and Class* 35(2): 57–74.

Dean, M. (1994) *Critical and Effective Histories: Foucault's Methods and Historical Sociology*, London: Routledge.

Delanty, G. (1997) *Social Science: Beyond Constructivism and Realism*, Milton Keynes: Open University Press.

Denscombe, M. (1998) *The Good Research Guide*, Buckingham: Open University Press.

Dews, P. (1987) *Logics of Disintegration: Post-Structuralist Thought and the Claims of Critical Theory*, London: Verso.

Dews, P. (1989) 'The return of the subject in late Foucault' *Radical Philosophy* 51: 37–41.

Dikotter, F. (1992) *The Discourse of Race in Modern China*, London: Hurst.

Donald, J. and Rattansi, A. (eds) (1992) *'Race', Culture and Difference*, London: Sage/Open University Press.

Doyal, L. and Harris, R. (1986) *Empiricism, Explanation and Rationality: An Introduction to the Philosophy of the Social Sciences*, London: Routledge & Kegan Paul.

Dresser, M. (1986) *Black and White on the Buses: The 1963 Colour Bar Dispute in Bristol*, Bristol: Bristol Broadsides.

Dreyfus, H.L. and Rabinow, P. (1982) *Michel Foucault: Beyond Structuralism and Hermeneutics*, Brighton: Harvester Press.

DuBois, W.E.B. (1966) 'The conservation of races', in H. Brotz (eds) *Negro Social and Political Thought 1850–1920: Representative Texts*, New York: Basic Books.

DuBois, W.E.B. (1973) *Souls of Black Folk*, New York: Kraus-Thomson.

Duffield, M. (1989) *Black Radicalism and the Politics of De-Industrialisation: The Hidden History of Indian Foundry Workers*, Aldershot: Avebury.

Dummett, A. and Nicol, A. (1990) *Subjects, Citizens, Aliens and Others: Nationality and Immigration Law*, London: Weidenfeld & Nicolson.

Dunn, J. (1978) 'Practising history and social science on "realist" assumptions' in C. Hockway and P. Peltit (eds) *Action and Interpretation: Studies in the Philosophy of the Social Sciences*, Cambridge: Cambridge University Press.

Evans, R.J. (1997) *In Defence of History*, London: Granta.

Eze, E.C. (ed.) (1997a) *Postcolonial African Philosophy: A Critical Reader*, Oxford: Blackwell.

Eze, E.C. (ed.) (1997b) *Race and the Enlightenment: A Reader*, Oxford: Blackwell.

Fairclough, N. (1992) *Discourse and Social Change*, Cambridge: Polity.

Fay, B. (1987) *Critical Social Science: Liberation and its Limits*, Cambridge: Polity.

Fieldhouse, D. (1984) 'The Labour governments and the Empire Commonwealth 1945–51', in R. Ovendale (ed.) *The Foreign Policy of the British Labour Governments 1945–51*, Leicester: Leicester University Press.

Fields, B. (1990) 'Racism in America', *New Left Review* 181: 95–118.

Foot, P. (1965) *Immigration and Race in British Politics*, Harmondsworth: Penguin.

Foucault, M. (1974) *The Archaeology of Knowledge*, London: Tavistock.

Foucault, M. (1977) *Discipline and Punish: The Birth of the Prison*, Harmondsworth: Penguin.

Foucault, M. (1978) *The History of Sexuality Vol. 1: An Introduction*, Harmondsworth: Penguin.

Foucault, M. (1982) 'Afterword: the subject and power' in H.L. Dreyfus and P. Rabinow (eds) *Michel Foucault: Beyond Structuralism and Hermeneutics*, London: Harvester Wheatsheaf.

Freeman, G.P. (1979) *Immigrant Labour and Racial Conflict in Industrial Societies: The French and British Experience 1945–1975*, Princeton, NJ: Princeton University Press.

Fryer, P. (1993) *Black People in the British Empire*, London: Pluto Press.

Fuller, S. (1997) *Science*, Buckingham: Open University Press.

Furedi, F. (1998) *The Silent War: Imperialism and the Changing Perception of Race*, London: Pluto Press.

Gabriel, J. and Ben-Tovim, G. (1979) 'The conceptualisation of race relations in sociological theory', *Ethnic and Racial Studies* 2: 190–212.

Gamble, A. (1985) *Britain in Decline*, London: Macmillan.

Geddes, A. (1996) *The Politics of Immigration and Race*, Manchester: Baseline Books.

Gellner, E. (1973) 'Explanations in history', in J. O'Neill (eds) *Modes of Individualism and Collectivism*, London: Heinemann.

Gellner, E. (1985) *Relativism and the Social Sciences*, Cambridge: Cambridge University Press.

Geras, N. (1995) 'Language, truth and justice', *New Left Review* 209: 110–35.

Giddens, A. (1979) *Central Problems in Social Theory: Action, Structure and Contradiction in Social Analysis*, London: Macmillan.

Giddens, A. (1984) *The Constitution of Society: Outline of the Theory of Structuration*, Cambridge: Polity.

Gilroy, P. (1987) *There Ain't No Black in the Union Jack*, London: Hutchinson.

Gilroy, P. (1993) *The Black Atlantic: Modernity and Double Consciousness*, London: Verso.

Glass, R. and Pollins, H. (1960) *The Newcomers: The West Indians in London*, London: George Allen & Unwin.

Goffman, E. (1970) *Strategic Interaction*, Oxford: Blackwell.

Goffman, E. (1971) *The Presentation Of Self In Everyday Life*, London: Allen Lane.

Goldberg, D.T. (ed.) (1990) *Anatomy of Racism*, Minneapolis: University of Minnesota Press.

Goldberg, D.T. (1993) *Racist Culture: The Philosophy and the Politics of Meaning*, Oxford: Basil Blackwell.

Goldsworthy, D. (1971) *Colonial Issues in British Politics 1945–61*, Oxford: Clarendon Press.

Gordon, C. (ed.) (1980) *Michel Foucault: Power/Knowledge: Selected Interviews and Other Writings 1972–1977*, London: Harvester Wheatsheaf.

Gouldner, A.W. (1970) *The Coming Crisis of Western Sociology*, London: Heinemann.

Guibernau, M. (1996) *Nationalisms: the Nation-State and Nationalism in the Twentieth Century*, Cambridge: Polity.

Guillaumin, C. (1995) *Racism, Sexism, Power and Ideology*, London: Routledge.

Habermas, J. (1987) *The Philosophical Discourse of Modernity: Twelve Lectures*, Cambridge: Polity.

Hall, S. (1992) 'New ethnicities' in A. Rattansi and J. Donald (eds) *'Race', Culture and Difference*, London: Sage/Open University Press.

Hall, S., Critcher, C., Jefferson, T., Clarke, J. and Roberts, B. (1978) *Policing the Crisis: Mugging, the State and Law and Order*, London: Macmillan.

Halliday, M.A.K. (1978) *Language as Social Semiotic*, London: Edward Arnold.

Halliday, M.A.K. (1985) *An Introduction to Functional Grammar*, London: Edward Arnold.

Hammersley, M. (1992) *What's Wrong With Ethnography?*, London: Routledge.

Harding, S. (1987) 'Feminism and epistemology' in S. Harding (ed.) *Feminism and Methodology*, Milton Keynes: Open University Press.

Harding, S. (1991) *Whose Science? Whose Knowledge? Thinking From Women's Lives*, Milton Keynes: Open University Press.

Harding, S. (1997) 'Is modern science an ethnoscience? Rethinking epistemological assumptions' in E.C. Eze (ed.) *Postcolonial African Philosophy: A Critical Reader*, Oxford: Blackwell.

Harré, R. (1972) *The Philosophies of Science*, Oxford: Oxford University Press.

Harré, R. (1986) *Varieties of Realism*, Oxford: Blackwell.

Harris, C. (1987) 'British capitalism, migration and relative surplus population: a synopsis', *Migration* 1(1): 47–90.

Harris, K. (1984) *Attlee*, London: Weidenfeld & Nicolson.

Hayes, P. (1993) 'Transracial adoption: politics and ideology', *Child Welfare* 72(3): 301–10.

Hayes, P. (1995) 'The ideological attack on transracial adoption in the USA and Britain', *International Journal of Law and the Family* 9(1): 1–22.

Hekman, S. (1994) 'The feminist critique of rationality', in S. Hekman (ed.) *The Polity Reader in Gender Studies*, Cambridge: Polity.

Hennessey, P. (1992) *Never Again: Britain 1945–51*, London: Jonathan Cape.

Herrnstein, R. and Murray, C. (1994) *The Bell Curve: Intelligence and Class Structure in American Life*, New York: The Free Press.

Heywood, S. (1990) 'Putting race placement policy into practice', *Adoption and Fostering* 14(2): 9–10.

Hickman, M.J. (1998) 'Reconstructing deconstructing "race": British political discourses about the Irish in Britain', *Ethnic and Racial Studies* 21(2): 288–307.

Higham, J. (1994) *Strangers in the Land: Patterns of American Nativism 1860–1925*, New Brunswick, NJ: Rutgers University Press.

Hiro, D. (1971) *Black British, White British*, London: Eyre & Spottiswoode.

Hollingsworth, L.D. (1997) 'Effect of transracial/transethnic adoption on children's racial and ethnic identity and self-esteem: a meta-analytic review', *Marriage and Family Review* 25(1–2): 99–130.

Hollis, M. (1994) *The Philosophy of the Social Sciences: An Introduction*, Cambridge: Cambridge University Press.

Holmes, C. (1988) *John Bull's Island: Immigration and British Society 1871–1971*, London: Macmillan.

Holmes, C. (1991) *A Tolerant Country? Immigrants, Refugees and Minorities in Britain*, London: Faber & Faber.

Howard, A. (1988) *RAB: The Life of R.A. Butler*, London: Macmillan.

Hoy, D.C. (ed.) (1986) *Foucault: A Critical Reader*, Oxford: Blackwell.

Hughes, D. (1988) 'When nurse knows best: some aspects of nurse/doctor interaction in a casualty department', *Sociology of Health and Illness* 10(1): 1–22.

Hughes, J. and Sharrock, W. (1997) *The Philosophy of Social Research*, Harlow: Longman.

Hugill, B. and Mills, H. (1998) 'Duty that's more than skin deep', *Observer* 19 April 1998.

Humphry, D. and Ward, M. (1971) *Because They're Black*, Harmondsworth: Penguin.

Humphry, D. and Ward, M. (1974) *Passports and Politics*, Harmondsworth: Penguin.

Husbands, C.T. (1983) *Racial Exclusionism and the City: The Urban Support of the National Front*, London: Allen & Unwin.

Ingham, G. (1984) *Capitalism Divided? The City and Industry in British Social Development*, Basingstoke: Macmillan.

Jenkins, K. (1995) *On 'What Is History?' From Carr and Elton to Rorty and White*, London: Routledge.

Joly, D. (1997) *Haven or Hell? Asylum Policies and Refugees in Europe*, Basingstoke: Macmillan.

Jones, S. (1997) *In the Blood: God, Genes and Destiny*, London: Flamingo.

Joshi, S. and Carter, B. (1984) 'The role of Labour in the creation of a racist Britain', *Race and Class* XXV(3): 53–70.

Juss, S.J. (1993) *Immigration, Nationality and Citizenship*, London: Mansell.

Katznelson, I. (1976) *Black Men, White Cities: Race, Politics and Migration in the United States, 1900–30, and Britain 1948–68*, Chicago: University of Chicago Press.

Kay, D. and Miles, R. (1992) *Refugees or Migrant Workers? European Volunteer Workers in Britain 1946–1951*, London: Routledge.

Keat, R. and Urry, J. (1982) *Social Theory as Science*, London: Routledge.

Kirk, R. (1999) *Relativism and Reality: A Contemporary Introduction*, London: Routledge.

Kirton, D. (1996) 'Race and adoption', *Critical Social Policy* 16(1): 123–36.

Knowles, C. (1992) *Race, Discourse and Labourism*, London: Routledge.

Kohn, M. (1996) *The Race Gallery: The Return of Racial Science*, London: Vintage.

Lal, B.B. (1986) 'The "Chicago School" of American sociology, symbolic interactionism, and race relations theory', in J. Rex and D. Mason (eds) *Theories of Race and Ethnic Relations*, Cambridge: Cambridge University Press.

Law, I. (1996) *Racism, Ethnicity and Social Policy*, London: Prentice Hall/Harvester Wheatsheaf.

Layder, D. (1981) *Structure, Interaction and Social Theory*, London: Routledge & Kegan Paul.

Layder, D. (1985) 'Beyond empiricism: the promise of realism', *Philosophy of the Social Sciences* 15: 255–74.

Layder, D. (1990) *The Realist Image in Social Science*, London: Macmillan.

Layder, D. (1993) *New Strategies in Social Research*, Cambridge: Polity.

Layder, D. (1994) *Understanding Social Theory*, London: Sage.

Layder, D. (1997) *Modern Social Theory*, London: UCL Press.

Lipstadt, D. (1993) *Denying the Holocaust: The Growing Assault on Truth and Memory*, Harmondsworth: Penguin.

Lockwood, D. (1964) 'Social integration and system integration', in Z. Zollschan and W. Hirsch (eds) *Explorations in Social Change*, London: Routledge & Kegan Paul.

Lorimer, D.A. (1978) *Colour, Class and the Victorians: English Attitudes to the Negro in the Mid-Nineteenth Century*, Leicester: Leicester University Press.

Louis, W.R. (1977) *Imperialism at Bay: The United States and the Decolonisation of the British Empire 1941–45*, Oxford: Clarendon Press.

Lunn, K. (1989) 'The British state and immigration 1945–51: new light on the "Empire Windrush"', *Immigrants and Minorities* 8: 161–74.

Macey, M. (1995) '"Same race" adoption policy: anti-racism or racism?', *Journal of Social Policy* 24(4): 473–91.

Malik, K. (1996) *The Meaning of Race: Race, History and Culture in Western Society*, London: Macmillan.

Manicas, P.T. (1987) *A History and Philosophy of the Social Sciences*, Oxford: Blackwell.

Martin, L., Gutman, H. and Hutton, P. (1988) *Technologies of the Self: A Seminar with Michel Foucault*, Amherst: University of Massachusetts.

Maynard, M. (1994) '"Race", gender and the concept of "difference" in feminist thought', in H. Afshar and M. Maynard (eds) *The Dynamics of 'Race' and Gender: Some Feminist Interventions*, London: Taylor & Francis.

McClintock, A. (1995) *Imperial Leather: Race, Gender and Sexuality in the Colonial Context*, London: Routledge.

McRoy, R.G. (1989) 'An organizational dilemma: the case of transracial adoptions', *The Journal of Applied Behavioural Science* 25(2): 145–60.

Miles, R. (1982) *Racism and Migrant Labour*, London: Routledge & Kegan Paul.

Miles, R. (1989) *Racism*, London: Routledge.

Miles, R. (1993) *Racism After 'Race Relations'*, London: Routledge.

Miles, R. (1994) 'Explaining Racism in Contemporary Europe' in A. Rattansi and S. Westwood (eds) *Racism, Modernity and Identity*, Cambridge: Polity.

Miles, R. and Phizacklea, A. (1984) *White Man's Country: Racism in British Politics*, London: Pluto Press.

Miller, J. (1993) *The Passion of Michel Foucault*, London: HarperCollins.

Ministry of Labour (1948) *Workers From Abroad*, London: Ministry of Labour & National Service.

Moore, R. and Wallace, T. (1975) *Slamming the Door: The Administration of Immigration Control*, London: Martin Robertson.

Morgan, K.O. (1984) *Labour in Power 1945–51*, Oxford: Clarendon Press.

Mouzelis, N. (1991) *Back to Sociological Theory: The Construction of Social Orders*, London: Macmillan.

Mouzelis, N. (1995) *Sociological Theory: What Went Wrong? Diagnosis and Remedies*, London: Routledge.

Mouzelis, N. (1997) 'Social and system integration: Lockwood, Habermas, Giddens', *Sociology* 31(1): 111–19.

Nairn, T. (1981) *The Break-Up of Britain*, London: Verso.

New, C. (1995) 'Sociology and the case for realism', *The Sociological Review* 43(4): 808–27.

Newton, S. and Porter, D. (1988) *Modernization Frustrated: the Politics of Industrial Decline Since 1900*, London: Unwin Hyman.

Norris, C. (1993) *The Truth About Postmodernism*, Oxford: Blackwell.

Norris, C. (1996) *Reclaiming Truth: Contribution to a Critique of Cultural Relativism*, London: Lawrence & Wishart.

Norris, C. (1997) 'Why strong sociologists abhor a vacuum: Shapin and Schaffer on the Boyle/Hobbes controversy', *Philosophy and Social Criticism* 23(4): 9–40.

Omi, M. and Winant, H. (1994) *Racial Formation in the United States: From the 1960s to the 1990s*, New York: Routledge.

Outhwaite, W. (1987) *New Philosophies of Social Science: Realism, Hermeneutics and Critical Theory*, London: Macmillan.

Outlaw, L.T. (1996) *On Race and Philosophy*, London: Routledge.

Owen, D. (1994) *Maturity and Modernity: Nietzsche, Weber, Foucault and the Ambivalence of Reason*, London: Routledge.

Palme Dutt, R. (1954) *The Crisis of Britain and the British Empire*, London: Lawrence and Wishart.

Park, R.E. (1950) *Race and Culture*, New York: The Free Press.

Patterson, S. (1963) *Dark Strangers: a Study of West Indians in London*, Harmondsworth: Penguin.

Pawson, R. (1989a) *A Measure for Measures: A Manifesto for Empirical Sociology*, London: Routledge.

Pawson, R. (1989b) 'Methodology', in M. Haralambos (ed.) *Developments in Sociology: An Annual Review*, Ormskirk: Causeway Press.

Pawson, R. and Tilley, N. (1997) *Realistic Evaluation*, London: Sage.

Perkmann, M. (1998) 'Social integration and system integration: reconsidering the classical distinction', *Sociology* 32(3): 491–507.

Phillips, D.Z. (1996) *Introducing Philosophy*, Oxford: Blackwell.

Phizacklea, A. and Miles, R. (1980) *Labour and Racism*, London: Routledge & Kegan Paul.

Pilkington, E. (1988) *Beyond the Mother Country: West Indians and the Notting Hill White Riots*, London: I.B. Tauris.

Pittman, J. (1997a) 'Postphilosophy, politics and "race"', in E.C. Eze (ed.) *Postcolonial African Philosophy: A Critical Reader*, Oxford: Blackwell.

Pittman, J.P. (ed.) (1997b) *African-American Perspectives and Philosophical Traditions*, London: Routledge

Pleasants, N. (1999) *Wittgenstein and the Idea of a Critical Social Theory*, London: Routledge.

Popper, K.R. (1972) *Objective Knowledge: An Evolutionary Approach*, London: Oxford University Press.

Porpora, D.V. (1987) *The Concept of Social Structure*, New York: Greenwood Press.

Porpora, D.V. (1989) 'Four concepts of social structure', *Journal for the Theory of Social Behaviour* 19(2): 195–211.

Porter, S. (1993) 'Critical realist ethnography: the case of racism and professionalism in a medical setting', *Sociology* 27(4): 591–609.

Pretorius, D. (1993) 'The social origins of failure – morphogenesis of educational agency in the Cape Colony', unpublished Ph.D. thesis, University of Warwick.

Rabinow, P. (ed.) (1984) *The Foucault Reader*, Harmondsworth: Penguin.

Ramazanoglu, C. (ed.) (1993) *Up Against Foucault: Exploration of Some Tensions between Foucault and Feminism*, London: Routledge.

Ramdin, R. (1987) *The Making of the Black Working Class in Britain*, Aldershot: Gower.

Rattansi, A. (1992) 'Changing the subject? Racism, culture and education', in J. Donald and A. Rattansi (eds) *'Race', Culture and Difference*, London: Sage/Open University Press.

Rattansi, A. (1994) '"Western" racisms, ethnicities and identities in a "postmodern" frame', in A. Rattansi and S. Westwood (eds) *Racism, Modernity and Identity on the Western Front*, Cambridge: Polity.

Rex, J. (1983) *Race Relations in Sociological Theory*, London: Routledge & Kegan Paul.

Rex, J. and Tomlinson, S. (1979) *Colonial Immigrants in a British City: A Class Analysis*, London: Routledge & Kegan Paul.

Richards, B. (1987) 'Family, race and identity', *Adoption and Fostering* 11(3): 10–13.

Richmond, A.H. (1961) *The Colour Problem*, Harmondsworth: Penguin.

Robbins, B. (1997) 'Sad stories in the international sphere: Richard Rorty on culture and human rights', *Public Culture* 9: 209–32.

Rorty, R. (1989) *Contingency, Irony and Solidarity*, Cambridge: Cambridge University Press.

Rose, G. (1995) *Hegel Contra Sociology*, London: The Athlone Press.

Rose, N. (1989) *Governing the Soul: The Shaping of the Private Self*, London: Routledge.

Rose, S., Kamin, L.J. and Lewontin, R.C. (1984) *Not in Our Genes: Biology, Ideology and Human Nature*, Harmondsworth: Penguin.

Rosenau, P. (1992) *Postmodernism and the Social Sciences*, Princeton, NJ: Princeton University Press.

Rowe, J. (1990) 'Research, race and child placements', *Adoption and Fostering* 14(2): 6–8.

Rubinstein, W.D. (1993) *Capitalism, Culture and Decline in Britain 1750–1990*, London: Routledge.

Said, E. (1983) *Orientalism*, Harmondsworth: Penguin.

Said, E. (1993) *Culture and Imperialism*, London: Chatto & Windus.

Sayer, A. (1994) *Method in Social Science: A Realist Approach*, London: Routledge.

Sayer, A. (1997) 'Essentialism, social constructionism, and beyond', *The Sociological Review* 45(3): 453–87.

Scott, J. (1990) *A Matter of Record: Documentary Sources in Social Research*, Cambridge: Polity Press.

Segal, L. (1990) *Slow Motion: Changing Men, Changing Masculinities*, London: Virago.

Sharrock, W.W. (1987) 'Individual and society', in J. Anderson, J. A. Hughes and W. W. Sharrock (eds) *Classic Disputes in Sociology*, London: Allen & Unwin.

Shotter, J. (1993) 'Psychology and citizenship: identity and belonging', in B.S. Turner (ed.) *Citizenship and Social Theory*, London: Sage.

Simpson, P. (1993) *Language, Ideology and Point of View*, London: Routledge.

Sinfield, A. (1989) *Literature, Politics and Culture in Postwar Britain*, Oxford: Basil Blackwell.

Sivanandan, A. (1981) 'From resistance to rebellion: Asian and Afro-Caribbean struggles in Britain' *Race and Class* XXIII, (2/3) 111–52

Skeggs, B. (1997) *Formations of Class and Gender*, London: Sage.

Smaje, C. (1997) 'Not just a social construct: theorising race and ethnicity', *Sociology* 31(2): 307–27.

Small, J. (1991) 'Ethnic and racial identity in adoption within the UK', *Adoption and Fostering* 15(4): 61–8.

Small, S. (1994) *Racialised Barriers: The Black Experience in the United States and England in the 1980s*, London: Routledge.

Smith, G. (1987) *When Jim Crow Met John Bull: Black American Soldiers in World War II Britain*, London: I.B. Tauris.

Solomos, J. and Back, L. (1995) *Race, Politics and Social Change*, London: Routledge.

Soper, K. (1993) 'Productive contradictions', in C. Ramazanoglu (ed.) *Up Against Foucault: Explorations of Some Tensions Between Foucault and Feminism*, London: Routledge.

Soper, K. (1995) *What is Nature? Culture, Politics and the Non-Human*, Oxford: Blackwell.

Stepan, N. (1982) *The Idea of Race in Science: Great Britain 1800–1960*, London: Macmillan.

Taylor, C. (1985a) *Human Agency and Language: Philosophical Papers 1*, Cambridge: Cambridge University Press.

Taylor, C. (1985b) *Philosophy and the Human Sciences: Philosophical Papers 2*, Cambridge: Cambridge University Press.

Thompson, J.B. (1990) *Ideology and Modern Culture: Critical Social Theory in the Era of Mass Communication*, Cambridge: Polity.

Tiratsoo, N. and Tomlinson, J. (1993) *Industrial Efficiency and State Intervention: Labour 1939–51*, London: Routledge/LSE.

Trigg, R. (1985) *Understanding Social Science*, Oxford: Blackwell.

Trigg, R. (1993) *Rationality and Science: Can Science Explain Everything?*, Oxford: Blackwell.

Triseliotis, J. (1991) 'Inter-country adoption: a brief overview of the research evidence', *Adoption & Fostering* 15(4): 46–52.

Tucker, W.H. (1994) *The Science and Politics of Racial Research*, Urbana and Chicago, IL: University of Illinois Press.

WING (1985) *Worlds Apart: Women Under Immigration and Nationality Law*, London: Pluto Press.

Wacker, F.R. (1983) *Ethnicity, Pluralism, and Race: Race Relations Theory in America Before Myrdal*, Westport, CT: Greenwood Press.

Ware, V. (1996) 'Island racism: gender, place and white power', *Feminist Review* 54: 65–86.

Webster, Y.O. (1992) *The Racialization of America*, New York: St Martins Press.

Weiner, M. (1981) *English Culture and the Decline of the Industrial Spirit*, Cambridge: Cambridge University Press.

Williams, M. (2000) *Science and Social Science*, London: Routledge.

Willis, P. (1977) *Learning to Labour: How Working Class Kids Get Working Class Jobs*, Farnborough: Gower.

Witte, R. (1996) *Racist Violence and the State*, London: Longman.

Young, R. (1990) *White Mythologies: Writing History and the West*, London: Routledge.

Index